BITTER MILK

Madeleine R. Grumet

BITTER MILK

Women and Teaching

The University of Massachusetts Press   Amherst

Copyright © 1988 by
The University of Massachusetts Press
All rights reserved
Printed in the United States of America
Set in Linotron Sabon by Keystone Typesetting
Printed by Thomson-Shore, Inc.
and bound by John H. Dekker & Sons
Library of Congress Cataloging-in-Publication Data
Grumet, Madeleine R.
  Bitter milk : women and teaching / Madeleine R. Grumet.
    p. cm.
  Bibliography: p.
  Includes index.
  ISBN 0–87023–612–1 (alk. paper.). ISBN 0–87023–613–x (pbk. : alk.
paper)
    1. Women teachers—United States.   2. Education—United States—
Curricula.   3. Teachers—United States—Psychology.   4. Sex role—
United States.   5. Feminist criticism—United States.   I. Title.
LB2837.G78 1988
371.1'0088041'09—dc 19   87–22679
                                                                CIP

British Library Cataloguing in Publication data are available.
Acknowledgments for permission to reprint selections under copyright and of
the first appearance of earlier versions of portions of this book are given on the
last printed page.

For my parents,
Frances Friedman Rotter and Norman Rotter

Contents

Acknowledgments

Acknowledgment provides the emblem for the project of this text. Lodged right in the middle of this term that we extend to honor the people who have influenced and cared for us, is the word "knowledge." An acknowledgment is an admission. It makes explicit what is tacit, or sometimes denied, in every scholarly monologue: none of us knows alone. And so these acknowledgments are a specific instance of the general project of this book: to name the relations that generate knowledge.

I acknowledge these people with gratitude and affection: Joan Stone, Jean Elshtain, Dick Martin, Mary O'Brien, Biddy Martin, Ayala Gabriel, Selma Greenberg, Margaret Zaccone, Betty Drysdale, Margaret Davidson, Dirk Wilmot, Marianne Wilder-Young, John Burns, Bill Pinar, Jo Anne Pagano, Dee Martin, Wendy Deutelbaum, Paula Salvio, Ann McBurney, Carolyn Proga, Jane McCabe, Elizabeth Keim, Marie-France Etienne, Nel Noddings, Wendy Atwell, Lynn Gordon, Dan O'Connell, Jim Crenner, Elena Ciletti, John Willinsky, Marta Zahaykevitch, and, of course, my husband, Gerald, and children, Amanda, Jason, and Jessica.

Preface

In Sri Lanka, young women sometimes experience psychotic responses to adolescence as they struggle with the ambivalence provoked by the separation from their families. In *Medusa's Hair* the anthropologist Gananath Obeyesekere tells us that these periods of distress are called "dark night of the soul" experiences. He describes a ritual tonic that the afflicted girls drink to release them from their trouble. It is called bitter milk and is a mixture of milk and crushed margosa leaves, the same bitter potion that mothers apply to their nipples when they wish to wean their babies.

Bitter milk, fluid of contradictions: love and rejection, sustenance and abstinence, nurturance and denial. I first heard Obeyesekere speak at the University of Rochester years ago, and the phrase has stayed with me ever since, for it contains the contradictions of my work and of the work of many other women and men who teach. I have written this book to explore these contradictions. In this text I am attempting to understand what teaching means to women. Women constitute the majority of all public school instructional personnel; nevertheless, our experience of this work is hidden. You will not find it in the volumes that record the history and philosophy of education. You will not find it articulated in teacher education texts or administrative handbooks. It is hidden from our students, our colleagues, even from ourselves. Its absence is not a mere oversight. Nor is it that we have been so busy doing it that we haven't taken the time to think about it. There is something about the task itself, the way it wedges itself into our lives, the way we place it somewhere between our work and our labor, our friendships and our families, our ambition and our self-abnegation, that has prohibited our speaking of it.

Sometimes it seems to me that it is everything that could possibly matter to us.

My maternal grandparents were both teachers though somewhat reluctant ones. My grandmother liked to play the piano and sing, and she taught music to the elementary students of P.S. 2 in New York City from 1910 to 1912 or 1913. Family lore has it that she referred to her students as "my little worms," a term that may have been more endearing in the early days of this century than it seems today. My grandfather, too, taught school. My mother remembers him collecting clothing to bring to his poor students. He is said to have been a good teacher, intense and theatrical, but he gave it up to go into the insurance business where, in search of social status, he found financial ruin. My mother studied business in college but returned to school after my brother and I had gone to college and did years of coursework so that she could teach in the primary grades. She taught in what we called an open classroom in the seventies and brought her extraordinary sensitivity and vitality to her students, gift-wrapped in learning centers, darkrooms, theatrical spectaculars, menageries, and quilting bees. I, well I was an English major at Barnard College, and I needed work to do when I graduated so I enrolled in the education program, which required little more than the student teaching I did at the Fieldston School, where I found students and colleagues I loved. Generations, stumbling in and out of this work. In *Psychoanalysis and Feminism* Juliet Mitchell points out that even matrilineal societies are not by definition, or by historical evidence, matriarchal. Similarly, if teaching came to me through my mother-line, it still came burdened with the legacy of patriarchy. It never provided the main source of income for my grandparents, my parents, or my family, and it was not until I returned to graduate school in the seventies that I was to claim it, to acknowledge its relation to my life, and to study that relation.

My graduate degree is in curriculum theory. It is a field both theoretical and practical. We study what goes on in schools and draw on the interpretive disciplines to help us make sense of it. Our work diverges from the studies of the sociologists, historians, and philosophers of education, because we expect to use our understanding to influence what goes on in schools either through teacher education or through curriculum criticism and innovation. Curriculum expresses the desire to establish a world for children that is richer, larger, more colorful, and more accessible than the one we have known. Perhaps it originates in what Sartre has called "negation," the creative refusal of human consciousness that says, "not this, but that." Perhaps it begins with a gesture to the future, with pulling back the curtain, opening the window, letting in more light. And then, too soon, we look at the window rather than through it, and negation collapses into prescription. I am not suggesting that this contraction of hope into resignation is inevitable, for it is an expression of historic and particular oppositions, the individual and the community, the family and the economy, the transcendental and the embodied, desire and renunciation.

Drawing from psychoanalytic and Marxist methods of analysis, curriculum theorists have worked with a dialectical model of the way that curriculum mediates between person and world. These approaches struggle to avoid the materialism of the accounts that portray the known as determining the knower, or the idealism that imagines the knower to determine what is known. The curriculum, in this conception, becomes tentative and provisional, a temporary and negotiated settlement between the lives we are capable of living and the ones we have.

So the curriculum that we study is the presence of an absence. Present is the curriculum, the course of study, the current compliance, general education, computer literacy, master teachers, the liberal arts, reading readiness, time on task. Present is the window. Absent is the ground from which these figures are drawn, negation and aspiration. Absent is the laugh that rises from the belly, the whimper, and the song. Suppressed is the body count, Auschwitz, Bhopal; even the survivors, the *hibakusha* of Nagasaki and Hiroshima, are invisible. Absent is the darkness and the light.

In the seventies we identified what was absent with what was called the hidden curriculum and stalked the culprit through the school, studying the language, testing, and textbooks of the classroom to reveal the hidden curriculum, crouching there behind the classroom door, like Polonius. We sorted curriculum into manifest and latent content. Manifest were the ideologies of participatory democracy, the melting pot, and achievement produced by effort and intelligence. Latent were opportunity determined by social class and the replication of labor/management relations in the classroom and the school. Many of my male colleagues became fascinated with the discovery that Daddy Warbucks was everywhere. They faithfully repeated Marxism's phallocentrism, identifying the forms and conventions of the public world and of its laboring men as the only significant influences on the development of the next generation. These preoccupations recapitulated the Marxist refusal, brilliantly revealed in Mary O'Brien's book, *The Politics of Reproduction*, to recognize the work that women contribute to child rearing as real, honest-to-goodness labor. More importantly, these theories provided a critique of patriarchal systems of education and production that sustained the very terms and prejudices of the system that they were attempting to criticize: Schooling was still being described in terms of production, and reproduction was limited to the analysis of the constitution of the next cohort of laborers.

This critique of reproduction planted procreation on the very assembly line it was trying to dismantle. The experience of family life was understood as a set of relations that had evolved to support the relations and values of the workplace. Manipulated and duped by the "system," parents apparently relinquished their children to schools that denied them knowledge, self-understanding, social mobility, economic security, and training for participation in democracy. Nevertheless, this account never adequately explained the willingness of parents, generation after generation, to send their children to these schools. It certainly did not acknowledge the willingness of the very authors of these critiques to enroll their own babes each September.

In the chapters that follow we will reverse this flow of influence from the public to the domestic by exploring the motives that are generated in the politics of the family and in the projects and intentionality that constitute male and female gender identities. The goal of this reversal is not merely to disrupt the male dominated discourse about how things work, although that accomplishment would in itself be gratifying. The goal of this reversal is to suggest that there are motives that support public schooling that are generated in the sexual/gender system of the family. Although this system cannot be isolated from the economy, it cannot be collapsed into it either, particularly because the marketplace and the academic discourses of collective experience such as economics and history are themselves generated to transcend the limits of domestic and familial affiliation and experience. If both schooling and the family are understood as epiphenomenal to the economy and the workplace, then they are only arenas for the subordination of children to the status quo and are forever fortified against our transforming theory and practice. But if at least some of the motives that we bring into our work as educators can be understood and acknowledged as issuing from our genderization and reproductive projects, then the argument that the school has a dynamic function in mediating the public and domestic oppositions in our culture is persuasive, inviting those who care for children in homes and schools to be the very agents of this transformation.

Entering the field of curriculum theory as a grown-up woman, deeply involved in the care of our three children, I was somewhat astonished to discover that only the public activities and interests of men were being studied as significant sources of contemporary education. Despite my identification with the Left's interest in social justice, somehow their serenade to society left me no part to sing. The experiences of family life, of bearing, delivering, and nurturing children, were absent from this discourse. Silent too was the language of the body, the world we know through our fingertips, the world we carry on weight-bearing joints, the world we hear in sudden hums and giggles. Many of us turned away from the generalizations and methods of social science as we sought a method and a language to draw these worlds into curriculum theory. We turned to literature, to theater, to history to recover specificity and contradiction, evidence that education was a human project that we all actively sustain. For, if the world we give our children is different from the one we envisioned for them, then we need to discover the moments when we, weary, distracted, and conflicted, gave in, let the curtain fall back across the window, and settled for a little less light.

For data we turned to autobiographical accounts of educational experience. For methods of analysis we turned to psychoanalytic, phenomenological, and feminist theories. As we study the forms of our own experience, not only are we searching for evidence of the external forces that have diminished us; we are also recovering our own possibilities. We work to remember, imagine, and realize ways of knowing and being that can span the chasm presently separating our public and private worlds.

Women who teach make this passage between the so-called public and private worlds daily. And, as I shall argue later on, that is also what we teach children to do. The ten chapters that follow have been written to study this passage. They go back and forth between the experience of domesticity and the experience of teaching, between being with one's own children and being with the children of others, between being the child of one's own mother and the teacher of another mother's child, between feeling and form, family and colleagues.

The text is arranged in a pattern that mirrors this argument. The first and last chapters address the familial relations that fall under the category of reproduction, a frame designed to emphasize the relations of reproduction and their importance to educational theory. The chapters closest to this margin are those that address women's work in schools, and the juxtaposition is chosen to accentuate the dialectical relation of our public and private meanings. The middle chapters are the ones most directly concerned with curriculum, that provisional ground that I am naming as our mediating space, the place where we can heal.

These chapters were written during a period of seven years. When I started writing them I was thirty-eight years old and starting my work in the Education Department at Hobart and William Smith Colleges. Our eldest child Amanda was thirteen, Jason was eleven, and Jessica, our youngest, was eight. I remember how I would wait for the school bus in the afternoons to bring them home and release me from the word processor. Their arrival, their presence, interrupted my work and made it possible. As I gather and revise this work for publication today, the children are all living away at school. I hope that you can still hear them, banging doors, calling to each other, to me, coming and going as you read these pages. Their presence in this work, no matter how subtle, is what this book is about.

When I first presented "Conception, Contradiction, and Curriculum" (Chapter 1) at a conference sponsored by the *Journal of Curriculum Theory*, I suffered the feeling that I had betrayed my child by describing my memory of her birth in a paper that I read to strangers. No audience response, no matter how receptive, could have pleased me, for by crossing the boundary between what I cherished in my family life and this work I do in the public world, I felt that I had desecrated the privacy and utter specificity of my relation to my children. At the same time I believed, and still believe, that by withholding information about that relation from the public discourse of educational theory we deny our own experience and our own knowledge. Our silence certifies the "system," and we become complicit with theorists and teachers who repudiate the intimacy of nurture in their own histories and in their work in education.

So I have chosen to let my own experience surface in this text. Because the experience that I refer to here, the experience of nurturing children within a marriage of twenty-six years appears conventional, I run the risk that you will read it prescriptively and take the project of reproduction to refer only to the procreative and nurturant activities grounded in the mythical "nuclear family." I worry that the reference of this text will be taken to exclude men and women who do not have children, or to exclude adopting parents, or single parents. When I refer to the "family" there is always the danger that we will forget that the family is a social, historical, and cultural construction. There is always the danger that the "family" will be construed as a natural rather than a social construction, even that its most sentimentalized, confining, and oppressive characteristics will be seen as necessary. On the other hand, if we speak of "family" only as an ideologically determined construct, as if none of us ever had one, we replicate the flight from the family in the politics of knowledge and turn away once again from home, from the place where we were most thrilled, most afraid, most ashamed, and most proud. Then again we slide into the discourse of political theory, cognitive theory, and educational history, and our experience as children, as women, and as parents gathers up its convictions and its questions and quietly leaves the room. The conversation continues, animated and noisy, until coats are reclaimed, farewells are made, and only then is our absence noted with some surprise and less regret.

I risk misinterpretation and anchor these arguments in examples drawn from my own experience of childhood and parenting because I am convinced that if only a theoretical presentation of these issues were offered, we would literally "overlook" the ways that each of us is implicated in them and the ways that our own practices as educators are motivated by them. It is the deviation of our own reproductive histories, mine and yours, from these theoretical formulations that opens the gap for new theory to fill.

The first chapter, "Conception, Contradiction, and Curriculum," presents the object relations theory that provided the bridging language needed to bring psychoanalytic and epistemological relations into one discourse. It sets out the relationship of curriculum to reproduction that is extended into the rest of the text. Chapter 2, "Pedagogy for Patriarchy: The Feminization of Teaching," was written to ground this theory in the history of teaching. Marxist and psychoanalytic perspectives are brought to bear on that moment in the nineteenth century when the work of educating the young passed from men to women. "Feminism and the Phenomenology of the Familiar" (Chapter 3) offers a reading of a contemporary teacher's texts of educational experience, drawing the themes presented in the structural arguments of the first chapter and the historical narrative of the second into the language of the world where we all live and work.

Part Two, the middle section of the text, addresses our experience of schools and teaching. It is in these chapters that the arguments concerning women's experiences of reproduction and nurture meet the forms and politics of curriculum. Chapter 4, "Where the Line Is Drawn," explores the passage from domestic to work spaces in teachers' lives and offers a sketch for the kind of school space that will support the art of teaching. "My Face in Thine Eye, Thine in Mine Appeares" (Chapter 5) presents a phenomenology of the look in parenting and pedagogy and a critique of its position in psychoanalytic theory and epistemology. "On Teaching the Text" (Chapter 6) extends this critique of the look in pedagogy by examining its trajectory in traditional approaches to teaching literature. Closing Part Two, "Bodyreading" (Chapter 7) celebrates the possibility of another approach to literacy, one that does not collapse into idealism but honors the body, the community, and the performance of knowledge.

Whereas Part One explores the gender differences between men and women and theorizes about their implications for curriculum, Part Three explores the differences that separate women from each other, differences rooted in the loyalty of maternal commitments to children and differences that evolve as daughters strive to differentiate themselves from their mothers. In this third section, I work backward, speaking first to our daughters, then to our sisters, and finally to our mothers. "Redeeming Daughters" (Chapter 8) nominates the lying daughter to displace the innocent son as education's icon of the child redeemer. "Other People's Children" (Chapter 9) takes up the relation that a woman has with children who are not her own and the politics of her response to the parents of the children she teaches. In Chapter 10, "The Empty House: Furnishing Education with Feminist Theory," I accept and attempt to fulfill Virginia Woolf's invitation to think back through our mothers so that we may find forms to shape and express what have, heretofore, been private visions. The text comes full circle in this last chapter, for if our curriculum choices are motivated by our responses to our experiences of reproduction, being the children of our parents and the parents to our children, then this chapter argues that we need to acknowledge what we and our sisters know about nurturance and to bring that knowledge into the deliberations that shape the form and purpose of public education.

As I reread these chapters, I can recall the situations that provoked their rhetoric. I can hear the shift from the first chapters, where the project was to interrupt the male discourse of my field with accounts of epistemology and curriculum drawn from the experience of reproduction and domesticity, to the chapters inviting my female colleagues to locate their reproductive histories in their teaching and theory. At the outset the opposition of male and female experience, ways of knowing, and educating is emphasized. Later chapters address our capacity to mediate this opposition through teaching and curriculum. If the voice that initiates this discourse is embattled and somewhat lonely, the process of this work has been its comfort, leading me to the discovery of the new scholarship on women and to the friendship of feminist scholars. The confidence of the final chapters testifies to the pleasure and promise of their company.

I know that, although this is a book about women, it is also a book about men. I know that when it celebrates the presence and affection of my mother, my daughters, and my friends I am also celebrating the care and commitments of my father, my husband, my son, and many of the men who are wonderful teachers and with whom I am proud to share my work. The designation of teaching and nurturance as the work of women in this text is necessary in order to avoid the emulsifying and idealist standard of androgyny, which distracts us from the analysis of our experience of reproduction by stripping it of gender. And, had I attempted to write a more general discourse, then I fear that issues that are particular to women's experience would inevitably slide under the discourse, weighted down by centuries of talk about education dominated by the history and preoccupation of male experience. I know that the transformation of the school into the middle place that I envision invites the most loving and creative expressions of masculinity and femininity. In our homes and in our families, many of us have learned to make a private peace in this battle of the sexes. There is more work to do before we can extend that respect for relation and concern for children that animate and dignify our private lives into the classrooms of the public school and the academy.

Finally, the fundamental argument of this text is that knowledge evolves in human relationships. These essays are merely partial inscriptions of what I have discovered in two conversations. The first discussion started with my mother, Frances Rotter, and although I cannot recall its initial exchanges, I do know that much of what I know and feel about my experiences of schooling I discovered from telling her about them and from the sense she made of what I told her. That conversation continues and blends with the one I hold with Joan Stone, my friend and colleague, as we make sense together of our work as mothers and as teachers. Talking with Joan, I scribbled the scheme for "Conception, Contradiction, and Curriculum" on the back of a conference program as she and I drove home from Albany to Rochester one wet spring, talking our way across the hills of routes 5 and 20, talking our way to the bitter wisdom of this sweet work.

Part One

1 Conception, Contradiction, and Curriculum

I suspect that I am about to present a feminist argument, and that's not easy. A feminist argument is unavoidably convoluted:

It is the argument of whoever is fed up with being a "dead woman"—Jewish mother, Christian virgin, Beatrice beautiful because defunct, voice without body, body without voice, silent anguish choking on the rhythms of words, the tones of sounds, without images; outside time, outside knowledge—cut off forever from the rhythms, colorful, violent changes that streak sleep, skin, viscerals: socialized, even revolutionary but at the cost of the body; body crying, infatuating but at the cost of time; cut-off swallowed up on the one hand the aphasic pleasure of childbirth that imagines itself a participant in the cosmic cycle, on the other, sexuality under the symbolic weight of law, (paternal, familial, social, divine) of which she is the sacrificed support, bursting with glory on the condition that she submit to the denial of nature, to the murder of the body.[1]

This is a secret that everybody knows. It is body knowledge, like the knowledge that drives the car, plays the piano, navigates around the apartment without having to sketch a floor plan and chart a route in order to get from the bedroom to the bathroom. Maurice Merleau-Ponty called it the knowledge of the body-subject, reminding us that it is through our bodies that we live in the world.[2] He called it knowledge in the hands and knowledge in the feet. It is also knowledge in the womb. Eve knew it, but she let on and was exiled from Eden, the world of divine law, for her indiscretion.[3] We, her daughters, have kept silent for so long that now we have forgotten that knowledge from and about the body is also knowledge about the world. The project of this text is to draw that knowledge of women's experience of reproduction and nurturance into the epistemological systems and curricular forms that constitute the discourse and practice of public education. It is an argument drawn from the experience in my own life that is most personal and at the same time most general as it links me to those who share my sex and gender and those who also acknowledge reproductive responsibility for the species. The argument takes off from a commitment in my life for which I accept responsibility with no doubts, hesitations, or second thoughts—parenting—and lands in a field of utter confusion: curriculum. What I hope to show is that the relation between this certain beginning and doubtful end is not accidental but inevitable, the end determining the beginning and the beginning the end.

The reproduction of society, its class structure, cultural variations, institutions, is currently a dominant theme in the sociology of education. Gramsci's concept of hegemony has caught our interest, for it articulates what the experience of our daily lives has led us to suspect, that the forms of our social and individual existences are not merely imposed upon us but sustained by us with our tacit if not explicit consent.[4] I want to take this term, "the reproduction of society," literally.

Now, it is not a new idea that schooling transmits knowledge or that education reproduces culture. But like so much of our language, this phrase, "reproduction," has traveled so far from home that we cannot even tell what part of the country it is from. Curriculum has provided safe shelter for these linguistic orphans so long as they relinquish their specificity and identification with their historical and social sources as they enter the discourse of the academy. I am not advocating that we withhold our hospitality from them, but I am suggesting that it is within their interest and ours that we connect these phrases to their roots and, in so doing, take their figurative function literally. Metaphor matters. If our understanding of education rests on our understanding of the reproduction of society, then the reproduction of society itself rests on our understanding of reproduction, a project that shapes our lives, dominating our sexual, familial, economic, political, and, finally, educational experience.

I want to argue that *what is most fundamental to our lives as men and women sharing a moment on this planet is the process and experience of reproducing ourselves.*

There are two phrases contained within this proposition that I wish to situate within my own understanding. They mark the intersections of action and reflection in my own experience that have generated the themes of this paper. The first is this word "fundamental." I confess to being constantly drawn to the lure of this word. When I was in graduate school, Husserl's call "back to the things themselves" was compelling, drawing me into his phenomenological texts and rigorous, if elusive, method.[5] The method promised clarity, a way of cutting through the thick, binding undergrowth that covers the ground of daily life to reveal a clear path. In 1972 when I went back to school, my children were three, seven, and eight years old, and clear paths were well hidden by the debris of sneakers, play dough, and cinnamon toast and interrupted by endless detours to nursery schools, grocery stores, and pediatricians. In those years, when there was a high probability that at any given moment one of the children was either incubating or recuperating from an ear infection, I found Husserl's stance of the disinterested observer, bracketing the natural attitude, a posture to be practiced and mastered. I am suggesting that there is a dialectical relation between our domestic experience of nurturing children and our public project to educate the next generation. It is important to maintain our sense of this dialectic wherein each milieu, the academic and the domestic, influences the character of the other and not to permit the relation to slide into a simplistic one-sided causality. The presence of the children was just one expression of my situation at that time, coinciding with other themes of my early thirties. It coincided with being the age of my own parents as they appear to me in memories of my own childhood. It coincided with my husband's professional development and our sense of economic security, which offered the family a brief respite from the pursuit of social mobility and class status until the children would be required to derive their sustenance from their own labor rather than ours. It coincided with what was for me a much more difficult bracketing of the natural attitude, the choice not to have more children.

Though any and all of these biographic issues may be probed to understand their relation to this search for the fundamental that kept me riveted to the chair by the dining room table, digging through the dense, often impenetrable passages of Husserl, Merleau-Ponty, and Sartre, they are not the explicit content of this discourse. The dining room table became the locus of this research not because its design was conducive to meditations on eidetic form but because of its proximity to the life world being carried on in the adjoining kitchen. I summon these scenes here because, although I may not directly address them again, they are currents that run through this text, linking the metaphors of epistemology and curriculum to the motives that choose and organize them. I present the passage through these rooms as an alternate route for the argument of this chapter and as a reminder of the many levels of experience that constitute the conceptual order that we employ here to inform, confront, and mystify each other.

This chapter, too, continues this search for the fundamental. The children, the work, the mother, the student are several years older, and the detours are different. The frequent trips to the grocery store have fallen into one "humungous" (as the kids say) trip a week, but the frequency has been retained by daily trips to Geneva, New York, where I go to teach. The path is not any clearer for the passage of time, and every route is a detour. "Back to the things themselves" no longer provides an adequate slogan for the project. The cadence of the command falls too decisively on the things themselves, encouraging an idealism fascinated with essential forms.

The search for origins has capitulated to the pursuit of mediations. The world "as given" is never received as such. The world we have is constituted in the dialectical interplay of our freedom and facticity. What the stripping away of phenomenological reductions reveals most clearly is not the things themselves but the conditions, relations, perspectives through which their objectivity evolves.

If the fundamental is an epistemological chimera, it is also a political ploy that promises cohesion but delivers domination. The fundamental is suspect if it suggests a single way of addressing the project and process of reproduction. To be a gendered human being is to participate in the reproductive commitments of this society, for reproduction is present as a theme in human consciousness without providing a norm for human behavior. Male or female, heterosexual, homosexual, bisexual, monogamous, chaste, or multipartnered, we each experience our sexuality and attachments within a set of conditions that contain the possibility of procreation. Our identities incorporate our position relative to this possibility. They encode our assent, or our refusal, our ambivalence, our desire, our gratification, or our frustration. Whether we choose to be parents or to abstain from this particular relation to children, the possibility of procreation is inscribed on our bodies and on the process of our own development. Even if we choose not to be a parent we are not exempt from the reproductive process, for we have each been a child of our parents. The intentions, assumptions, emotions, and achievements of educational practice and theory are infused with motives that come from our own reproductive histories and commitments. What is fundamental is not the nuclear family of an orange juice commercial enjoying a suburban breakfast in the family room. What is fundamental is that although there is no one way of being concerned with children, we cannot deny our responsibility for the future whatever form our projects of nurturance assume.

CONCEPTION

Stephen Strasser's concept of dialogic phenomenology more closely approximates the notion of the fundamental that this text addresses.[6] For Strasser, what is fundamental is the interpersonal basis for human experience, and so the primary question is no longer how one comes to constitute a world but how a world evolves for us. The very possibility of my thought, of consciousness, rests upon the presence of a "you" for whom I exist. My thought is a moment suspended between two primordial presences, the "you" who thinks me, and the "you" whom I think.

> My affirmation of the "you" must transcend all doubt for me; it must be characterized as the "primordial faith" upon which all my further cogitos rest. For the nearness of the "you" is a primordial presence, one that makes me believe that relations with other beings also are meaningful. My turning-to a "you" is the most elementary turning-to, one that causes my intentionality to awaken. In short, only the "you" makes me be an "I." That is why, we repeat, the "you" is always older than the "I."
> This principle holds for every aspect and all levels of human life. Husserl speaks of primordial faith in connection with the "being given" of the things that are experienced. It is precisely through the mediation of a "you" that I know at all that there are things worth touching, tasting, looking at, listening to. A "you" teaches me also that there exists reality which can be manipulated, "utensils" destined for particular use (Heidegger), matter which I must modify in my work (Marx). Without the active-receptive interplay with a "you" I would not know that my existence has a social dimension (Merleau-Ponty). . . . My "thinking"—no matter what one may mean by it—is never a sovereign act. I cannot think without attuning the mode of my thinking to that which must be thought.
> . . . But because the "you" is the "first thinkable" I must in the first place attune my thinking to the being of the "you." We may even say that generally speaking, my thinking comes about because there is a "you" that thinks and invites me to a thinking "response." It is the "you" that makes it clear to me for the first time that thinking is possible and meaningful. This also shows the finite, social, and historical character of my cogito.[7]

When Strasser asserts that it is not only the original intentional object but intentionality itself that is generated through human relationships, he is in effect acknowledging that the very ground of knowledge is love. This bonding of thought and relation is consummated in our word "concept." It is derived from the Latin phrase *concipere semina*, which meant to take to oneself, to take together, or to gather the male seed. In this etymology both the child and the idea are generated in the dialectic of male and female, of the one and the many, of love.

What is most fundamental to our lives as men and women sharing a moment on this planet is the process of reproducing ourselves. It is this final phrase, reproducing ourselves, that contains multiple meanings for me. First there is the obvious meaning that refers to the biological reproduction of the species. Then there is the reproduction of culture, the linking of generations, each conceived, born, and raised by another, parenting by extending the traditions and conventions with which it was parented. But by situating reproduction in culture we need not collapse it into the habits, aversions, and appetites that testify to the persuasions of ideology. For reproducing ourselves also brings a critical dimension to biological and ideological reproduction by suggesting the reflexive capacity of parents to reconceive our own childhoods and education as well as our own situations as adults and to choose another way for ourselves expressed in the nurture of our progeny. It is this last, critical interpretation of the phrase that I wish to address here because I see curriculum as expressing this third intention. Curriculum becomes our way of contradicting biology and ideology. The relationship between parent and child is, I suggest, the primordial subject/object relationship. Because these initial relationships are mediated by our bodies and by history, distinct masculine and feminine epistemologies have evolved. Although the initial stages of the parent/child relationship are influenced by the biological processes of conception, gestation, birth and breastfeeding, the epistemologies that evolve from them do more than merely mirror the biological bonds; they intertwine them with subjective aims representing the power of the human species to negate biology with culture. Hence, these male and female epistemologies and the curricula that extend them into our daily lives stand in a dialectical relation to the original terms of the parent/child bond.

Subjectivity, objectivity, epistemology: Abstraction falls from these terms like a veil, blurring their relation to the men and women who create them, believe them, and use them. We forget that they are lifted from our loins and lungs, from our labor and our love and our libido. And we forget that they in turn pervade our breath, lust, fears, joy, and dreams. The very word "epistemology" is drawn from the Greek word for understanding, *episteme*, and is extended into the word "epistles," or letters that Paul sent to the apostles. In contrast to *gnosis*, a Greek word denoting the immediate knowledge of spiritual truth, epistemology refers to knowledge that is intersubjective, developed through social relations and negotiations. I am interested in understanding the ways in which epistemological categories of subject and object and their implied relations are rooted in the psychosocial dynamics of early object relations as they are experienced by both children and parents. The three interpretations of reproduction—the biological, the ideological, and the critical—never exist independently of one another, and although my discussion of them will be organized in the order just given, often you may hear all three voices.

It is within the infant's social relationships that the terms "subject" and "object" first evolve. Derived from psychoanalysis and cultural anthropology, object relations theory investigates the genesis of personality in the interplay of the aggressive and libidinal drives seeking satisfaction and the social relationships that surround the infant and in which it participates. In *The Reproduction of Mothering* Nancy Chodorow declares that object relations theory eschews both instinctual and cultural determinism. Instead of portraying a passive subject, driven by biology or hypnotized by culture, object relations theory presents biology and social relationships as themes that influence consciousness without subsuming it.[8] Chodorow shows us how the infant transforms the relationships in which he or she participates into psychic structure through the processes of fantasy, introjection, projection, ambivalence, conflict, substitution, reversal, distortion, splitting, association, compromise, denial, and repression.[9] The relationship of curriculum to the experience of the birth and nurturance of children will not proceed, you will be glad to learn, with my psychosexual history, or yours, dear reader. There would be no point in making reference to our own situations, for it is obvious that there are no remote, authoritarian fathers, no binding, seductive mothers among the readers of this feminist study of education. The analysis is structural and thematic and, as such, abuses the specificity of each of us even as it respects our privacy and defenses.

Yet there is one moment I would remember, the day following the birth of my daughter, my first child, when my skin, suffused with the hormones that supported pregnancy, labor, and delivery, felt and smelled like hers, when I reached for a mirror and was startled by my own reflection, for it was hers that I had expected to see there. Over and over again we recapitulate and celebrate that moment, even as we struggle to transcend it.

The child is mine. This child is me. The woman who bears a child first experiences its existence through the transformations of time and space in her own body. The suspension of the menstrual cycle subordinates her body's time to another, contained and growing within her. The pressure of labor and the wrenching expulsion of the infant (the term "delivery" must have been created by those who receive the child, not those who release it) physically recapitulate the terrors of coming apart, of losing a part of oneself. The symbiosis continues past parturition, as the sucking infant drains her mother's swollen breasts of milk, reasserting the dominance of the child's time over the mother's as lactation and sleep as well respond to the duration and strength of the child's hunger and vigor.[10]

In contrast, paternity is uncertain and inferential. Supported and reinforced by the intimacy and empathy of the conjugal relationship, the experience of paternity is transitive, whereas maternity is direct. Paternity, always mediated through the woman, originates in ambiguity. Subject/object relations as experienced on the biological level of the reproduction of the species are concrete and symbiotic for mothers, abstract and transitive for fathers. If the "other" to whom the biological individual is most closely related is the child, then the definition of subjectivity as that which is identical with myself and of objectivity as that which is other than myself originates in an experience of reproduction that differs for men and women. So long as it is women and not test tubes who bear children, conception, pregnancy, parturition, and lactation constitute an initial relation of women to their children that is symbiotic, one in which subject and object are mutually constituting.[11]

It is important to acknowledge at this point that I am not assuming that all women experience the identification or that all men experience the ambiguity associated here with the anatomical and biological conditions for reproduction. The response to these conditions will vary for different cultures and specific individuals according to the interaction of these conditions with the physical environment, division of labor, organization of families, ritual and legal customs, and so on.

"This child is mine, this child is me" is an index of relation that will
vary with every speaker. What it means to be mine, to be me, depends
on the way each speaker knows herself. The maternal ego reaches out
to another consciousness that is of her and yet not in her, and self-
knowledge grows in this process of identification and differentiation
with this other, this child, "my child." The process of thinking through
the world for and with the child invites a mother to recollect her own
childhood and to inspect the boundaries of her own ego. Indeed, as
Vangie Bergum's study of women's experiences of becoming mothers
suggests, the extension of a mother's own ego identity to another who is
her child is a doubling that fosters and intensifies reflexivity.[12]

But what of the mother who is a child herself? Or the mother who is
exhausted from the care of too many children, or from strenuous or
monotonous work, or from malnutrition? And what about the mother
who has been raped or abandoned? "This child is mine, this child is
me" is a lullabye sung and chanted, whistled and hummed, keened and
whispered, almost, maybe never, uttered.

In order to investigate the interaction of biology and culture in our
milieu, I shall turn to the work of Nancy Chodorow, whose book, *The
Reproduction of Mothering*, investigates the patterns of parenting that
are dominant in our culture. Chodorow's patterns may not provide the
score for my song of motherhood or for yours. But the tune of her
theory may remind us of our own perhaps unsung tunes and theories.
That is the way that general interpretations function in psychoanalysis.
The dramas that Freud offered us, Jürgen Habermas points out, were
not intended as literal portrayals of our family relations, or as tem-
plates for their development.[13] They provided narratives against which
the scenes and accounts of the analysand's experience could be perceived in their specificity *and* in their difference. Chodorow's schematic
presentation of object relations is a magnificent contribution to those
of us who work to understand the relation of gender to the symbol
systems that constitute knowledge, curriculum, and schooling. Her
work, which describes the constitution of the gendered human subject
coming to form in relationships that contain the objects of the child's
love and thought, has given us a subject/object schema that permits us
to analyze, criticize, and, it is hoped, transform the subject/object
relations that organize curriculum and the disciplines.

At the outset of her argument, Chodorow suggests that, even as the
biological determinants of mothering have lessened as birth control
and bottle feeding have become established, biological mothers have

come to have ever-increasing responsibilities for child care. Her observation is reinforced by Bernard Wishy's historical study of child nurture in American culture, which indicates that as urban industrialization drew fathers away from home and the household ceased to be the primary economic unit, the responsibility for moral, social, and emotional development of children devolved upon the women who stayed home to care for them.[14] Our own time has accentuated this process. The economy's demand that working parents be mobile has isolated child nurture from extended kin, isolating mothers and their children from the aunts, uncles, and grandparents who may formerly have shared the tasks and pleasures of nurturance.

These social and economic developments support Chodorow's thesis that the infants of both sexes, though polymorphous and bisexual at birth, as in Freud's view, are immediately introduced into a social field in which they become predominantly matrisexual. Gender identity, which has evolved by the age of three, becomes a precondition for the oedipal crises, and it is the preoedipal relationships of the boy or girl child that, Chodorow argues, are most significant in influencing ego structure, gender, and, ultimately, patterns of parenting in succeeding generations. When mother is the primary caretaker of her infant, the preoedipal attachment to her precedes the infant's attachment to his or her father and influences it profoundly. Peaking during the first half-year, the infant's symbiotic relation with its mother is upset by the asymmetry in their relation. For the infant there is only the mother, whereas for the mother there are others: husband, other children, the world. She is the first object, the "you" in Strasser's dialogic *cogito*, and it is within the tension produced by her intermittent presence and absence that the infant evolves as a subject. It is at this developmental juncture that Chodorow distinguishes the mother's response to her sons from her response to her daughters. Acknowledging the sexual gratification that the mother experiences suckling and tending to children of both sexes, she notes that the mother identifies with the daughter but, perceiving her son as sexually other, more closely monitors her contact with her male child:

> Correspondingly, girls tend to remain part of the dyadic primary mother-child relation itself. This means that a girl continues to experience herself as involved in issues of merging and separation, and in an attachment characterized by primary identification and object choice. . . . A boy has engaged and been required to engage in a more emphatic individuation

and a more defensive firming of ego boundaries. . . . from very early then, because they are parented by a person of the same gender, girls come to experience themselves as less differentiated than boys, as more continuous with and related to the external object world and as differently oriented to their inner object world as well.[15]

The achievement of masculine gender requires the male child to repress those elements of his own subjectivity that are identified with his mother. What is male is "that which is not feminine and/or connected with women."[16] This is another way in which boys repress relation and connection in the process of growing up. Girls, on the other hand, need not repress the identification with their mothers. Whereas the dyadic structure of preoedipal parent/child relations is extended into the male oedipal period, with the male child transferring his identification from mother to father and repressing the internal preoedipal identifications, the female oedipal crisis is less precipitous and decisive. The dyadic relationship with her mother is sustained rather than repressed, and the father is introduced as a third element, creating what Chodorow calls a relational triangle. For both boys and girls, the father, who is more immersed in the public world, represents an external presence, often called a "reality principle," although that term expresses the very denigration and marginalization of the preoedipal relation that we are trying to rescue from centuries of oblivion and sentimentalization. Identification with the father presents the girl with a means of dealing with the ambivalence she experiences as the intense identification with her mother threatens to subsume her own autonomy. Nevertheless, because that ambivalence, also shared by the male child, is not accompanied by the dramatic repression that accompanies the incest taboo in the male oedipal crisis, the female child sustains the intuitive, emotional, and physical connectedness that the male represses, and for her, external objectivity becomes an alternative postoedipal object relation rather than a substitute for the powerful and emotional experiences of early childhood, which she retains as well. The reciprocity and mutual dependency of a concrete subjectivity, here bonded to the child and a concrete objectivity, the preoedipal other, who is the mother, are sustained for the postoedipal girl; and a more abstract objectivity associated with the external world and the father becomes a third term that mediates the mother/daughter, subject/object relationship.

This story of palpable presence and shadowy absence, of turning to and turning away, is and is not my story. Over and over again it contradicts the intimacies of my own childhood. It obscures my mother's energy and activity in the public world just as it erases my father's attentiveness and care. He walked with me in the dark morning hours when I would not relinquish the world for sleep. She gave speeches and came home late after the meeting, her eyes glowing, showing me the beautiful pin that she had been given to recognize her achievement. The theory fails to notice the photo in our album of my son, sleeping on my husband's chest, and the presence of their father's humor and inflections in our daughters' voices. These moments of familial specificity achieve meaning for me as they both confirm and contradict the relations that Chodorow describes. My father's participation in my infant care, my mother's leadership were both achieved in opposition to the politics of separation and connection that Chodorow presents. Furthermore, the meaning of their actions cannot be separated from this contradiction, for it was in opposition to those norms that my mother talked and my father walked. And sometimes the actors themselves, located somewhere between connection and separation lose their grasp of their own experience. My mother puts my father on the phone to talk to the landlord. My father never talks about his business at home. My son asks about my work and reads my papers, but he is careful not to mention that the research that he is citing in his college classroom was written by his mother.

I reclaim the specificity of my own gender formation as I read these memories of identification and differentiation through the lens of pre- and postoedipal politics. I begin to grasp the dialectic that makes me a particular personality who is, nevertheless, a woman. Because education mediates this passage between the specificity of intimate relations and the generalities of the public world, because cognition requires perpetual negotiation between general concepts and specific perceptions and intuitions, our understanding of our work as educators is enhanced when we grasp the interplay of the general and the specific in the constitution of our own gender identities.

Theory is cultivated in the public world. It is an interpretive and speculative enterprise that the community undertakes to make sense of our collective past, present, and future. Theory grows where it is planted, soaking up the nutrients in the local soil, turning to the local light. A theory of education that is cultivated in the academy, the library, or the laboratory accommodates to its environment. For educational theory to comprehend the experience and implications of reproduction we must generate a dialectical theory that gathers data and interpretation from both the public and the domestic domains.

Psychoanalytic theory abandons mothers and children at the very moment when we make room for Daddy. Though the presence of the father is gathered into the symbolic representation of the third term in the object relations of both mother and child, the entrance of the father and the world he brings with him need not be construed as obliterating the world that mother and child have shared. Too often psychoanalytic theory portrays the mother/child symbiosis as undifferentiated, as if mother and child spent the early days of infancy plastered up against each other, allowing no light, no space, no air, no world to come between them. Mother/child interaction, as the research of Daniel Stern has shown us, is a much more dynamic and differentiated relation than classical psychoanalytic theory would suggest.[17] This is not to dismiss the significant contribution to the life of the mother and the life of the child that the father, the friends, the world provide. A relation to this third term is achieved by both mother and child through their shared history of attachment and differentiation. What we have to remember, however, is that the father does not create the world although he may enrich and extend it.

In constructivism the symbolic status of the world is acknowledged as the construct that evolves from the interacting and mutually constituting reciprocity of subject and object.[18] Underneath every curriculum, which expresses the relation of the knower and the known as it is realized within a specific social and historical moment, is an epistemological assumption concerning the relation of subject and object. In an attempt to understand how we come to have and share a world, the various epistemologies relegate differing weights to consciousness and facticity. Each epistemology offers a negotiated peace between these two competing terms to account for this intersubjective construct, this ground of all our cognitions, "this world." Materialist epistemologies favor facticity; idealist epistemologies favor consciousness or mind. Whereas both materialist and idealist epistemologies permit the third term to collapse into one or the other poles of the dyad, the constructivist epistemology of Piaget retains the third term as constituted simultaneously by the interaction of the two and as constituting them in turn. Whereas constructivism mirrors the configurations of the symbiosis of the mother/child bond, and the extension of that continuity beyond the oedipal crisis in the mother/daughter relationship, the tenuous father/child bond and harsher repression of the mother/son preoedipal bond reflect the dyadic structure of materialist and idealist epistemologies.

The shift between dyadic and triadic epistemologies marks the contradictory moment that transforms the structure of conception into the structure of curriculum. The paternal relation is first constituted in three terms, as the father's relation with the child is mediated by the mother. The paternal compensation for this contingency is to delete the mother, to claim the child, and to be the cause, moving to a two-term, cause/effect model, where the father is the cause and the child his effect. The original maternal relation, on the other hand, is dyadic, and it is through the process of differentiation as mother and child grasp the world in which they found each other that the third term appears. So where constructivism may represent a preoedipal past for masculine epistemology, it suggests a postoedipal future for feminine epistemologies. This conclusion is mirrored in the collaborative research of Belenky, Clinchy, Goldberger, and Tarule. They develop five categories to describe the epistemological perspectives held by the women they interviewed:

> *Silence*, . . . women experience themselves as mindless and voiceless and subject to the whims of external authority; *received knowledge*, . . . women conceive of themselves as capable of receiving, even reproducing knowledge from the all-knowing external authorities but not capable of creating knowledge on their own; *subjective knowledge*, . . . truth and knowledge are conceived of as personal, private, and subjectively known or intuited; *procedural knowledge*, . . . women are invested in learning and applying objective procedures for obtaining and communicating knowledge; and *constructed knowledge*, . . . women view all knowledge as contextual, experience themselves as creators of knowledge, and value both subjective and objective strategies for knowing.[19]

This study of women's ways of knowing settles on constructivism as the epistemology that celebrates the creativity and responsibility of the knower as well as the context and relations within which knowing takes place and comes to form. Within their developmental argument, these authors make it clear that the constructivist position is an achievement, earned as women bring together the parts of their experience that the politics of gender, of family, school, and science, has separated. What I have called masculine epistemology may be found in their categories of received and procedural knowledge and the silence that their politics produces.

Masculine epistemologies are compensations for the inferential nature of paternity as they reduce preoedipal subject/object mutuality to postoedipal cause and effect, employing idealistic and materialistic rationales to compensate as well for the repressed identification that the boy has experienced with his primary object, his mother. The male child who must repress his preoedipal identification with his mother negates it, banishing this primary object from his own conscious ego identity. As his mother is not he, objective reality also becomes not he, and his own gender, more tentative than that of the female, is constituted by the symbolic enculturation of his culture's sense of masculinity, a conceptual overlay that reinforces his own sense that his subjectivity (that preoedipal maternal identification) and objectivity (that primary object, mother) are alienated from each other. Chodorow's point is that masculine identification processes stress differentiation from others, the denial of affective relations, and categorical, universalistic components of the masculine role, denying relation where female identification processes acknowledge it. She concludes that both as infants and as adults, males exist in a sharply differentiated dyadic structure, females in a more continuous and interdependent, triadic one.

If psychoanalytic theory has given too much power to the father, it has taken too much power from the son. The harshness of the son's repression of his preoedipal relation to his mother, though necessary for the development of male gender identity, may be somewhat diminished if that mother is not portrayed as a cloistered recluse, wallowing in regressive fantasies. The mother who is in the kitchen and in the world may nurture both sons and daughters for whom male and female, private and public, knowing and feeling are not so harshly dichotomous and oppositional.

Although Chodorow acknowledges the contributions of biology to the infant's matrisexual experience and subsequent maternal symbiosis, she maintains that the oedipal crisis is culturally specific. She demands that we acknowledge culture, the organization of families and labor, as responsible for the oedipal crisis, which in Freudian theory is attributed to a biological determinism of shifting zones of libidinal expression. For Chodorow the interpretive shift from biology to culture is significant for it acknowledges human agency, assuming that, if biology makes us, we make culture. Culture, she claims, is not a species characteristic but evolves as a response to the repressions demanded by those social relations that prevail in a particular era and milieu. Chodorow argues that the object relations she describes are sustained by a highly rationalized economic system of capitalism that draws men away from parenting and into institutions that require behavioral obedience and an orientation to external authority, thus reinforcing the repressions of the preoedipal experience. Such an argument coincides with the work of critical theorists such as Herbert Marcuse and Christopher Lasch who argue that mass culture, media, and the glorification of the adolescent peer culture have undermined the role of the father as a palpable authority in a child's life, vitiating the oedipal struggle and the autonomy that is the reward of the child who survives it.[20]

Although we must acknowledge the resemblance of this profile of contemporary culture to the world we know, I find its analysis skewed in the weight it gives to the labor and love of the fathers in determining the character of our culture and world. This scheme suggests that the female, domestic, and maternal influence prevails in our time as a consequence of patriarchal default and continues to represent the consequences of female influence as regressive, binding the children left to us to infantilized, undifferentiated, and narcissistic futures. The broad strokes that paint sociology's portrait of culture necessarily present its surface, most visible, and accessible structures for its total reality. The very clarity of the structural scheme that has permitted the generative analogies we draw between object relations and epistemology may mislead us, if it overwhelms us with a description of our situation that is too coherent. In a culture such as ours, where the symbol systems that dominate our social worlds are most often designed, distributed, and credentialed by men, it is not surprising that a sociological portrayal, locating itself in a description of our common situation, depicts a patriarchal order.

An attempt to provide a more complex and dialectical sense of culture is suggested in a study such as Julia Kristeva's *About Chinese Women*, which combines history and sociology to examine the cataclysmic changes in Chinese culture and their impact on the lives of Chinese women.[21] Kristeva describes an era in Chinese history that parallels the preoedipal period of psychological development in the West. Her analysis is interesting because it suggests that despite the 8,000-year-old repression of a putative matrilineal and matrilocal culture, contemporary Chinese women may be able to draw upon the deep streams that have run through their history, linking them to a cultural and historical epoch in which preoedipal symbiosis and continuity of internal and external structures were political realities rather than psychological repressions. Of course, the comparison that I make between Kristeva's and Chodorow's portraits of culture also marks the location of my own perception, as I find the one that deals with my own culture too general because I am so familiar with its complexities and am persuaded by the study of the culture so distant from me.

CONTRADICTION

Although our culture may lack the matriarchal history that might reveal our latent possibilities and the perspectives to reassure us that all is not lost and we have a past ready to reclaim, within us resides the power to imagine, if not remember, the negations of the conditions of our existence.[22] I think we attempt to accomplish this negation in the worlds we construct for our children. The contradiction is not merely altruistic, designed for them, for it also extends the projects of our own development as adults trying to extricate ourselves from our own childhoods and our own children. Unlike other organisms we do not spawn and die. We not only survive the birth of our children, but from the moment of their conception, their time and ours intermingle, each defining the other. Biology and culture influence our contemporary categories of gender and attitudes toward parenting as well as our epistemologies and curricula. This study of women and curriculum is claiming a space in culture for the women who care for children other than the great empty void assigned to us by the absent fathers and homesick sociologists. It presents a reading of curriculum that attributes the motive of differentiation to the mothers rather than the fathers, whose bureaucracies and collusions extend their own wishes to own and be owned. And if Kristeva finds in archaic Chinese history a female consciousness and promise of transformation contained, yet present, in collective memory, I suggest that our revolutionary female consciousness is lodged not in the recesses of time, but in the work that women do daily teaching children in classrooms.

While claiming, even flaunting, the preoedipal symbiosis of mother and child, we must be suspicious of portrayals of that primal relation that disqualify it as a way of knowing, of learning, of being in the world. If we bury our memories of this relation we knew as children and again as mothers under language, under law, under politics, and under curriculum, we are forever complicit in patriarchal projects to deny its adequacy, influence, and existence. Kristeva maintains that our culture and codes of communication contain not only the linguistic rules and conventions that constitute our postoedipal symbolic systems but also the imagistic, inflected, and gestural semiotic codes that signal the continued presence of our preoedipal pasts in our adult experience.[23] Similarly, the method of this discourse invites us to read the work of women in classrooms as a text of our repressions and compromises. It invites us to read the texts of educational experience and practice as semiotic as well as symbolic systems. Curriculum is a project of transcendence, our attempt while immersed in biology and ideology to transcend biology and ideology. Even in the most conventional scene of classroom practice we can find traces of transformative consciousness, no matter how masked in apparent compliance and convention. This perception invites us to refuse to run the classroom like a conveyance, designed to transport children from the private to the public world, but to make it instead a real space in the middle, where we can all stop and rest and work to find the political and epistemological forms that will mediate the oppositions of home and workplace.

CURRICULUM

The assertion that curriculum is motivated by our projects to transcend the biological and cultural determinations of our reproductive experience seriously undermines the assumption that curriculum design is a rational activity resting on needs assessments, systems analyses, or values clarification. The degree to which our support for open schooling, back-to-basics, moral education, or minimum competency testing is lodged in the relationships of our infantile psychosexual milieu is the degree to which our choices are overdetermined and our praxis vitiated. It would be simple if the relationships were direct, if schooling were just one great funnel into which we poured the entire social, emotional, political contents of our lives. Instead, rather than merely replicating the society from which they spring, schools contradict many of the dominant social and familial themes in our society. The history of education in this country provides countless instances of institutional, curricular, and epistemological configurations that emerge to contradict a particular condition in the culture. The famous "Olde Deluder Satan Law," passed in the Massachusetts Bay Colony in 1647, empowered the minister to compel illiterate children to attend his lessons so that they could learn to read Scripture and be saved. It did not merely reflect the colonists' religious fervor and commitment to the Bible. It also revealed the decline of the colonists' religious fervor and commitment to the Bible. It was compensatory. The very notion of childhood itself, argue both Aries and Wishy, is also compensatory, for it endowed youth with the innocence and protection that adults, adjusting to pluralistic urban centers, lacked in their own daily experience.[24] We do not have to turn back to fourteenth-century Europe or the Massachusetts Bay Colony to discover contradictions. The democratic ethos of American schooling, equality of opportunity leading to social mobility based on achieved rather than ascribed characteristics, belies the actual commitments of the upper and middle classes to retain their class status and the function of the schools in support of their privilege. Racial integration and busing contradict racial distrust and antagonism.[25] Essentialist and "Great Books" curricula contradict our immersion in the imagery of contemporary video, our cultural pluralism, and our infatuation with technology.

Because schools are ritual centers cut off from the real living places where we love and labor, we burden them with all the elaborate aspirations that our love and labor are too meager and narrow to bear. Contradicting the inferential nature of paternity, the paternal project of curriculum is to claim the child, to teach him or her to master the language, the rules, the games, and the names of the fathers. Contradicting the symbiotic nature of maternity, the maternal project of curriculum is to relinquish the child so that both mother and child can become more independent of one another.

Nevertheless, when negation is collapsed into a simple antithesis, a polar contradiction of one extreme by another, the alternative is as restricting as the condition it strives to repudiate. Just as the mother may succumb to the pleasures of sensuality or the shallow comfort of individualism, the father is also menaced by the contradictions he employs to negate conditions of paternity. As a parent the father contradicts the inferential and uncertain character of his paternity by transforming the abstraction that has been felt as deficiency into a virtue, into virtue itself. Co-opting the word, and transforming it into the law, the fathers dominate communal activity. Tying procreation and kinship to the exchange of capital, the fathers master the pernicious alchemy of turning people into gold, substituting the objectification of persons for the abstraction implied by paternity and amplified by technology and capitalism. The project to be the cause, to see the relation of self and other as concrete, is expressed in monologic epistemologies of cause and effect, of either/or constructions of truth, and of social science that denigrates the ambiguity and dialectical nature of human action to honor the predictability and control of physical and mechanistic phenomena.

Who are these fathers? They are our sons. They are the children the incest taboo estranges from their mothers, repressing their symbiotic experience of connection and identification with the other, the mother, the first object and the conditions of their own sense of self. They are the ones for whom gender identification requires a radical negation that violates the mutual dependency of child and parent, of subject and object. (Hence the "null hypothesis" of social science, which assumes there is no relation between variables and requires substantial quantification before a "significant" relation can be asserted.) Split off from identification with his mother, his primary object, the boy's later identification with his father is supported by his growing capacity to symbolize, to associate signs with experience, genitals with gender, words with power. As a man he will seek to reestablish the connectedness of infancy through work and culture and family; and if he can escape the depersonalizing, bureaucratic alienation of work and the positivistic, objectivizing dehumanization of culture—both of which combine to estrange him from his family—he may succeed. Masculine epistemology reflects this search for influence and control. It is oriented toward a subject/object dyad in which subject and object are not mutually constituting but ordered in terms of cause and effect, activity and passivity.

Masculine curriculum reflects this epistemology, contradicting the ambiguity of paternity, in forms differentiated by class interests. Though more closely identified with class status than women, men of all classes hope to engage in work that will be acknowledged as productive. They seek to be acknowledged as agents, who can claim the crop, the engine, the legal code, the party, the cure, the peace as theirs. For those engaged in manual labor the product, if not fragmented beyond recognition by the assembly line or trick shift, is concrete and tangible. For white-collar workers it becomes more abstract: the plan or the report, or the paycheck. For others it becomes an investment portfolio, an office with a window, a two-year improvement in reading scores. The product, material or symbolic, is public and can be traced, if not to a particular individual, then to the group to which he lends his name.

Competency testing, back-to-basics, and teacher accountability were the expressions of this process/product paradigm in the curriculum trends of the 1970s.[26] They accompanied the historical development of increasing bureaucracy and rationalization of the means of production and, in particular, the repudiation of the educational initiatives of the "sexties," rife with sensuality, ambiguity, rebellion against the paternal order. In the eighties fundamentalist assaults on the curriculum have sought a totalitarian solution for the family's incapacity to reproduce its world view in its children. The attempt to control and shape the child through schooling is also present in the recent criticisms of schooling that have appeared in the proliferating "school reports" of this decade. These documents reinforce the authority of the traditional disciplines and the rationalization of the workplace in their curriculum proposals, demanding higher standards, fewer electives, reliance on the literary canon, more homework, better use of time, merit designations for staff, and higher salaries. No longer rationalizing schooling as the path to success for the entrepreneurial "self-made man" in an era when small business has given way to the corporation, it is the economic prosperity of the Nation, no less, that is depicted in some of the reports as resting on the quality of instruction in schools. As we lose ground in our competition with other countries for international markets and military technology because of the greed and mismanagement of corporate production and trade agreements, blame is deflected from the men who establish these policies onto the women who teach the children who fail.[27]

For all the simplistic positivism of the programs of the seventies and the proposals of the eighties, there is a courage in their paternalism that I celebrate. There is courage in their assertions, however self-serving, and in those who designed them. There is courage in their willingness to address the future and to try to shape its character. They are political.

In contrast, even though the curriculum reform that grew out of the counterculture movement of the seventies was a serious political response to the arbitrary and abstract politics that brought us the Vietnam atrocities and Watergate, its open classrooms, alternative schools, and interdisciplinary curricula came to be seen as attempts to retreat from the world rather than as projects to redesign it. The curriculum of the open classroom mirrors the characteristics that Chodorow identifies as characteristic of women's work rather than men's.[28] Whereas men's work in the office or the factory is contractual, delimited in time, organized around a defined progression toward a finite product, women's work is nonbounded and contingent on others.[29] Women's work is seen as maintenance, repeated in daily chores required merely to sustain life, not to change it.

Ironically, the child-centered philosophy of the open school, the curriculum movement that might have extended the vigor and specificity of maternal nurturance from home to classroom, shifted the stasis attributed to women's work and lives to children. Rachel Sharp and Anthony Green argue that the ethos that supported the individuation of the child was the expectation that, left to his or her own developmental agenda, the child would express an inner nature, realizing what she or he *is*.[30] But they maintain that this ontological view of the child that honors what the child is, rather than what the school will make him become, ultimately served to sustain class differences, masking that teleological agenda and allowing it to function even more efficiently than it had in the traditional setting because its assumptions were no longer explicitly articulated. Their critique suggests that the maternal, ontologic ethos of such schools, its commitment to the "whole child," and apparent willingness to honor the specificity of each child's background and developmental level, masked the patriarchal teleologic project to protect class distinctions and advance the interest of the middle class that proceeded unimpeded by the new "familial" organization and ambience of the classroom. Because the innovations in curriculum often stopped at the classroom door and did not penetrate programs of evaluation or credentialing, the acceptance that they extended to the individual child trapped the poor child in a repertoire of behaviors that did not conform to the standards set to recognize and celebrate middle-class culture. Oblivious to the far-reaching epistemological and political implications of this approach to schooling, the teachers who had transformed their classrooms into places of active exploration and group process failed to create the political and ideological structures required to sustain and enlarge the movement. It disappeared almost as quickly as it came, leaving an empty terrarium, Cuisenaire rods, and an occasional learning center in its wake.

The degree to which schooling continues to imitate the spatial, temporal, and ritual order of industry and bureaucracy indicates the complicity of both men and women in support of paternal authority. That pattern becomes even more obvious in the social arrangement of faculty within schools, where male administrators and department chairmen dominate female teaching staffs, who, secretive and competitive, vie for their fathers' approval while at the same time disregarding the rational schemes and programs that emanate from the central office in favor of a more contextual, idiosyncratic curriculum of their own. Docile, self-effacing, we hand in our lesson plans, replete with objectives and echoes of the current rationale, and then, safe behind the doors of our self-enclosed classrooms, subvert those schemes, secure in their atheoretical wisdom, intuitive rather than logical, responsive rather than initiating, nameless yet pervasive. The programs stay on paper, the administrators' theory barred from practice, the teachers' practice barred from theory by the impenetrable barriers of resistance sustained by sexual politics.

Dorothy Dinnerstein argues that so long as primary parenting remains within the exclusive domain of women, both men and women will seek and support the paternal order as a refuge from the domination of the mother.[31] She maintains that from the early years in which mother is the source of all satisfaction as well as its denial, the audience for our humiliations as well as our triumphs, the supporting, inhibiting, protecting, abandoning agent through whom, and despite whom, we discover the world, we retain a rage at our own dependency and disappointment. The sons *and* the daughters turn to the fathers for relief, they who seem free of her dominion, substituting paternal authority for the maternal order.

It is the female elementary schoolteacher who is charged with the responsibility to lead the great escape. At the sound of the bell, she brings the child from the concrete to the abstract, from the fluid time of the domestic day to the segmented schedule of the school day, from the physical work, comfort, and sensuality of home to the mentalistic, passive, sedentary, pretended asexuality of the school—in short, from the woman's world to the man's. She is a traitor, and the low status of the teaching profession may be derived from the contempt her betrayal draws from both sexes. Mothers relinquish their children to her, and she hands them over to men who respect the gift but not the giver.

Who are these teachers? They are our daughters. Because mothers bear so much of the weight of parenting, as Dinnerstein has pointed out, we are very powerful figures for our children. That power would seem less threatening if it were not confined, however, to the domestic sphere. The discrepancy that children experience between their mother's influence in their home, compared to her influence in the public world, must undermine their comfort and confidence in maternal strength. Though their own intimate experience of her power is not diminished, it becomes suspect if it appears to be confined only to the forms of domestic nurturance. Whereas the sharper repression of the symbiotic tie permits her son to feel safe from her, the stronger identification of the daughter increases her vulnerability, and she turns to her father to escape the maternal presence that threatens to subsume her. Dinnerstein maintains that "both men and women use the unresolved early threat of female dominion to justify keeping the infantilism in themselves alive under male dominion."[32] The infant's rage, projected onto the mother, is reinforced by the disappointments and denials encountered in adult life, whereas the child's aspirations for autonomy along with the enduring desire for dependency are transferred to the father. Identification with paternal authority becomes a spurious symbol of autonomy, while the acquiescence it requires satisfies the unresolved desire to be managed and deny responsibility.

Kim Chernin's study of mother/daughter relationships in *The Hungry Self* suggests another motive for the daughter's emigration to the father's world. Chernin explores the daughter's identification with her mother's experience of stasis, frustration, and disappointment. She sees daughters struggling with their sense of their mothers' unrealized ambitions, unexpressed talents. So the daughter who flees may be attempting to escape her memory of maternal dominion as she simultaneously attempts to compensate her mother for her disappointments by achieving what was denied to her.[33]

The lure of patriarchy is an index to the enduring power of the mother/daughter bond. The symbiotic, concrete, polymorphic, preoedipal attachment of mother and child links our lives across neighborhoods, time zones, and generations. As the woman creates the child, the child completes the woman. Particularly in Western culture, where female sexuality is acknowledged and tolerated only in its capacity for procreation, motherhood bonds sexuality and gender. It legitimizes desire. It permits the woman to reclaim her body and her breasts from their status as erotic objects hitherto perceived only in their capacity to attract and seduce man. It dissolves the stigma of menstruation, inherited from the Old Testament, in the glory of creation. It releases the woman from the guilt of her secret sexuality as it repudiates the myth of the Virgin impregnated by the Word. As the child realizes his or her form within the woman, the woman realizes her form through the child. They constitute each other, subject and object dependent upon each other for both their essence and their existence. Chodorow endows this somewhat idealistic portrait of intersubjectivity with its erotic life when she argues that whereas the male reexperiences the preoedipal intimacy with his mother through coitus with a woman, the female ultimately reexperiences that bond not through the sexual relation to the male but in the intimacy she experiences with the child.[34] This dialectical interdependence obtains not only in the early months of the child's life but throughout its development, for the mother is able to differentiate from the child only insofar as the child is able to differentiate from her. The facticity and freedom of both mother and child are contingent upon their relationship. Psychoanalytic theory celebrates both maternal absence and maternal presence as the basis of ego development. It is argued that it is only in the mother's absence that the child begins to perceive his or her own selfhood so that their intermittent separation is the basis for the first identification of self. Yet the converse is also true. For the willingness and capacity for separation rest upon the prior and anticipated satisfaction of the child's needs for intimacy, dependence, and nurturance. The developmental needs of both mother and child simultaneously sustain and contradict the concrete, symbiotic origins of their relationship. A feminist epistemology reflects this dialectical dependence of subject and object.

Although the presence of open, nongraded classrooms seemed to suggest that a feminine epistemology had penetrated the patriarchal pedagogues of elementary education, the movement has collapsed, its foundations eaten away by technological methods that subvert it as well as by an ethos of individualism that has drained it of social promise and political power. This educational initiative finally failed to address the dilemma that has always plagued public education: the tension between addressing the needs of each individual student and developing the cohesion and identity of the group that contains that student. The project of differentiation that supports ego boundaries and personal strength is too often translated into a laissez-faire individualism that surrenders a vision of the world we might share to a project of individual development that repudiates intersubjectivity and interdependence.

Bonded, interminably, it would seem, to her mother and then to her child, the woman who survives the demands of these relationships to work in the world as a curriculum theorist, school administrator, or teacher is often engaged in the project of her own belated individuation and expression. Furthermore, as I shall argue later, our relations to other people's children are inextricably tied to our relation to our own progeny, actual and possible, and to the attribution of rights and influence that we attribute to that affiliation. If it is our relation to our own children that is contradicted by the curriculum we develop and teach, we must remember that what we develop we teach not to our own but to other people's children. It is with them that the contradictions between the woman's own experiences of childhood and mothering and the curricula she supports appear. Convinced that we are too emotional, too sensitive, and that our work as mothers or housewives is valued only by our immediate families, we hide it, and like Eve, forbidden to know and teach what she has directly experienced, we keep that knowledge to ourselves as we dispense the curriculum to the children of other women. Bonded to the other in a nurturant but inhibiting symbiosis on the species and cultural level, feminine curricula reverse the patterns of species and sociocultural relations emphasizing an asocial and apolitical individuation. It is this monologic intentionality that Kristeva fears will vitiate the hidden, presymbolic power that resides within feminine experience. She fears that we sell out: we escape the binding preoedipal and postoedipal identification with our mothers by identifying with our fathers, striving for access to the word and to time; or we repudiate the dialectic of sexuality, obliterating the other in a fascistic and totalitarian mimicry of power; or we sink into a wordless ecstacy, back into the preoedipal maternal identification, mystical, melancholic, sullen, and suicidal—Virginia walking into the river. Kristeva's warning:

> To refuse both extremes. To know that an ostensibly masculine, paternal (because supportive of time and symbol) identification is necessary in order to have some voice in the record of politics and history. To achieve this identification in order to escape a smug polymorphism where it is so easy and comfortable for a woman here to remain.[35]

Bearing epistemologies and curricular projects that contradict both our psychosocial development as sons and daughters and our procreative experience as fathers and mothers, we find ourselves as trapped in the activity we claim as conscious intentionality as we have been in the overdetermined, repressed experience of our early years. This compensatory and simplistic pattern of opposition demeans the dialectic, a title it hardly deserves. To qualify for that designation we would need to interpret our reproductive experience (procreation and nurturance) and our productive practice (curriculum and teaching) each through the other's terms, not obliterating the differences between them but naming their contradictions and reconceiving our commitment to the care and education of children. It is a dialectic that strives not to obliterate differences in a shallow, totalitarian image of equality but to sustain them and work for their integration.

Feminist social theory directs us to reorganize our patterns of infant nurturance, permitting fathers to assume significant nurturant activities and an intimacy with their children that will preclude the harsh, deforming repression of the rich and powerful preoedipal experience. The felt presence of both mothers and fathers in the infant's world may diminish the crippling dichotomy of internal and external, dream and reality, body and thought, poetry and science, ambiguity and certainty. These domestic arrangements clearly remain fantasy unless supported by the economic, religious, and legal systems in which we live. The task when viewed in the structural complexity of our social, political, economic situation appears herculean. Only when we suspend the despair that isolates us from our history and our future can our reproductive capacity reclaim the procreative promise of our species, not merely to conceive but to reconceive another generation.

We, the women who teach, must claim our reproductive labor as a process of civilization as well as procreation. We can continue to escort the children from home to the marketplace as did the *paidagogos*, the Greek slave whose title and function survive in pedagogy, or we can refuse the oppositions and limits that define each place and our love and work within them. The task is daunting. This book contains its contradictions. These words, for all their intensity, have been sifted through the sieves of academic discourse. The very institutions that I repudiate for their perpetuation of patriarchal privilege are the ones within which I have found the voice that tries to sing the tune of two worlds. This writing has been interrupted and informed by driving the kids to the pool and to soccer practice, by the laundering of sweaty sports socks and mildewed beach towels, by the heat of the summer sun and the soft summons of the night air. As I end this chapter, I am

tempted to celebrate both it and myself. But I am chastened by Kristeva:

> To be wary from the first of the premium of narcissism that such integra-
> tion may carry with it: to reject the validity of the homologous woman,
> finally virile; and to act, on the socio-political, historical stage, as her
> negative: that is, to act first with all those who "swim against the tide," all
> those who refuse—all the rebels against the existing relations of produc-
> tion and reproduction. But neither to take the role of revolutionary (male
> or female) to refuse all roles, in order on the contrary, to summon this
> timeless "truth"—formless, neither true or false, echo of our jouissance,
> of our madness, of our pregnancies—unto the order of speech and social
> symbolism. But how? By listening, by recognizing the unspoken speech,
> even revolutionary speech; by calling attention at all times to whatever
> remains unsatisfied, repressed, new, eccentric, incomprehensible, disturb-
> ing to the status quo. A constant alternation between time and its "truth,"
> identity and its loss, history and the timeless, signless, extra-phenomenal
> things that produce it. An impossible dialectic; a permanent alternation;
> never the one without the other. It is not certain that anyone here and now
> is capable of it. An analyst conscious of history and politics? A politician
> tuned to the unconscious? A woman perhaps . . .[36]

2 Pedagogy for Patriarchy:
The Feminization of Teaching

Eye yami nkalawanda chidyila hanjila
I am the lion who eats on the path

Wukama kankanta wutaleng'a mwewulu
You sleep on your back, you look into the sky

Chala chankumbi kusemina chiyimbi
Nest of the marabout stork where a black kite lays eggs

Ewina wantoka kusemina chitombu
Hole of a mamba where a (harmless) lizard lays eggs

Inyamwadyi wantukileng'a
Novice's mother, you used to revile me

Leta mwaneyi nikwang'ijekeli
Bring me your child that I may mistreat (him)

Mwaneyi nayi
Your child has gone

Mwan kamwanta wafwana musuka
The son of a chief is like a slave.[1]

This is a song of circumcision translated by Victor Turner in his study of *Mukanda*, an Ndembu ritual that achieves the reversal of the natural order as it takes male children from women and gives them to men.[2] In the song creatures are displaced from their natural habitats. The natural order is contradicted when the chitombu, a harmless lizard, dispossesses a venomous mamba of its hole. The kite abandons the heights it favors for the nest of the earth-hugging stork of the river plains. The eggs of these creatures will be deposited in strange nests and will yield the life that stirs within them to alien guardians. Turner attributes the song's imagery to the antagonism of men toward mothers in a matrilineal society.[3] Hostility between mothers and circumcisers is made explicit in the last four lines of the song, which assert that the novices will be separated not only from their mothers but also from their familial and class identifications, merging into a community of peers supervised by male elders. Throughout the ritual there is abundant evidence that this event marks the transfer of male children from matriarchy to patriarchy. Novices may not cry out for their mothers, but they may call out for their fathers. Mothers are banished from the circumcision site, as are all females. During the three to four months of the novice's seclusion, those mothers who prepare food for the novices are prohibited from having sexual intercourse by the threat that their sexual activity will prevent their sons' wounds from healing properly. Turner reads *Mukanda* as a systematic repudiation of maternal sexuality, nurturance, and influence:

> From being "unclean" children, partially effeminized by constant contact with their mothers and other women, boys are converted by the mystical efficacy of ritual into purified members of the male moral community, able to begin to take their part in the jural, political and ritual affairs of Ndembu society. . . .
>
> Matriliny is the principle governing the persistence of narrow local units through time. It is a principle of cardinal importance in Ndembu society and it is ritualized in a great number of contexts. Nevertheless, in Mukanda emphasis is laid on the unity of males, irrespective of their matrilineal connections. The father-son tie assumes special prominence and is almost regarded as representative of the values and norms governing the relationships of the widest Ndembu community.[4]

Turner's analysis of the ritual underscores the themes of the song: the reversal of the reproductive order, hostility between mothers and the patriarchal order, and an ideal of equality binding young men to each other and to the patriarchal order. The transfer of sons in our culture from their mothers to their fathers recapitulates these same three themes in an elaborate and extended ritual that we call schooling. Strangely enough, we don't banish all women from the scene as the Ndembu do; instead, we employ many women, even many mothers, as the very agents who deliver their children to the patriarchy.

This is the contradiction that this chapter will explore: the feminization of teaching and the ways in which it has both promoted and sabotaged the interests of women in our culture. During the nineteenth century, teaching school changed from men's to women's work. The process of this change, its causes, and its consequences provides a knot that ties Marxist and psychoanalytic threads of feminist inquiry together with the histories of our current notions of pedagogy and curriculum. In her important essay, "Feminism, Marxism, Method, and the State," Catherine MacKinnon explores the mutual deprecations deployed by feminist and Marxist theoreticians, each bent on revealing the deficiencies of the other's conceptualization and study of women's powerlessness:

> Because marxists tend to conceive of powerlessness, first and last, as concrete and externally imposed, they believe that it must be concretely and externally undone to be changed. Women's powerlessness has been found through consciousness raising to be both internalized and externally imposed, so that, for example, femininity is identity to women as well as desirability to men.[5]

Yes, we too have our rituals, our purification and bonding ceremonies, as our tenured priests eagerly appropriate our histories and hopes to their paradigms and publications and papas (Freud or Marx). Is class the male compensation for the inferential nature of paternity, or is sexism a consequence of capital and class divisions? The very fascination with origin suggests an overdetermined need to name the source, a project that interminably repeats the reproductive project of patriarchy to link knowing the cause to being the cause. Satisfied to start in the middle rather than at the beginning, I will not pursue the question of origins here but will look instead at the time when women took up teaching and teaching took up women. In exploring both the economic conditions that shaped teaching at the time of industrialization and the meaning of that work to women as it provided a context for their own reproductive agendas, I hope to tell a story of teaching that accommodates both class and consciousness.

Schooling shares the liminal character of *Mukanda* by providing a passage from domestic and maternal nurturance to public institutions and patriarchal identifications. If we are to bridge the gap that divides the public from the private in our culture and in our consciousness, then we need to think of schooling as a time and place where those oppositions can be mediated and reconceived. To take sides in the Marxist, psychoanalytic dispute is to perpetuate the heterosexual contest that is the problem of this chapter. Rather than extending this ancient antagonism into my own method, I have attempted to find a middle way, bringing both Marxist and psychoanalytic approaches to bear on this work.

The study of curriculum as gender text has been advanced recently by those working in curriculum theory and in the disciplines.[6] In Chapter 1 I argued that correspondence theory was myopic in its preoccupation with those processes of schooling that support class structure and the relations of the workplace. In their attack on the hegemony of capitalist interests, the correspondence theorists (unwittingly perhaps) recapitulated the hegemony of masculine work and experience, blatantly ignoring the reproductive experience of mothers, daughters, and teachers.[7] Implicit in that argument was my surprise and outrage at the consistent and flagrant exclusion of female experience from the organization and life of schools, from the theories and methods of pedagogy, learning, and curriculum theory. This essay is an initial attempt to investigate the sources of this silence, to discover why the women who, by 1888, already constituted 63 percent of American teachers—90 percent in the cities—permitted the ethos of American schooling to violate their own experience of nurturance.[8] What follows is a brief analysis of the economic and social conditions of these women and of those who spoke for them. Unfortunately, their own voices are barely audible. Feminist history must recover their specificity.

The Era of Industrialization   The early decades of the nineteenth century saw the coincidence of major transformations in American culture. Most significant was the shift of capital and labor from agriculture to industry. In the 1820s, the residential and occupational structures of the population were changing rapidly. The war of 1812 had forced the nation to become more independent of Europe in manufacturing its own commodities, and it was during this antebellum period, 1815–60, that advances in the machine-tool industry made machines more accessible and manufacturing more extensive. Wages of skilled and managerial employees increased more rapidly than did wages of unskilled labor during this period of rapid industrialization. Immigration in the forties and fifties added to the pool of low-skilled workers, keeping their wages lower. As capital accumulated in the hands of those who built the new railroads and factories, income distribution became more highly differentiated, and a sharper class structure began to emerge.[9] Managers, professionals, and bureaucrats joined shopowners and small businessmen in a growing middle class that favored the homogenization of culture through common schools and the credentials those schools promised to their children. Redding Sugg maintains that although the workingmen's groups of the 1830s opposed initiatives that contributed to the wealth of the privileged classes, they supported common schooling, expecting that it would equip the children of all classes to compete for the new wealth of the industrial society.[10] David Nassaw argues, however, that the workingmen's faith in education should not be confused with support for the common school, and he cites their criticisms of its excessive discipline, restriction of physical activity, irrelevant curricula, and mindless faculty as well as their support for such alternative forms as their own reading rooms and libraries, mechanics' institutes, lyceums, and lecture series.[11] At the same time, ancient barriers of class and gender operated to sabotage an alliance between working-class men and women and women of the new middle class. The alienation of working-class men from the common school and the support of middle-class women combined to strengthen the grip that the men of the middle and upper classes were to have over the shape and ends of public education.

It was during this period of economic and population expansion, when the average wage of even the unskilled worker increased steadily at the rate of roughly 1 percent a year, that middle-class women of the northeastern United States found themselves transformed from being producers to being the consumers of the nation's goods. This shift from an active to a relatively passive role was accomplished within the span of one generation, for in 1800 this country, North as well as South, could still have been considered an agricultural nation whose common productive unit was the domestic household. There women had been engaged in making the food, cloth, and other commodities their families required—the fabled, but actual, age of homespun. Between 1820 and 1840 the number of people engaged in manufacturing increased 127 percent, whereas those in agriculture increased only 79 percent. By 1840, two-thirds of the 1,200 cotton factories in the United States were operating in the Northeast, and women were buying homespun instead of making it.[12] The cottage industries that had permitted women to work within their own homes diminished as machinery drew labor into factories. Douglas maintains that in the new urban industrial centers like Massachusetts and New York there was no place for independent women. They were excluded by the newly emerging medical profession and appeared less often on public records as artisans or small business owners. During this antebellum period, we see the household emptied out as productive activity is shifted to public spaces. Fathers go to work. Mothers go shopping. Children (and their older sisters) go to the common school. In both rural communities and these new urban centers, teaching provided one of the few occupations, other than domestic service and work in the textile mills, open to women.

From Loom to Classroom   This shift from production to consumption, from loom to classroom, is explored in Robert Bullough's study of teaching in St. George, Utah, in the 1860s.[13] His account provides insight into the motives that led Martha Cox, a young Mormon, to choose teaching as her "calling." Her journals confess to her youthful frivolity and reveal the discussion she has with a man in her community that turned her to teaching, a choice that resembles religious conversion more closely than it does career planning:

> Whenever it happened that I awoke in time to get off to school in the morning I went. If too much of the morning was spent in restoring the strength lost from the night before, I stayed home and prepared for the dance on the following night or wove a few yards of cloth as many people still held to home weaving. The routine of my life was that of every other girl in school. . . .
>
> The words fell on me solemn-like and prophetic and I pondered on them deeply. "What profit is there finally" I said to myself, "in all this round of never ceasing labor? . . . in weaving more cloth to buy more dresses. When my day is past—my warp and woof of life and labors ended and my body gone to rest in the grave. What is there to mark the ground of which I trod? Nothing" and (sic) the thought made me weep.[14]

Martha is counseled by her friend and former teacher "Brother" McCarty to "Plant in the minds of men and the harvest will be different."[15] Bullough offers us Martha's own account of her struggle to become a teacher, to continue her own instruction, and to begin her own school. She starts off teaching the young children, but soon her journals record her efforts to bring those "idle marble players, my street boys," into the classroom and to control them once there. In pursuit of that end, she attends the classes of another St. George teacher, Richard Horne: "This was the best school of the town and the teacher was my ideal of what a teacher should be. Good governing ability—he had perfect order and much method."[16] Martha repudiates frivolity and domestic labor and attempts to master the disciplining of boys in order to draw them into the moral order of men. She not only adopts a new form of work but also converts the joy, expressiveness, and sensuality of her youth into the rule, recitations, and repressions of the patriarchal school.

Even before the 1820s, women had worked intermittently as teachers in the public schools, especially during summer when most of the men were busy farming. The men who taught in these schools were often itinerants, working to finance their own college educations or preparation for the ministry or the professions. Their average salary was $15.44 per month (including board), whereas their female counterparts earned $5.38 for the same work.[17] Terms were short, irregular, often suspended. Both men and women recruited to teach in the late eighteenth century were young, single, and sufficiently free of family responsibilities to engage in this undependable activity.

The most apparent explanation for the preponderance of women moving into teaching in the antebellum period is that a plethora of job opportunities became available to those young men who chose not to labor on the farms. Thomas Morain argues, as well, that as the teaching profession became more organized and formal preparation was required through attendance at a normal school or at a teacher's institute, those young men who were just teaching for a while to get by were loath to invest either time or money to gain accreditation.[18] Although the young women rarely stayed behind the desk too long, they had fewer options and acceded to the training requirements as they evolved.

Even though at no one point in the antebellum period did teaching employ more than 2 percent of all white women aged fifteen to sixty in Massachusetts, Richard Bernard and Maris Vinovskis have concluded that one out of five women living in that state during this period taught school at some time in her life.[19] The magnitude of this contact with the classroom for young women bridging the time between adolescence and their own motherhood suggests that not only did females influence the character of teaching but also that teaching in these schools at this time may have influenced the character of their femininity. Though we may deplore this contagion of patriarchal culture, Catharine Beecher celebrated the female teacher as carrier: "The great purpose in a woman's life—the happy superintendence of a family—is accomplished all the better and easier by preliminary teaching in school. All the power she may develop here will come in use there."[20]

Strictures against marriage combined with paltry salaries limited this work to young, single people who could supplement their pay by "boarding around," the practice that required the teacher to live in the home of one of her pupils where she received food and shelter and constant surveillance. Earning 60 percent less than their male counterparts, female teachers soon began to teach winter school as well, for their lower salaries made them attractive to employers. In the 1830s and 1840s, immigration brought many new pupils to urban centers without appreciably raising the tax base, and this cheaper and plentiful labor force of women was employed to stretch the education dollar across a burgeoning population. Some women left to work in the textile mills, where their teaching experience brought them high regard and higher salaries. There was little incentive to choose teaching as a lifetime career as contracts were extended by local boards for only one term at a time and the positions of principal or assistant principal were definitely closed to women.

In 1888, an investigator reporting to the Association for the Advancement of Women declared that, whereas 67 percent of the teachers in the country were women, only 4 percent of those with administrative responsibility were women.[21] Nevertheless, as Sheila Rothman points out, by the eighties and nineties there was a surplus of qualified teachers, and many of those who had jobs had begun to hold on to them. In 1888, the average tenure for women teachers in Indianapolis was eight years, and 27 percent of the female staff had taught for more than a decade. This presence of a pool of committed female educators prepared to fill administrative assignments suggests that the persistent exaggeration of the female teacher's transience was an atavism of the early years that became more instrumental than descriptive as it was used to rationalize the exclusion of women from positions of administrative responsibility.

Lower salaries for women hardly required the myth of transience for justification. The very figures who led the common school movement and supported the employment of female teachers are on record as supporting their recruitment with the argument that they were less costly than men. In drawing up a plan for Iowa's infant system in 1855, Horace Mann promoted the employment of women with a rationale of frugality.[22] It was Catharine Beecher, the founder of the Central Committee for Promoting National Education, who argued for the rigorous intellectual preparation of female teachers and for their placement in the new schools of the western states. Nevertheless, she too justified lower salaries for women. In 1853, in a petition to Congress asking for free normal schools for female teachers, Beecher wrote:

> To make education universal, it must be moderate in expense, and women can afford to teach for one half, or even less the salary which men would ask, because the female teacher has only to sustain herself; she does not look forward to the duty of supporting a family, should she marry; nor has she the ambition to amass a fortune.[23]

So it would appear that in a state like Massachusetts, where the textile industry and massive immigration brought 37,000 Irish immigrants to the city of Boston in the year 1847 alone, the middle-class woman was simultaneously displaced from her position as an active, self-reliant participant in a self-sufficient household and employed as a low-salaried, temporary pedagogue. She was hired to proclaim and maintain the order and the innocence of that vanished household in the face of industrial urbanization and the centralization of authority in the state.

The common school movement and the feminization of teaching colluded in support of a program of centralized education that exploited the status and integrity of the family to strip it of its authority and deliver its children to the state. Horace Mann, celebrating his own material success in moving from a rural to an urban culture, saw the common school as providing the work ethos and character building that he attributed to the moral training of his family. As a Whig legislator in Massachusetts, Mann had been an active member of both the Boston Society for the Prevention of Pauperism and the Prison Discipline Society. In the legislature he had supported the establishment of a state hospital for the insane and legislation licensing liquor sales. Revisionist historians like Feinberg and Nassaw have argued that nineteenth-century school reformers, ignoring the inequities and disruption caused by the new industrial order and a privileged class that supported its own affluence, shifted the onus of poverty and disorganization onto the character of the poor.[24] Working-class, farming, and immigrant children became, by definition, unfit to participate in the national ethos of self-discipline and productivity without the ministrations of the school. Mann, tired of rehabilitating their fathers in the prisons and asylums of the state, moved to adopt the children and to substitute a common state paternity for a distinct and particularly familial one. He asserted that "men are cast-iron; but children are wax. Strength expended upon the latter may be effectual, which would make no impression on the former."[25] Nassaw offers this 1853 statement of the Boston School Committee as evidence of the state's explicit program to usurp parental privilege:

> The parent is not the absolute owner of the child. The child is a member of a community, has certain rights, and is bound to perform certain duties, and so far as these relate to the public, Government has the same right to control over the child, that it has over the parent. . . . Those children should be brought within the jurisdiction of the Public Schools, from whom, through their vagrant habits, our property is most in danger, and so, of all others, most need the protecting power of the State.[26]

If Mann represents a benevolent paternalism that functioned to strip actual fathers of their authority and parental privilege, Catharine Beecher's attempt to rationalize maternity and to describe, classify, and organize it and thus extend it to the school deprived maternal nurturance of the very intimacy, vigor, and specificity that distinguishes the mother/child bond. In the name of womanhood, Beecher's ideology of self-sacrifice undermined familial resistance to the culture of the state and the factory. The eldest daughter of Lyman Beecher, a Calvinist minister, Catharine clearly identified with his power. The disestablishment of the church had, as Ann Douglas argues, forced the ministers to look beyond state governance for social structures that would support their moral programs, and Kathryn Sklar locates the model for Catharine's manipulation of domesticity in the service of education in her father's use of the family in the service of religion.[27] Accordingly, Catharine Beecher argued for placing educational responsibility in the hands of women, maintaining their submissiveness and elevating feminine self-sacrifice, purity, and domesticity into moral superiority that could be dispensed in schools. The good daughter had found a way to advance women into the public sphere without disturbing the dominance of the patriarchal authority. In her provocative study of Beecher, Sklar argues that the most important property of this new domestic space was its capacity to integrate personal and national goals. It fostered uniform communities, molded socially homogeneous human beings, and produced a set of predictable habits among contemporary Americans. To shape this collective character and at the same time to defend the virtues of self-reliance, freedom of choice, and independence of mind required considerable effort and ingenuity. Beecher gave lectures in the major cities of the East, was a prolific author of books and articles addressing the arts of domesticity and the education of women, and was an influential member of the elite struggling to articulate an American ethos, numbering among her friends and relatives Harriet Beecher and Calvin Stowe, Henry Ward Beecher, the Boston intelligentsia, Sarah Hale, Lydia Sigourney, and Horace Mann. Sklar notes the role that gender played in this project of moral suasion and social cohesion:

> Catharine Beecher was among the first to engage in the contradictory task of both nationalizing and personalizing the American domestic environment. Like others so engaged, she found the key to her task in gender roles. The dichotomies of masculine and feminine identity could be orchestrated to agree with both a standardized cultural score and a specialized personal calling. Womanhood could be designed to engage all one's creative energies, yet simultaneously to smooth the edges of one's regional, lineage, or class identities and to articulate the similarities one shared with other women. The same could be done for American manhood. In a nation tentatively evolving new democratic forms, gender roles were an effective way to channel the explosive potential of nineteenth-century social change and bring it at least partially under the control of a national elite.[28]

The women who poured into the common schools lived out this contradiction under the banner of maternal love and participated in a process of denial that Ann Douglas has labeled "sentimentalism":

> Sentimentalism is a complex phenomenon. It asserts that the values a society's activity denies are precisely the ones it cherishes; it attempts to deal with the phenomenon of cultural bifurcation by this manipulation of nostalgia. Sentimentalism provides a way to protest a power to which one has already in part capitulated. It is a form of dragging one's heels. It always borders on dishonesty but it is a dishonesty for which there is no known substitute in a capitalist country.[29]

What the society denied to the women of the nineteenth century was a vigorous, active motherhood. With one hand it took away the men and the children, and with the other it bestowed the cult of motherhood, replete with a rhetoric of false praise. In her foreword to Friedrich Froebel's (1878) collection of instructive songs and games entitled *Mother-Play and Nursery Songs*, Elizabeth Peabody (who was also Horace Mann's sister-in-law) glorified this passage to submissiveness:

> The only perfect guardian and cherisher of free self-activity is the mother's love, who respects it in her own child by an instinct deeper than all thought, restraining her own self-will, and calling out a voluntary obedience (the only obedience worthy of the name), because it proceeds from hearts that "the forms of young imagination have kept pure."[30]

Mother and child would form the perfect vessel. Into the constricted routine of the mother's domestic isolation would be poured the clear fluid of the child's inexperience. The education for this cult of motherhood required the mastery of self-denial, as this excerpt from the journal of a ten-year-old Louisa May Alcott indicates:

A Sample of Our Lessons

"What virtues do you wish more of?" asks Mr. L.

I answer:

Patience,	Love,	Silence,
Obedience,	Generosity,	Perseverance,
Industry,	Respect,	Self-denial.

"What vices less of?"

Idleness,	Wilfulness,	Vanity,
Impatience,	Impudence,	Pride,
Selfishness,	Activity,	Love of cats.[31]

The reward of this self-discipline was to be the calling of Motherhood. Elizabeth Harrison, another promoter of Froebel's philosophies and of the kindergarten movement, gilded submissiveness with these false titles: Motherhood "demands of woman her highest endeavor. . . . It demands of her that she become a physician, an artist, a teacher, a poet, a philosopher, a priest. In return, it gives her an insight into science, into history—into art, into literature, into human nature."[32]

This sentimentality, this rhetorically inflated and practically deflated function of mothering, was not an isolated phenomenon. Childhood caught it as well; its symptoms were innocence and cuteness. It escorted immigrant populations to urban centers as if it could shield their women and children from the complexity and confusion that pluralistic cities brought to families coming from European villages or from the small towns and farms of rural America.[33] The profound rupture created by the shift from farm to city was never mended; nor was it left behind or outgrown. It too became part of urban life, glimpsed in the growing schism between public and private, work and home, men and women, adults and children. It was extended into the distinctions that developed between the culture of the home and that of the workplace and was expressed in the differing expectations of the men, women, and children who spent their days in those spaces. Women were detained in their kitchens and nurseries, and their exile was as extensive and efficient as the taboo that the Ndembu place upon the presence of women during *Mukanda*, banishing them to their cooking fires on the periphery of the ritual grounds. Douglas underscores the contradictions implicit in this ideal woman:

> She was to exert moral pressure on a society in whose operations she had little part, and to spend money—or have it spent on her—in an economy she could not comprehend. . . . The lady's function in a capitalist society was to appropriate and preserve both the values and commodities which her competitive husband, father and son had little time to honor and enjoy. She was to provide an antidote and a purpose to their labor.[34]

The contradictions implicit in this image of the ideal woman and the ideal mother were extended into the training and work of the ideal teacher. The intimacy, spirituality, and innocence that teachers and students were to inherit from the mother/child bond—the prototype of their relationship—collapsed into strategies for control. The ideal teacher was one who could control the children and be controlled by her superiors. In 1867 visitors to Boston's Emerson School noted its exemplary order: "Every pupil appears to be in anxious waiting for the word of the teacher, and when issued it is promptly obeyed by the class. The movements and utterances of the class are as nearly simultaneous and similar as they can be."[35] Compliance was the key to success for teachers as well as for students, as this report of the Boston School Committee in 1841 attests: "They [female teachers] are less intent on scheming for future honors or emoluments [than men]. As a class they never look forward, as young men almost invariably do, to a period of legal emancipation from parental control."[36]

In 1870, women constituted 60 percent of the nation's teachers; by 1900, 70 percent; by 1910, 80 percent.[37] Figures from the mid-1970s indicate that 67.1 percent of all teachers are women. (The percentages in elementary teaching are 87 percent; in secondary they are 48 percent.) Teaching had become the shelter of the educated woman. It was a refuge both familiar and alien, a boardinghouse where she didn't make the rules and didn't even have her own key. From those early days of industrialization when the first women took a turn at a day school or summer school session to their majority in the teaching corps today, women teachers have been weighted down by this attribution of passivity and self-abnegation. In 1795 the Reverend John Bennett published a book of essays entitled *Strictures on Female Education* in which he enunciated the doctrine of docility and denial that still, I will argue, misrepresents both the women and the work.

> Their virtues, exercised in solitude and springing purely from the heart, make no noise, and court no observation. Lavished chiefly on their children and their friends, they blaze not on the world, nor are they thought of dignity or consequence enough to embellish the recording page. Still let not these degrading fair ones despond. . . . Many are the statesmen they have raised by their secret magic, into fame; and whenever they are tempted to repine at the appearance of weakness and inferiority it becomes them to remember that their greatest strength lies in their "weakness," their commands in their "tears."[38]

This was the sentimentalism that served to mute this culture's acknowledgment of the bargains it had made with expansion and industrialization. It had bartered the City upon a Hill for sprawling settlements, had substituted religious pluralism and voluntary participation for a tight Calvinistic order, had abandoned its kitchens as well as its plows for mill towns and cities. The feminization of teaching became a form of denial as the female teachers in the common schools demanded order in the name of sweetness, compelled moral rectitude in the name of recitation, citizenship in the name of silence, and asexuality in the name of manners.

Well, the times have changed. Two world wars drew women into factories and offices; the Great Depression marked an era when employment possibilities for men contracted. As social science laid claim to the child and identified the devoted mother as a threat to normal social development, the early twentieth century brought an attack on the very maternal solicitude that the nineteenth century had valorized. Nevertheless, the contradictions that evolved in the nineteenth century between the doctrine of maternal love and the practice of a harsh and regimented authority, between women's dominance in numbers and our exclusion from leadership, between the overwhelming presence of women in classrooms and the continuing identification of men as the only persons with the capacity to know, are still present in the culture of schooling. It is at this juncture that this discussion must turn from social realism to examine the psychoanalytic implications of these social conditions. History can offer us the figures on the gross national product, the ratio of male to female teachers, and the rhetoric of the Bennetts, the Beechers, the Manns, and the Peabodys, but it cannot tell us how the experiences symbolized by these signs were integrated into the daily lives and understandings of the women who lived them.

INFLUENCE OF GENDER

Ann Douglas has suggested that the cruelest aspect of oppression is the "logic by which it forces its objects to be oppressive in turn, to do the dirty work in their society in several senses."[39] This is the logic we need to understand, for women, through our work as mothers, as students, and as teachers, have contributed our labor and our children to institutional and social organizations that have extended our own subordination and contradicted our own experiences of nurturance. It has been widely argued that schooling supports the dominance of men in society first by exaggerating those characteristics that distinguish male from female gender and then by gradually establishing success norms that favor males, linking their achievements and world view to ideologies that dominate both the economy and the state.

Studies of the differential treatment given to male and female children in elementary school and secondary school classrooms, of the images of adult males and females in school texts, and of the bias in counseling and professional advancement that functions to hold women to certain academic disciplines and certain professions all provide evidence of sexism and the imposition of restrictions placed upon an individual in response to his or her sexual identity.[40] If sexism refers to the response of society to a particular sexual identity, gender refers to that sexual identity as it is experienced, acknowledged, and owned by the individual. Because gender is more intimately intertwined with consciousness than sexism, it is more difficult to specify and more difficult to study. Because it is related to an individual's experience and understanding of her own sexuality, gender is embodied. I concur with

Jean Elshtain's assertion that the ego is first a body ego, a necessary condition of personal identity.[41] The sexual difference is not a mere anatomical decoration on the surface structure of personality but central to that personality's experience of the world. Elshtain quotes Peter Winch: "masculinity and femininity are not just components in . . . life, they are its mode."[42]

Because it is embodied, because we are in Merleau-Ponty's terms body-subjects, because the body is our basis for consciousness and ultimately for having a world, gender appears to be natural whereas sexism is merely social.[43] What appears to be "natural" acquires the status of being fixed. We often conceive of the natural order as that order of physical reality (including, remarkably enough, our own bodies) that exists somehow outside the perception, language, and explanation processes that created the category "the natural." Because we experience the twinge, the pulse, the spasm, the touch, before we have time to name them regret, anxiety, fear, or love, we imagine that the names are the epiphenomena determined by these visceral responses. Freud has taught us to recognize the reciprocity of libido and culture, each shaping the other, so that there is no nature outside of culture, no culture that is not linked to the body. His analyses have helped us to question and challenge those prerogatives and positions that we considered natural.

An analysis of teaching cannot ignore teaching's association with femininity. And the influence of femininity cannot be limited to the imposition of sexism, as a study of the restrictions placed upon teachers who are women would illustrate. A gender analysis of teaching must strive to depict how women who are teachers experience our femininity in schools and how our sense of gender, in turn, influences our pedagogy and the curriculum of our classrooms. In order to understand the consequences of the feminization of teaching that occurred during the nineteenth century, we will need to examine feminine gender as a category that expresses multiple relations among people and among institutions, being most suspicious when its characteristics appear most natural. Furthermore, it will be useful to identify those attributes of femininity and pedagogy that became associated with each other during the period of rapid industrialization and urbanization when women took over the classroom. Although many of the economic and social conditions that accompanied the feminization of teaching no longer obtain, pedagogy and curriculum still bear the character of this era, and we carry in our bodies, in our smiles, our spasms, our dreams, responses to a world that is no longer ours. The sex/gender system that is expressed in our classrooms through contemporary forms of curriculum, classroom discourse, gesture, and theater is an atavism that expresses church/state, school/family, social class, and sexual politics more appropriate to the 1820s than the 1980s. By noting the historical origins of our current practices we do not succeed in exorcising them.

In his Marxist study of literary forms, Raymond Williams distinguishes the dead from the living past when he points to the difference between "archaic" and "residual" traditions: Whereas the archaic is recognized as belonging exclusively to an era that has ended, the residual participates in the active cultural processes of the present.[44] Though that participation may accommodate to the dominant culture as it is incorporated into it, other aspects of that residue may exist in opposition to that culture. Teaching, as I shall argue in Chapter 4, "Where the Line Is Drawn," shares many aspects of aesthetic practice, and curriculum also shares this historical property of literary forms, bearing both the burdens and the unrealized aspirations of another era. By attempting to recover the reproductive projects of the women who made teaching women's work, we may find not only the compromises and distortions that they endured but also the intentionality contained in their pedagogy, waiting for our realization.

I want to explore the notion that these contradictions surrounding the teaching practice of the first women to enter the profession in the early 1800s may have mirrored the issues in the development of their sense of their own womanhood. The early nineteenth century, as we have seen, was a time when centralized capital, industry, and city life split work and home and drew fathers away from their families for long periods of time. Chodorow asserts that, born into this configuration, children of both sexes will be matrisexual. Whereas male children are required in the oedipal crisis to repudiate this primary identification with their mothers, female children often extend that sense of identification and intimacy well into adult life. Whereas males achieve a sense of autonomy from their mothers (albeit at the cost of their access to the fluid, emotional expressiveness that characterized the preoedipal bond), the females turn to their fathers to escape an identification with their mothers that is stifling and denies their own autonomy. It would appear that at the onset of this industrial era, we find mothers and daughters of the middle class penned up in the preoedipal privacy of the parlor.

Fact and Fiction   Whereas industrialization encouraged some middle-class families to limit family size in order to provide their offspring with greater educational opportunities, persistent high fertility rates reflected economic opportunity in both urban and rural areas. It is possible to speculate that young women entering teaching in the antebellum period were not rushing to the classrooms in an excess of passion for the young. It is probable that they were trying to escape the passivity and dependency that the feminine ideal and the cult of motherhood conferred upon its daughters—or they may have been seeking the world of work in order to escape the child-care demands of a large family of siblings. Bernard and Vinovskis's study of the occupations of fathers of Massachusetts normal school students in 1859 suggests that students attending coeducational schools more often had fathers who were farmers than did students attending the all-female schools, whose fathers were more often employed as artisans or managers.[45] We might speculate that these girls who attended the all-female seminaries are the ones who would be most eager to appropriate the power of their fathers through the process of their own education and work in the public world, especially if the productive power of their fathers had not been a reality of their daily lives, as it might have been for the daughters of the farmers. Ironically, this distribution of students in the coed and all-female schools suggests that it may have been the female school that was most influential in purveying a patriarchal curriculum and purpose. It is possible to imagine that the cult of maternal nurturance celebrated by Mann, Beecher, Peabody, and others was hardly the ambition of these students. D. H. Lawrence drew such a daughter for us in *The Rainbow*, a novel in which he sketched the impact of industrialization on the lives of a family in an English village.[46] When seventeen-year-old Ursula Brangwen graduates from high school, she loathes "the close, physical, limited life of herded domesticity."

> Calm, placid, unshakable as ever, Mrs. Brangwen went about in her dominance of physical maternity. . . .
>   There were battles. Ursula would fight for the things that mattered to her. She would have the children less rude and tyrannical, she would have a place in the house. But her mother pulled her down, pulled her down.

Ursula would try to insist, in her own home, on the right of women to take equal place with men in the field of action and work.

"Ay," said the mother, "there's a good crop of stockings lying ripe for mending. Let that be your field of action."[47]

Hating her mother bitterly, Ursula confronts her parents and accepts a position teaching in a distant town.

She dreamed how she would make the little ugly children love her. She would be so personal. Teachers were always so hard and impersonal. There was no vivid relationship. She would make everything personal and vivid, she would give herself, she would give, give, give all her great stores of wealth to her children, she would make them so happy and they would prefer her to any teacher on the face of the earth.[48]

The bitterness of the school, the resistance of the children, the cynicism of the teachers overwhelm her.

She was tortured by the voice of Mr. Brunt. On it went, jarring harsh, full of hate, but so monotonous, it nearly drove her mad: always the same set, harsh monotony. . . . It was horrible—all hate! Must she be like this? She could feel the ghastly necessity. She must become the same—put away the personal self, become an instrument, an abstraction, working upon a certain material, the class, to achieve a set purpose of making them know so much each day. And she could not submit. Yet gradually she felt the invincible iron closing upon her. The sun was being blocked out.[49]

Failure to keep her post in this prison house would haunt her forever.

She did not believe that she could ever teach that great, brutish class, in that brutal school: ever, ever. And yet, if she failed, she must in some way go under. She must admit that the man's world was too strong for her, she could not take her place in it; she must go down before Mr. Harby. And all her life henceforth she must go on, never having freed herself of the man's world, never having achieved the freedom of the great world of responsible work.[50]

After struggling for control, she thrashes a student who had defied her, subduing him after a desperate and vicious struggle.

Ursula would appeal no more to the headmaster, but when she was driven wild, she seized her cane, and slashed the boy who was insolent to her, over head and ears and hands. And at length they were afraid of her, she had them in order. . . . But she had paid a great price out of her own soul to do this. It seemed as if a great flame had gone through her and burnt her sensitive tissue. She who shrank from the thought of physical suffering in any form had been forced to fight and beat with a cane and rouse all her instincts to hurt. And afterwards she had been forced to endure the sound of their blubbering and desolation, when she had broken them to order. . . . Oh, why, why had she leagued herself to this evil system where she must brutalize herself to live? Why had she become a school teacher, why, why?

. . . She was not going to be put down, prevented from standing free. It was not to be asked of her, she could not take her place and carry out her task. She would fight and hold her place in this state also, in the world of work and man's convention.

She was isolated now from the life of her childhood, a foreigner in a new life, of work and mechanical consideration.[51]

Bearing the gift of maternal nurturance, Ursula enters the school and succeeds there only to the degree that she suspends nurturance and adopts control. Lawrence draws this issue to a critical moment by requiring his heroine to beat a recalcitrant and provocative student into submission. No stranger to passion, Lawrence is able to reveal the other side of maternal love in all its sordid vigor. Ursula's success violates her sensibilities, severs her sense of connection with the past by cutting her off from her own childhood as well as from her present as she splits teaching away from the rest of her life in order to endure. Lawrence's fiction makes no attempt to euphemize the dehumanization that is suffered by teacher and student alike, for it was Lawrence's project to give those passions a name that the sentimentalism of his era had silenced.

The Rainbow provides its protagonist and its reader with a truer image of teaching, I suspect, than we find in the records of those actually engaged in this endeavor. The journals of Cyrus Peirce, the principal of the first normal school in this country, founded in 1839 in Lexington, Massachusetts, under the sponsorship of Horace Mann, and of Mary Swift, his student, provide a double image of the classroom experience of the women introduced to teaching in the heyday of the common school. Peirce obviously had access to Mary's journal, but she, of course, had none to his. Peirce, we are told by Arthur Norton, editor of the volume, was an excellent disciplinarian: "As a beginner, he secured order after the usual fashion of the day—a liberal use of the rod. As a more experienced teacher, however, he abandoned flogging, and used moral suasion with equal success."[52] According to Norton, the normal school pupils were encouraged by Peirce to adopt this same method of moral suasion: "They must be moved by a *pure and lofty desire* of doing good. They must be intelligent, discerning. They must be firm, consistent, uniformly patient, uniformly kind."[53] Peirce's own reflections on teaching these normalites appear to be neither patient nor kind. Most of the journal is composed of his complaints. He finds the students ill-prepared in the common branches, lacking language, interest in studies, and a sense of order. He is annoyed when they want to go home but ends up wishing that many of them would. He describes them as a "lumpish set of scholars," lazy, distracted, frivolous.

> Monday, Dec. 14—a day which were it lawful, one would gladly blot from the school calendar.
> Heard one [of] my pupils this day talking about Combe's Physiology being "dry," "so dry." Dry! Combe's Physiology dry! If it were dry as a seared leaf, I am sure there is sap enough in her soft head to moisten it.[54]

I do not begrudge Father Peirce, as the girls called him, his exasperation. He was running a normal school for young women (many of whom were away from their own homes and families for the first time), was continually receiving visitors eager to take the pulse of this experiment, and was teaching reading, writing, arithmetic, astronomy, geometry, algebra, natural history and moral philosophy, mental philosophy, Combe's physiology, ancient geography, rhetoric, political economy, and botany as well as the principles of pedagogy and school governance (not to exclude mention of a topic called Ment. Excitement)—grounds for exasperation. Nevertheless, in his accounts of his lectures and in Mary Swift's copious notes on those lectures, there is no acknowledgment of his very real and justified distress. His frustration, almost desperation, is denied, and this mystification of the actual experience of teaching is extended into his presentation of the professional ethos to his impressionable students. Teaching is presented as pure altruism: "The question to be asked is, how the best good can be obtained by others and not ourselves."[55] He lists the desirable qualities of teachers as health, good standing in the community, a well-balanced mind "free from eccentricities and the infirmities of genius," deep interest in children, patience, mildness, firmness and perfect self-control, and a high sense of moral responsibility. Hassled, fatigued, desperate, he tells his students that "the work of education is the work of order. Order was Heaven's first law." Mary Swift dutifully records these lectures and many others without comment. Her only responses seem to have been expressed in the frequent headaches she reports.

Father Peirce, himself a former minister, compels compliance with a tedious and demanding regimen. The issues of resistance, defiance, and guilt that rage through his own journal are denied to his students, who are instructed to find within themselves a deep well of patience, obedience, self-abnegation, and loving-kindness. It is probable that the thousands of young women who taught in the common schools, with or without benefit of normal school education, accepted the rhetoric of nurturance, expecting to mollify the reluctant student with earnest affection and good intention. I suspect that the many women who must have failed either returned to their parents' homes or fled to the shelter of their husbands' kitchens, chastened and humiliated, interpreting their failure as proof of their own frailty, weakness of will, and essential incapacity to function in the man's world. The cult of maternal nurturance prohibited those who stayed behind the desk from confessing their rage, frustration, and disappointment to each other. The moralistic and impossible demand that women, without expressing anger or aggression, control children who were resisting a tightly repressive and tedious regime encouraged teachers to confuse the logical consequences of these harsh conditions for the failure of their own discipline, intelligence, and inspiration.

Sentimentality versus Reality   The predictable incapacity of the loving teacher to save society through the example of her own submissiveness led to an inevitable failure—a failure of moral fiber, a failure of femininity, a failure of professionalism. It is no wonder that those recalcitrant students who were reluctant worshipers at the altar of maternal love (otherwise known as the tedious and strict classroom of the common school) were branded as deficient, if not pathological, in order to share this burden of blame. As Catharine Beecher assumed meekness and orderliness to be essential properties of femininity, so teachers were quick to stigmatize those students who were not meek and orderly with class and ethnic and racial deficiencies. Blind to the class specificity associated with this ideal of feminine gender and with its denial of eroticism, of anger, of ambition, women of all classes who ventured into teaching must have experienced the collision of their needs, personalities, and expectations with this feminine version of the Protestant ethic. We find the doctrine of self-control and denial of emotions extended into those traits listed as desirable in the 1928 *Common-wealth Teacher-Training Study*:

Traits which serve as example to pupils. Striving systematically to set pupils a good example; exercising self-control in the face of irritation; being polite and courteous to impolite pupils; being on time when pupils are detained by other teachers; setting an example of openmindedness by setting prejudices aside.

Traits involved in winning of pupils' respect. Keeping one's temper, re-pressing anger, irritation, desire to punish; not waiting for pupils to start something, taking initiative, seizing opportunities to show command of the situation; avoid confidences, maintaining reserve, preserving dignity without being unfriendly.

Traits involved in maintaining friendly relations with pupils. Taking gen-uine personal interest in pupils' problems; listening to pupils' grievances, expressing sympathy at appropriate times; being tactful with pupils who are antagonistic; doing good turns for pupils, being generous and for-giving toward petty offenses; keeping cheerful, looking happy when feel-ing otherwise; indulging in good natured kidding within proper limits; dropping classroom manners out of class.[56]

For those seeking independence from maternal authority, the pater-nal authority of the principal, the normal school instructor, the minis-ter on the Board of Visitors offered an attractive if chimerical alterna-tive. The urge to gain paternal approval may have undermined the support that the normalites were prepared to extend to each other, as it was paternal sanction that promised their continued presence in the world of work rather than a collective spirit and solidarity.

The father/daughter relation of the department head, principal, or superintendent to the teacher functioned to deny their eroticism and extend her infantilization. The cult of maternal nurturance ignored female sexuality, oblivious to the erotic gratifications of maternity and the sensual and sexual life of the young women it kept under constant surveillance. The teacher was expected to banish sensuality from the classroom and from her life. The repudiation of the body was a blight that fell upon the curriculum as well, severing mind from body and draining the curriculum of the body's contributions to cognition, aes-thetics, and community as realized through its capacity for sensuality, for movement, and for work.

I have argued that our reproductive projects are contradicted and extended into curriculum as we, men and women, look to education to reverse our initial relations to our children. Women, intertwined with our children and our mothers in biologically and emotionally symbiotic relationships, have seen education as differentiation, a gradual growth in independence. Men, troubled by the inferential character of paternity, have sought to extend their claim on the child through strategies of influence and control.

An ironic reversal may have been operating for the male educational administrators and theorists as well as for the female practitioners. Sugg suggests that Horace Mann's preference for female teachers and an ideal of gentle, loving influence was a reaction against the harsh Calvinism of Nathanael Emmons, the powerful minister of his boyhood. Associating Emmons's severity with pure intellect, Mann preferred to match the "milk and gentle manners of women to the tenderness of childhood."[57] It is possible that the feminization of teaching was originally located at the crossroads of masculine and feminine projects to rectify their own object relations. Cut off from their mothers by the harsh masculine authority of church and fathers, theorists like Mann sought the reclamation of mother love by promoting women as teachers of the young. Overwhelmed by the presence of their mothers, women entered teaching in order to gain access to the power and prerogatives of their fathers.

This thesis, which suggests the desire of the male to reclaim the early preoedipal intimacy with his mother, was dutifully inscribed in Mary Swift's journal as she took notes at the Middlesex County School Convention, which she attended on December 26, 1839, in Waltham, Massachusetts. The notes that follow were taken from Horace Mann's address to that assembly: "Special Preparation a Pre-requisite for Teaching." Mann moves from his reference to family resistance to the common school to the praise of women as teachers of young children. The transitional utility of their feminine graces is revealed in the pedagogical practices he prescribes.

> Many are unwilling to send their children to the public schools, because they are subject so much to the town.—They ask; why is all this interference in schools, the choice of books, times of attendence, &c. The[y] consider the school committee as an obtrusion—They say are not the children our own?—These questions are honestly put, and should be soberly answered.—Children are carried forth by the tide of nature and will soon be men; they will soon have the rights of citizenship, & will become blessings or curses, to society.—The world receives them as they

are and has no option to accept or reject. . . . In merchandise we pay for an article, and we expect it to be good; if it is not we have a right to return it.—On the contrary after twenty one years from birth society must receive him.—In this state a far larger number of females are employed than males; the proportion being about three to two.—In Prussia, the reverse is true.—They are best for young children—They have much feeling, & if not exerted it must lie dormant—Is she not fitted to commence the first work in the Temple of Education?—After a child's mind has become tough, then let it be subjected to the firm grasp of the masculine hand. Why then should woman put off her form of Seraph, and assume the [ways] of man? To be the former of a great mind, is as much greater as to be creator, instead of created. . . . The fact that success depends on practise is shown by the teaching of brute animals.—Two things are necessary for a teacher; a knowledge of the properties, qualities & powers of the mind, and the means of controlling them. . . . "Train up a child in the way he should go" is this same principle as train means drill.—Every teacher should have a tact at explanation, but it is not to be used too often. . . . He should know how to touch the right spring, in the right manner, & at the right time.[58]

So male educators invited women into the schools expecting to reclaim their mothers, and the women accepted the invitation and came so that they might identify with their fathers. Accordingly, female teachers complied with the rationalization and bureaucratization that pervaded the common schools as the industrial culture saturated the urban areas. Rather than emulate the continuous and extended relation of a mother and her maturing child, they acquiesced to the graded schools—to working with one age group for one year at a time. Rather than demand the extended relation that would bind them over time to individual children, they agreed to large group instruction where the power of the peer collective was at least as powerful as the mother/child bond. Deprived of the classical education that most of the males who organized the schools enjoyed, normalites accepted the curriculum as bestowed, and deviations from it remained in the privacy of the classroom and were not presented to principals or committees of visitors.

In the 1970s Dan Lortie's research identified these three themes within the ethos of American classroom teachers: individualism, conservatism, and presentism.[59] The familial and economic situations of the young women who took over the classrooms provided the context for all three of these conditions. The motive to differentiate themselves from their mothers and from the cult of maternal nurturance encouraged individualism. The motive to identify with their fathers encouraged a conservatism that accepted the epistemological and social configurations of schooling as given. The exclusion from administrative positions discouraged career planning and encouraged the acceptance of short-range goals and identification with the immediacy of the classroom context.

What a view, even cursory, of contemporary schools suggests is that the feminization of teaching and the cult of maternal nurturance did little to introduce the atmosphere of the home or the integrity and specificity of the mother/child relationship into schools. Dominated by kits and dittos, increasingly mechanized and impersonal, most of our classrooms cannot sustain human relationships of sufficient intimacy to support the risks, the trust, and the expression that learning requires.

Furthermore, the gender contradictions, the simultaneous assertion and denial of femininity, have served to estrange teachers of children from the mothers of those children. Instead of being allies, mothers and teachers distrust each other. Bearing credentials of a profession that claimed the colors of motherhood and then systematically delivered the children over to the language, rules, and relations of the patriarchy, teachers understandably feel uneasy, mothers suspicious. Their estrangement leaves a gap in school governance that the professional administrators, the state, and textbook publishers rush in to fill. Until teachers and mothers acknowledge the ways in which schools perpetuate the asymmetry in class privilege and gender that is present in both the home and the workplace, they will not interrupt the patterns of their own complicity.

The promise that women would bring maternal nurturance into schools was sheer sentimentality, as it denied both the aspirations of the common school movement and the motives of those women who came to its classrooms in order to escape the horrifying isolation of domestic exile. Similarly, the ethos of equality associated with the common schools repeated the sentimental denial of the class identities and affiliations of the women who were teachers. The cult of motherhood was primarily a middle-class ethos. It did not include nor did it countenance the interests of the classes that industrialization and immigration were creating within the nation. Helpless to raise our own class status through our work, female teachers may be the least-equipped persons in our society to show students how to bridge the distance between effort and social status.

The feminization of teaching is hardly a process that confirms the rhetoric of Horace Mann, Catharine Beecher, or Cyrus Peirce. We need to read Mary Swift's other journal, the one she didn't hand in to Father Peirce. We need to acknowledge that, even as we celebrated their maternal gifts, we have required women to draw children out of the intimacy and knowledge of the family into the categorical and public world. We have burdened the teaching profession with contradictions and betrayals that have alienated teachers from our own experience, from our bodies, our memories, our dreams, from each other, from children, and from our sisters who are mothers to those children. Perhaps it is time for women who call ourselves educators to question our participation and practice in the schools. We might start with the questions Virginia Woolf asked in 1938:

> The questions that we have to ask and to answer about the academic procession during this moment of transition are so important that they may well change the lives of all men and women forever. For we have to ask ourselves, here and now, do we wish to join that procession, or don't we? On what terms shall we join that procession? Above all, where is it leading us, the procession of educated men? . . . Let us never cease from thinking,—what is this "civilization" in which we find ourselves? What are these ceremonies and why should we take part in them? What are these professions and why should we make money out of them? Where in short is it leading us, the procession of the sons of educated men?[60]

The optimism of the industrial era has since dissipated in the steam of the soup kitchens, but the common school endures. Its assaults on the family, on nurturance, and on domesticity linger in PTA meetings reduced to planning the Teacher Recognition Day luncheon, in the space and time of the school day, in the substitution of "individualized" busywork for problem solving and communication. Its misogyny flourishes when school failure is attributed to divorce rates, working mothers, and single-parent families.

Woolf's questions are not new to teachers. They are implicit in the resistance to administrators and experts who pontificate on topics in education but spend no time in classrooms. When Woolf's suspicions are translated into a defensive passive resistance by uneasy teachers, they lead us into emotional and intellectual stasis and reinforce our isolation from the community and from each other. When we attempt to rectify our humiliating situation by emulating the protectionism and elitism of the other "professions," we subscribe to patriarchy's contempt for the familiar, for the personal . . . for us. But if we seem immersed in this civilization, we must remember too that we are the mistresses of its ceremonies. Stigmatized as "women's work," teaching rests waiting for us to reclaim it and transform it into the work of women.[61]

3 Feminism and the
Phenomenology of the Familiar

In 1972 Colin Greer characterized historiography from
"E. P. Cubberly to Lawrence Cremin, from 1900 to 1965," as "filiopie-
tist, parochial and narrowly institutional."[1] Accusing the history of
education of masking the conservatism of schooling in the myth of the
"American Dream," Greer called for a revisionist account that would
address the actual practice of education and not merely the claims of its
theorists and apologists. He called for a history that would incorporate
the experience of those the school did not serve: its dropouts rather
than its valedictorian, its teachers rather than its superintendent. As
social historians work from documents that challenge the speeches and
reports of the Pooh-Bahs and potentates, problems of interpretation
proliferate. Multiple accounts demand that we reconcile the endurance
of cultural myths with accounts of experience that contradict them.
When cultural myths persist in the very journals, letters, and shopping
lists of those whose interests they appear to contradict, interpretation
becomes even more difficult.

But the present is hardly more transparent to our inquiring gaze than
the past. We have all come to form within the very forms we wish to
study. And so it is difficult to separate the well-taught consciousness
from the consciousness that teaches. If we ask women who teach to talk
about their work in the language that dominates the discourse of
schooling, we invite language that celebrates system and denies doubt,
that touts objectives and denies ambivalence, that confesses frustration
but withholds love.

That was also the language, Ivor Goodson and Stephen Ball argue,
that dominated research studies of teaching. "In the 1960s teachers
were shadowy figures on the educational landscape, . . . represented in
aggregate through imprecise statistics or . . . viewed as individuals only
as formal role incumbents mechanistically and unproblematically re-

sponding to the powerful expectations of their role set."[2] As sociologists turned to case studies and ethnomethodology to grasp both subjectivity and its situation, curriculum theorists too turned from the systems assumptions of the Tyler rationale to bring the specificity and creativity of human consciousness to the discourse of schooling. Sharing the revisionist persuasion that the study of schooling required new texts and methods of interpretation, reconceptualist curriculum theorists James Macdonald, Dwayne Huebner, Maxine Greene, and Michael Apple addressed the epistemological and ontological assumptions, material and social interests, present in curriculum practice and research.[3] Calling out, talking out of turn, these critics invoked Heidegger, Sartre, and Habermas, bringing existentialism's repudiation of the familiar and critical theory's exposure of its motives to the language of curriculum and teaching. As their work evoked the whispers and melodies of language we could not hear, it filled us with nostalgia for a world we have never known.

Although William Pinar also cited the poets and philosophers to support his critique of role theory and of schooling's dehumanizing process of socialization, he extended his critique into a method for writing and reading texts of educational experience that located alternative codes and visions for curriculum within the daily experience of teachers and students.[4] In our work with autobiographical texts of educational experience, Pinar and I have substituted hermeneutics for the positivism of the social sciences that still dominate curriculum research.[5] As we concur with Richard Rorty's claim that hermeneutics has displaced epistemology by providing another politic for scholarship that refuses the dichotomization of subject and object, we invite endless problems of interpretation, not as impostors at the banquet planned for the truth but, indeed, as the guests of honor.[6]

As I continue to work with teachers' autobiographical texts, I continue to worry about the narrative forms that contain and shape them and the interpretive methods I use to understand them, and I tinker with them like a technician.[7] I look through the lens of feminist theory to find shadows sliding across the face of texts that, given our current ideologies, seem clear and thus persuasive.

For the source of light, like human knowledge, is always situated, here or there, rising or setting, or just breaking through as the clouds pass. The figure is never fully illuminated. Light moves through time as well as space, and so clear seeing is burdened with all the limitations of human consciousness, always situated in spatial perspectives and temporal phases. Furthermore, our work, no matter what its form, is not the seeing itself but a picture of the seeing. Some of us become fascinated with our own light equipment, checking our meters, our spots, our kliegs and gels, and we stumble into the diffuse light of our life worlds like Sartre's actor Kean, who, leaving the deep shadows and brilliant lights of the theater, is dismayed to find how flat real light is.[8]

So it is the shadow of the experience of teaching that we pursue here, hoping that as we catch a glimpse of its distortions and of the ground on which it falls, mingling the human figure with roots, rocks, curbs, and stairwells, we shall address the relation between what appears and what is hidden in autobiographical accounts of teaching. And because so many teachers are women working in the shadows cast by the institutions of the public world and the disciplines of knowledge, I read their narratives to draw our life worlds out of obscurity so we may bring our experience to the patriarchal descriptions that constitute our sense of what it means to know, to nurture, to think, to succeed. Finally, I look through phenomenology to read the intentionality in these texts, seeking meaning not only in story but also in the dance of the body-subject through the prereflective landscape nestled in the shadows of the text.

You may have noticed that people wince when a colleague announces an interest in phenomenology. Sometimes they wince because they do not know what the word means and, confusing it with phrenology, they fear a laying on of hands. Sometimes they wince at the effort of not losing one of its many middle syllables along the way of utterance. But when our colleagues know what the word is they never wince. For a wince is an involuntary expression of pain, a crinkle of vulnerability around the eyes, a fleeting impulse to fold up your face like an accordion. Those in the know rarely wince. Forewarned and defended, they act as if they have nothing to fear and open their eyes and raise their eyebrows as if phenomenology were merely an amusing, if oddly irrelevant, distraction. But they can't fool us. They are terrified, for what phenomenologists do is not only an assault on the methodology of the social sciences; phenomenology displaces the very world that social science addresses. After all, if I designate the ground of my inquiry as the life world, you can imagine what you're left to work with.

If we are strict constructionists in the tradition of Husserl, we sweep away the work of traditional social science as if it were a heap of leftover assumptions. If we are loose constructionists following Heidegger, we are contemptuous of our colleagues' positivism and display our engaged inquiries as evidence of our superior sensibilities and humanity. No wonder we are not popular.

Lest it sound as if I am describing pretensions that I do not share, let me be clear that this is my story too. When I was in graduate school, social science was the ground against which I located and established my own position. Then I was a strict constructionist, taking delight whenever I could detect an errant assumption dipping below the hemline of the positivists' surveys and chi squares. When I tired of playing coroner to their corpses, I too turned to the life world, quickly loosening my interpretation of the *epoche* so that I could do something with it. So I am arguing that phenomenology originates in acts of negation as we repudiate the methods of social science and of institutional knowledge.

The word "institution" comes from the Latin verb, *instituere*, which means "to set up." The root of that verb is the same as the root of stature and state. It is *stare*, meaning "to stand." And it is our upright posture, argues Erwin Straus in "The Upright Posture," that privileges sight instead of touch, an imposture of rationality that ranks structural abstraction above textured detail as the highest achievement of human cognition.[9] Now, as a partial response to the Sphinx who asks, "What walks on four legs in the morning, two legs in the afternoon, and three legs in the evening?" we can, with Oedipus, reply that the child is the four-legged creature, close to "Mother Earth" and to the sensuality of "pronecreation."[10] Children and the women who bear them have never had the status of men, excluded from the institutions, the standards, and the state that insure patriarchal privilege. And, as Mary O'Brien has shown in her critique of political thought, women do not even appear in the theories constructed to deconstruct the institutions, the standards, and the state.[11] Only men, according to Hegel and Marx, can attain second nature, the rational culture of the upstanding citizen. That consciousness is achieved through labor, and neither theorist, O'Brien argues, is willing to recognize the work that women contribute to child rearing as real, honest-to-goodness, social, material labor.[12] This exclusion is supported by Freud, as well, in his assumption that women, less scarred by the desire, castration fear, and ultimate identification with power that emerges from the male oedipal crisis, would identify with society only provisionally, failing to develop the collective superego that brands male consciousness with a C for citizen.

Although classic idealism, the Enlightenment, monotheistic traditions of Judeo-Christian thought, and Victorian sublimations can all be invoked to explain the limits of these theorists' imagination of female consciousness, it is interesting to note a similar theme in contemporary curriculum theory. Fascinated by the factory and the corporation, the so-called Left in curriculum theory reduced reproduction to education's generation of laborers. Their reproduction story was a story about how factories and corporations and schools came together to make people, a correspondence version of the Immaculate Conception. Ultimately embarrassed by the passivity attributed to teachers, students, and their families by this process/product paradigm, they discovered resistance, which, when stripped of its romantic associations with Sartre, Camus, and grade-B World War II movies, usually meant lying down on the job.

Entering the field in the midseventies, a grown-up woman filled with the sights and sounds and needs of my three children, I was struck with the absence in theory, research, and practice of the commitments, logic, and contradictions that plague female consciousness. It was still the Sphinx's world of four-legged and two-legged creatures; babies and animals cavorted in it in the morning, men took over in the afternoon. What of the women who cared for the babies but were neither as up nor as right as their upright men? Like the child, like the wild, women, we are told, are supposed to be context-dependent, hugging the horizontal. At what cost did we uphold the curriculum as teachers? Through what repressions did we subordinate our own experience of reproduction, of labor, of value, of relation to the institutions, the standards, the state? Accordingly, I was drawn to phenomenology's texture and presence, too short, or bent, to appreciate systems theories, the structure of the disciplines, behavioral objectives, or other tall tales that towered over curriculum theory in the seventies.

Phenomenology took me home and extended the horizons of educational theory to embrace the passion, politics, and labor of reproduction. I was not the only one of us to turn to the life world of the family to understand the child and our own understandings of education. For many of us the family is the place of feeling. There sound and touch compete with sight. Sensual, engaged, caring, it appears to offer us a first nature much richer than the culture of the public world, and we fall to the task of describing it with earnest effort.[13] Because the family is the first nature for all of us, because its politic is threaded through our bodies, separating ourselves from our assumptions about our mothers, our fathers, our own children, our spouses, is like separating ourselves from breath, from hunger, and from sleep. The very act of description is a naming that splits the fusion of intimacy into words for the stranger. And the memory of that primal intimacy is under language, burdened with the weight of loss and the disguises of repression. Here is the methodological dilemma this chapter addresses. How do we grasp the life world of family relations and of reproduction without falling into the sentimentality of the immigrants who can only remember how wonderful everything was in the old country? Tied to the constraints of the phenomena—that which appears to consciousness—how could the phenomenologist cope with the sentimentalism that so sweetens our sense of reproduction that we can neither discern its ingredients nor metabolize it in our theory?

Now, it is reasonable to assume that feminists and phenomenologists share a common project to describe subject/object relations with a clarity that dispels ideology. The phenomenologist is committed to showing how subjectivity and objectivity are reciprocal, constituting both person and world. Phenomenology's search for the ground of knowledge and meaning always leads to reflection on the relation of the knowing subject to the object of consciousness. Feminism's hospitality to object relations theory is drawn from the understanding that the development of gender is not an isolated process but intrinsically related to and contingent upon the processes of becoming a knowing subject in a particular set of relations filled with desire, need, and love. Meredith Skura suggests that the distinction between psychoanalysis and phenomenology may no longer be as clear as it once was:

> Psychoanalysis began as a study of the instincts, then widened to include defensive battles about instinct, and has gone on to encompass the whole person and his relation to the natural and social world. Analysts are now interested in tracing the emergence of the whole "self" and sense of reality, from its earliest infantile archetypes to its current phenomenology.[14]

The family should be the obvious place for such studies, and we would expect to find phenomenologists and feminists huddled around the kitchen table, but in the last few years we have seen feminists rushing from the family just as phenomenologists were rushing toward it. We have avoided crashing into each other because we have defined our discourses as mutually exclusive. Feminists see phenomenology as naively apolitical and its exclusion of psychoanalytic theory as a refusal to acknowledge desire in the constitution of knowledge, communication, and gender. Phenomenologists see feminists as ideological, imposing a political or psychoanalytic determinism on their accounts of "the things themselves." We have much to learn from each other. Phenomenology can correct a feminist's temptation to lie to herself about feeling and affiliation in order to deny the constraints of attachment. The feminist can correct the phenomenologist's refusal to remove the veils of repression that psychoanalytic theory has revealed.

For the family, the child, are, finally, like the institution, setups. The phenomenologist cannot crawl back there on four legs, for it is a romantic fantasy that desires such a recapitulation of wordless intimacy. Nor can we stand on two legs, like an upright anthropologist in the midst of the kitchen, dividing the contents of the refrigerator into the raw and the cooked. The riddle of the Sphinx leaves one more option. What walks on four legs in the morning, two legs in the afternoon, and three legs at night? The third leg, like the old man's cane, must mediate the dichotomies that have divided us from our theory and from our experience. It is the old man, softer, wiser, not so upright, who knows like a woman. Women are three-legged creatures; neither babies nor men, women need a dialectical phenomenology that moves back and forth between the world as it appears to us and the world we refuse to see. We need a mediating method that stretches between lived phenomena and an ideology of family life to help us diminish the distance between the private and public poles of our experience. For the world we feel, the world we remember, is also the world we make up. The place that is familiar can be the place where we are most lost. That is what Emily Dickinson understood in this letter written in the spring of 1883 soon after the death of her mother:

Dear Friend,
. . . All is faint indeed without our vanished mother, who achieved in sweetness what she lost in strength, though grief of wonder at her fate makes the winter short, and each night I reach finds my lungs more breathless, seeking what it means. . . .

> Fashioning what she is,
> Fathoming what she was,
> We deem we dream—

And that dissolves the days
Through which existence strays
Homeless at home.[15]

THE TEXT

Existence strays through three autobiographical accounts written by the teacher Jane McCabe.[16] In the philosophy of education course that I was teaching, Jane and the other graduate students had each been asked to provide three narratives of events or moments in their lives that they associated with the phrase "educational experience." We had read Joan Didion's essay, "On Keeping a Notebook," together and had taken her distinction between *what happened* and *what it means to me* as the space that these stories would fill.[17] Fidelity rather than truth is the measure of these tales.[18] But fidelity does not imply being faithful to a continuous and consistent ego identity. William Earle urges us to think of the composing ego as an index rather than an identity.[19] The "I" of autobiographical consciousness, he tells us, is an index to a subjectivity that is always open to new possibilities of expression and realization.[20] The "I" is the location of a stream of possibilities. So there is no search for the hypostatizing and romantic ego themes of the sixties, no genuine, authentic, real, deep-down selves we seek in these texts. Altieri celebrates this repudiation of idealism in Nietzsche, whose autobiographical narratives were constructed, Altieri argues, to expose idealizations constructed to deny responsibility for the sense we make of ourselves, our work, our world:

> Thus traditional philosophy can be seen as a willful attempt to posit a principle of authority which one then appears to discover as an objective principle for controlling the will. If this situation is to be even partially changed, the philosopher must turn from truth to truthfulness. Truthfulness provides an immediate state of personal expression. Thus it affords a measure of the relation between thinking and existential conditions because it tests the powers ideas confer for living a certain kind of life. Philosophy, and autobiography, must prove their worth as forms of power. And one basic index of power is how fully one can consciously "become what one is"—Nietzsche's subtitle—precisely by avoiding the delusions of ideal truths and noble rational selves in pursuit of those truths. To the extent that fantasies of power go unacknowledged or get denied on unspecified methodological grounds, ideas of reason are the

most pernicious enemy to true thinking and to the possibility of people taking responsibility for themselves. By pursuing ideals one stages oneself as what one is not.[21]

If subjectivity is invited to be multiple, varied, and still coherent, objectivity, that which is related to yet other than consciousness, is also fluid. Categorical meanings are suspended wherever possible in the composing process, of these narratives for we are seeking not an illustration of our categories but the dialectical interplay of our experience in the world and our ways of thinking about it. In this way the literary narrative that is autobiography resembles the social event that is curriculum: Both function as mediating forms that gather the categorical and the accidental, the anticipated and the unexpected, the individual and the collective. The gap or error or surprise that erupts in the midst of the well-made text is what deconstructionists seek, not to embarrass the author of the erratum but to demonstrate that the power of the person, the text, the meaning, is spurious when we impute to it an utterly consistent, exclusive, bounded, and delineated logic.

Separated from the world, from other people and other texts, such meanings, whether they emerge as persons or texts, can be easily objectified, bound, named, possessed, bought, and sold. Their separateness is necessary to their commodification. These days "teacher thinking" is a hot number. But if the text is to display teacher thinking for the thought of the teacher, for her reflection and interpretation, rather than for someone else's utilization and marketing, then the gaps, the contradictions, the leaks and explosions in the text are invitations to her own self-interpreting and self-determining reading.

It is the ambiguity of self-determination that initiates Jane McCabe's first story.

July 1980. Sunapee, New Hampshire

Free, white and twenty-one! I remember those words my grandfather used implying the world was his oyster. I remember him as not a very free spirit but rather a seeker of independence in thought as well as deed. He used to paint lovely free-form birds on the walls of the back room of his farmhouse—always blue and never attached to anything. I invariably glanced at them on my way through the room, taken with their fluidity and the fact that my own grandpa could, would, do such a thing. And, he used to smell of the molasses he sheeted by the panful on the hay in the barn. He sat for hours on the front porch, cool and still.

These reflections were a part of that July day as I sat on the steps of the timeworn cabin by the lake. My youngest son was napping contentedly in the crib, which I considered musty and not as clean as I would have wished. I rationalized that clean sheets from home would protect him. My older sons were boating and fishing with their father. Alone at last. Time for me to do just what I pleased. I'd waited for months, expectantly, for this time warp as I'd plowed through reading groups, PTO meetings, piles of laundry, oil changes, and diaper changes.

The steps smelled of creosote. I wondered if the oily residue would stain my jeans. They were incredibly comfortable and I hoped so. A little stain might allow me to hold fast to this moment in time. Blue jays chattered in the evergreens. I wondered what kind of trees they were. They made a dancing filigree against the warm blue of the sky. I've been told that blue is a cool color—I felt it to be warm and comfortable. Something rustled in the grasses at my feet. Out of the clear sky came a light plane to land without a bounce. As it motored the length of the lake I remembered another plane years ago in my childhood—a different place and a different time but one with evergreens, water, and quiet.

The undulating waves created by the plane lapped at the stones and caused the old dock to creak and groan. The water was crystalline. The light, disturbed by the movement of the water, was hypnotic, dappling the lake bottom brown and gold. The tranquil surface was dimpled by a dandelion parachute as it landed in the water. It soon looked like seaweed swaying to the cadence of the waves. Gradually it rode ripple by ripple to the shore. I wondered if that puff of fluff carrying a hope of life would fulfill its destiny or merely rot away. I looked at the pine cones at my feet. What would be their fate? And the spider at my side? And how about the worms hidden in the black dirt in the can on the bottom step? White snowflaky blotches spread on the top of the dirt—milk my son said the worms needed. They couldn't possibly know their purpose in life unless they were male and female and that was their immediate interest. The confines of a can wouldn't necessarily interfere with that, or are worms hermaphroditic? The quiet was numbing.

I have no idea how long I sat there, quite some time I'm sure, but suddenly a restlessness came about me. I felt compelled to check my somnolent son and scan the horizon for a familiar face. I paced through the cabin, baked gingerbread in a battered and rusted pan, put buttercups on the table in a red and black-rimmed glass.

I found myself provoked with myself. I'd been waiting for time for me. Time to sit cool and calm and think out some of the dilemmas of life. I thought nothing through and sought refuge in activity. There I was in perfect contradiction.

Jane chooses the suspended moment to catch her own intentionality at work. The horizons of the narrative stretch into history and zoology as culture and nature are invoked to frame a few moments of thought. The story is framed by labor, her grandfather's and her own. Trying to find her own freedom, the writer recovers the path of her own gaze as she looks from trees to sky to seaplane, from waves to light to dandelion destiny. Her meditation on purpose offers posterity to pine cones, serendipity to spiders, and will to worms, a teleological version of nature that abandons her to a question somewhat like Freud's "What does woman want?" The sensual mapping of the narrative could be read to confirm the first nature of the female. We move from sight, the idealistic images of the grandfather's birds, "free-form," "never attached to anything," to touch, as detachment surrenders to the wish that the oily residue of the steps will stain her jeans and as the meditations on the telic character of life are displaced by baking gingerbread. "Earth's the right place for love," Frost tells us, and Jane too, it would seem, confirms this position as she moves her eyes from the horizon and returns to care, to making things, to domestic labor, immediate, context-specific, perishable.[22] The phenomenological display of the scene as it appears to consciousness invites the collusion of this story with the attribution of field dependence to female consciousness. But this reading of the text is undermined by the idealism of its icon. The freedom of the bluebird image is shown to be apocryphal by its containment on the farmhouse wall. And if this world was Grandpa's oyster, it too was clamped shut, neatly hinged and locked up tight as a farmhouse on a winter night. And whatever internal visions of detachment oysters may entertain, they, like the worms in the can, are somewhat internally attached, for they too are hermaphrodites, changing their sex to provide sperm and eggs in an orgy of self-sufficiency that sustains their isolation. Even free, white, and twenty-one are all freedoms that rely on a history of exclusion to be perceived. They imply a recent, if not chimerical, evasion of racism, ageism, and, probably, sexism.

The conclusion of this story portrays her desire for the other. First she checks the sleeping child (for her benefit or his?) and then scans the horizon, she tells us, for a familiar face—husband, children. Sexuality is connection, and rather than being a form of dependence and containment it is a form of freedom. The desire for the other is a restlessness that liberates its subject from the oyster shell, the can of worms, the claustrophobic farmhouse, and the isolation of idealism's detached meditations. The disassociations of thought and activity, association and independence, desire and strength, are the themes in the heterosexual division of gender, themes that are lived by this writer but can be obscured if the reading she receives rushes to the world as it appears.

The second story is a story of teaching. It takes place six years earlier than the first. The order of the stories is established by the writer. I read them accordingly.

Fall 1974. Colebrook Consolidated School, Colebrook, CT.

I had substituted in the Colebrook School, often enjoying this classroom. Two walls of windows, one facing south. The room felt warm. I recall feeling cold in the gym, the hall, or other rooms, but this one always was warm. The bulletin boards were all the same—blue background with children's papers mounted neatly on red. The desks tidily in rows, the room shipshape. It smelled of paste and crayons. I could hear the clock tick away the seconds and the heat bang in the pipes.

This day is different. I am no longer a substitute. Now this is my classroom to share with twenty-one expectant little faces. Last year was my first year of teaching and I survived sixth-graders. Now I'm teaching my dream, first grade. Today is my first formal observation. Mrs. Burnham will come, impeccably dressed, yellow pad in hand, to sit, observe, and write for an hour. Will I measure up? Will the children show growth? Will they be at ease? Will I?

My place will be behind the new half-round table. The table came at my request to provide what I hoped would be face-to-face teaching. Plans in duplicate. Interest centers set—a short vowel tape, beads and pattern cards, Indian vests to make from paper bags, leaf rubbings, and boardwork neatly written. If there was more I cannot remember.

The room looks different. The bulletin boards are all different colors. One has stories, one has art work, another an arithmetic project; the last is for the children to decorate for fall. It is a hodgepodge of leaves and seeds and milkweed fluff that drifts around the room. The desks are in groups basically arranged by the children. Would this be acceptable? Too much disorder?

The lessons were going well. The children were busy. Steven turned his chair over, which was par for the course. He interrupted to tell me his father was like a teddy bear—all furry, but he had freckles even on his tummy. I caught Mrs. Burnham's eye and we smiled. The children went to her to show their work. As I glanced around the room I felt passable.

Paul came to me. He opened his mouth to speak and threw up—all over the half-round table, books, papers, and me. He turned to repeat his illness and there on the floor in the middle of the vomitus were his false teeth. Paul was a very special child. Before I could reach him he had picked up his teeth and fled to the bathroom. I wiped off his shoes. He was cleaner than I. We went to the nurse's office as I bid the others to "sit tight." Thank God the nurse was there. I hailed a janitor with a can of sweetly malodorous stuff to throw on the mess. I returned to the moans and groans of twenty youngsters threatening to be sick. I surveyed the room, Mrs. Burnham waiting expectantly, and twenty miserable children. I ordered everyone in line. What we all needed was fresh air and exercise, recess.

My evaluator ended up staying all morning. As she started to leave several of the crew felt compelled to gather around her, hugging and begging her to stay. She told them she would count to three and they must let go because she had work to do. In her eyes was unmistakable hope. I was struck with the thought that she didn't know all the answers. She counted. It worked. Her exit was graceful.

I can remember little of what transpired from that recess till noon when I sat at my desk, the class gone to lunch. I still reeked of sickness, my slacks were damp. The art project we had after reading was incomplete—shreds of paper littered the floor. The geraniums bloomed on the windowsill. I was conscious of the clock ticking and the pipes banging. For the first time that I can recall I felt comfortable with teaching. Whatever that morning had been was what teaching was for me—at that point in time.

This narrative celebrates the constructed world. The power to shape, to be the source, is announced in every detail of order and design. Coming after the first story where order is suspect and drifting intolerable, this story asserts the second birth that is curriculum. If second nature is designed to provide a collective consensus, the rule, the rationale, the form, then this room is its icon. And so we see our writer turn to it from making gingerbread, from waiting for the men to return from sea. She is the captain of this "shipshape" room—until Paul vomits. All the divisions so carefully marked and ordered in the classroom as it appears collapse into this eruption of body, of intimacy, into the public space. The half-round table to permit just so much contact disappears as she cleans Paul's shoes. This illusion of the children's separateness, confirmed in the spatial presentation of their expectant faces, sans bodies, sans belches, sans sound, sans everything, collapses as Paul's teeth, his power to bite, to eat, to speak, land at her feet. She finds shelter in the euphemism "special child." It is a convenience that permits her to subordinate her revulsion, her desire to name him, to keep him other. The evaluator can leave. She escapes with a number game. Order regulates her comings and goings. But our writer remains, reeking, damp, and her closing lines repudiate the idealism of her opening scene and the futility of constructing a world that denies intimacy. What teaching was for me becomes a practice mediating first and second nature, a three-legged walk through women's work.

The third story brings us back to 1962 where the body question is her own.

Spring 1962. Chardon High School, Chardon, Ohio

I was a high school freshman then, acutely aware of myself, in some ways perhaps as ego-centered as a two-year-old and conversely painfully aware of those around me.

That day as I hurried from gym to Latin class I was aware of my hot sweaty body and the fact that I was required to wear my winter coat between the buildings which encompassed the two events. The former was the high school, a yellow-brick edifice with brown-red heavy metal double doors. The latter was the same yellow-brick double-doored affair but an elementary school into which classes, swelled by the baby boom, necessarily spilled. I was ambivalent about going to the elementary school. My mother taught there and was both a comfort and a vexation. It was a step down but I did enjoy the Latin classes there. They were taught by a young man whom I held in the highest regard. He was learned, demanding, and he liked my green tweed, raccoon-collared winter coat. He always wore loafers, white shirts, and a tie and preferred browns and greens. I'm sure he was my first love. We were reading Caesar. When I was to return to rework part of Caesar in a college class I could never see what I had even found palatable about the works.

As I entered the classroom that day perspiration rolled down my back. The collar of my yellow blouse was stuck to my neck. My clothes felt twisted and tight. I resented the fact that gym class ran late and I was the only one who had to change buildings. As a genetic endowment my face has always had the propensity to be very red when I am overheated or embarrassed. That day I could feel my face beaming like Rudolph's nose. The fact that class had begun didn't help. The atmosphere was hushed, books open, heads bent to task. When questioned about my tardiness my excuse was mumbled as I slipped amoebalike into my chair. I struggled to find my place in the frayed blue Caesar, pushing damp hair off my face and searching for a writing utensil. When I was told by the instructor that my face resembled a shiny red Christmas ornament disarray dissolved into total confusion and I was sure red had given way to purple. What was to come next didn't serve to reinforce self-confidence.

As I translated at the board I simply could not remember how to spell January. Did it have an *r* in it as did February? The chalk dust felt abrasive, the green board unbounded. Confusion melted into panic. I felt tears smart in my eyes as I retreated to my place. Glenn, seated next to me, whispered that January did not have an *r* in it and I returned to correct my error. My translated passage stood correct, a breeze drifted through the open side door, and the remainder of that class has drifted somewhere into the oblivion of the past.

After class the day seemed balmy as we walked back to the high school. Glenn and I chatted. He conjectured as to why I had put an *r* in January. We reminisced about a third grade in a red-brick building and a teacher as straight and gray as an elm. She always dressed in gray, always with a white collar or blouse and always smiling. We remembered her reading *Cinnabar the One O'Clock Fox* to us and telling us about a "rat" in "separate" and how we would rue the day we misspelled February in January. It was comforting to share those memories and to recall that teacher and to have some possible logical reason for my idiocy at the board.

Ego and body are conflated here, as the writer presents herself as a four-legged creature overwhelmed with sensuality and the shame that accompanies it in the place called school. Her mother's presence in the school is described as a vexation and a comfort. She steps down to the classes taught by the upright man, torn between the past and her desire to repudiate her own body, the body of her mother, the world of her mother, for the ghost of this Roman emperor and his autumnal deputy. Body strains against clothes and finally encompasses all constraints and slips, amoebalike, into her chair. Regression plunges back through the phylum into the shapelessness of primordial life rather than acknowledge the infantile identity of daughter, baby daughter to this mother who teaches in this school. Redness associated with Christmas intensifies the association with infancy as the Christ child, the link between woman, sexuality, and the spirituality that subsumes them both, is established. Chaos erupts when she cannot spell January. Janus, the first month of the year, marks the beginning and the ending. He is liminal deity, this Janus, two-headed, looking backward and forward. Accordingly, Janus is the presiding spirit of gates or doors, and we remember that both the high school and the elementary school are double-doored affairs. The phenomenal reading of the story gives us a text of adolescent self-consciousness, infatuation, shame over sexuality. It is enunciated in the taken-for-granted drama of heterosexual attraction, as she is drawn to the young male Latin teacher and comforted by a boy her own age. The relations of women to each other, of girls to their mothers, to their female teachers, are obscured by this reading as they are obscured by our culture, and it is feminist theory that returns those relations to this text, to our understanding of the process of engenderization and the differentiation, betrayals, and denials with which it is accomplished.

Does the *r* in February belong in January? In Latin *februarius* stands for the feast of purification held on the fifteenth of the month, entailing a ritual involving fire and smoke. Her confusion is accompanied by redness, by heat. A breeze enters the room once she has corrected the error and February's *r* is removed from January on Glenn's counsel. Only as they leave the elementary school setting of the Latin lesson and walk back to the high school does the day seem balmy. The cause of the confusion is then identified as another female teacher, "always dressed in gray, always with a white collar or blouse and always smiling." This standard-bearer of the patriarchy delivers the logical reason by inverting maternal logic, displacing intimacy and the female identification. The feminist reading is not the one that phenomenology discovers. It is under cover. It must be dragged up through associations, etymology, through the denial of human history and human relationship. That is what Lacan and Freud mean when they say that coming to know and coming to be gendered are one and the same process. The differences that mark us as male and female and shape our consciousnesses are patterns extended through our perceptions of the phenomenal world and inscribed in the philosophies, ideologies, and pedagogies that constitute our culture. The women who would teach to provide a path to a richer, fuller sense of human possibility and agency must read the shadows of their stories to recover their intentionality. In order to understand our own experiences of teaching we must truly stand under them in those places where the bluebirds never fly.

Part Two

4 *Where the Line Is Drawn*

My father used to paint. Not often. On vacations, mostly. The painting that still hangs over the couch in my parents' living room, the one with the rowboat sheltered by the shore and the canopy of branches, he painted when we all camped out on an island in Lake George. It was the same vacation when my brother learned to tie his shoelaces and we listened to the news from the Democratic convention that repudiated Richard Russell. He used oils and a palette knife, sculpting the light on the water into hollows where my terror of the dark lake that surrounded us and my trust in him met and nestled.

I don't remember him talking about painting very much, only about trying to get the light right. That canvas, or the one of the barn on the distant hill that he worked on years later, probably falls into the pastoral idealism of the back-room bluebirds that Jane's grandfather gave her. The lake and the farm do not offer images of the world he struggled with on the subway or of the fatigue and anxiety that would bring him home, tight-lipped and quiet, after work. Situated in the landscapes, the sun-drenched barn and the tethered rowboat, their shadows and light, explore the courage and limits of human enterprise. At the same time the project was never utterly separate from the life of the family. Images of otherness, they are sacred testaments of unspeakable tenderness and love of the world. You just had to be there to know for sure that they are also about my brother learning to tie his shoes.

Like the worlds of so many men, my father's was zoned. He moved between our home in Brooklyn, the "place" on First Avenue, the island in the lake, and as he crossed the lines that separated home and work and vacation he sensed, perhaps, the subjectivity that detached from each situation and stayed with him, the commuter. Is it that subjectivity, like the leftover subway token found in the pocket of an old jacket, that funds his art? And is it that currency that Jane McCabe lacks when she turns from her lake to bake gingerbread and check the baby? Hear Marcuse:

> Art is committed to that perception of the world which alienates individuals from their functional existence and performance in society—it is committed to an emancipation of sensibility, imagination, and reason in all spheres of subjectivity and objectivity. The aesthetic transformation becomes a vehicle of recognition and indictment. But this achievement presupposes a degree of autonomy which withdraws art from the mystifying power of the given and frees it for the expression of its own truth. Inasmuch as man and nature are constituted by an unfree society, their repressed and distorted potentialities can be represented only in an *estranging* form. The world of art is that of another *Reality Principle*, of estrangement—and only as estrangement does art fulfill a *cognitive* function; it communicates truths not communicable in any other language; it *contradicts*.[1]

FINDING FORM

The things of art stand away from the world that surround them. The text is, literally, bound; the painting framed. The play ends to applause. The dance ceases. The sweep of marble reaches just so far. Whether the boundaries are the definitive dramatic dimensions prescribed in Aristotle's *Poetics* or the problem to be solved in a performance piece from the 1970s, somewhere in space and time the line is drawn.

Because the things of art have form, they invite perception and can be described. Because the things of art are deliberately bounded in space and time, they are set off from the tools of trade, the bird's song, the neighbor's complaint, and the funeral cortege. Anthropologists, philosophers, and art critics regularly inspect the boundary that distinguishes art from life, seeking to understand them both. They examine the objects that fall to either side of the line as well as the allegiances and manners of those who identify with each territory. They are most intrigued when the border drawn between art and life, due to frequent or infrequent crossings, falls into disrepair, requiring negotiation, judgment, and specification. The art of teaching invites this inspection of its boundaries and territory, for if teaching is an aesthetic experience, it is also a form of labor and an accommodation to bureaucracy. It is both subject to and extends social control in schools designed by and for professionals.

The school day with its lessons and communal rituals, costumes, flags, and dramatis personae seems to move to the pulse of aesthetic time and to fill the frame of aesthetic space. Curriculum is, after all, artifice, deliberately designed to direct attention, provoke response, and express value; it reorders experience so as to make it accessible to perception and reflection. The study of life in schools draws upon aesthetic theory to reveal the essence of educational experience and to illuminate the relation of curriculum to the rhythms of history and biography and to lived spaces of home, factory, and church.[2]

None of us, neither teacher nor artist, dwells on one side of the line or the other. Even though aesthetic objects and aesthetic experience are spread out on the other side of the boundary from the places where money, supper, and trouble are made, the artist regularly passes back and forth between the actual and the possible, and we are, all of us, commuters.

If I am a teacher, I rise early. It may still be dark. I check to see if my children are up. I made their lunches last night. My eldest can't find her shoes. My youngest worries that I will forget to sign her permission slip for the field trip. I worry that I will dash out of the house and leave the stencil that I need for my second-period class in the typewriter. Maybe it will be light when I get to school. Maybe there will be no homeroom announcements, and I can slip out to run off the stencil. Maybe there will be a fire drill and second period will self-destruct. Maybe the entire morning will be drenched in bleary anxiety, filtered through chalk dust, recorded only in the incomplete circles my coffee cup leaves on the cover of my grade book. Or maybe the winter sun will shine with a summer's heat and on the very day that we are reading Frost, the world will exhibit its essential paradox in mud and snow and they will feel metaphor seep through the soles of their shoes and know it from the ground up.

The point is that to be an artist is perpetually to negotiate the boundary that separates aesthetic from mundane experience. The degree to which the crossing is difficult or the voyager suspect varies with the values of a culture, its conception of work, community, nature, gender, and family. I want to explore what it means to take up teaching as an art at this place and at this time. For some years I have relied upon aesthetic forms to study educational experience. I have used autobiography to disclose the student's understanding of education, scanning her narrative for a point of view, for a logic of action, a theory of cognition, for the detail that suggests motives hardly whispered in the text. I have employed theater to portray the public events that curriculum becomes, the shifting status of actors and audience, the relation of intention to improvisation, of text to action.

A metaphor for educational experience will illuminate some aspects of educational practice and leave others in shadows. A metaphor will influence not only what is described but also the form the description takes, its knowledge claims, and the response of those who attend to it. The selection of these metaphors for educational experience combines observation with hope. They serve as emblems for a good deal of educational practice while providing an ideal toward which that practice might move.

Now, it is not obvious what it is we are talking about when we refer to aesthetic experience as a metaphor for education. Arguments about what is beauty, about the relationship between art and reality, are threaded through the recorded history of human thought. The following propositions do not exhaust the definition of aesthetic experience. Drawn from the philosophical writings of Johan Huizinga, Susanne Langer, F. David Martin, and Herbert Marcuse, these statements address those features of aesthetic experience that I find most pertinent to teaching.[3] They concern form: its relation to the fluidity of experience and to the community of persons who create, perceive, and respond to it.

1. Participation in aesthetic experience is voluntary.
2. Aesthetic experience is bounded in time and space.
3. Aesthetic experience is not subordinated to instrumental purposes.
4. Aesthetic forms express knowledge about feeling.
5. Aesthetic forms express an implicit acquiescence or resistance to social and political conventions.
6. The meaning of aesthetic forms is constituted in the dialogue that takes place between the artist's work and its audience.

It is necessary to provide a conceptual skeleton for the discussion that follows, and for the past few years it has been important to identify the assumptions and values of aesthetics in order to articulate an alternate theory of learning and instruction and to defend it against behaviorist and technical approaches to schooling.[4] Even if we could, with some certainty, outline the elements of an ideal conception of aesthetic form, practice, or experience, we could never provide a portrait of the ideal artist. Who would be our model? There are, after all, only real artists and real teachers. We need to be reminded that the real artists and the real teachers who created and distributed the symbolic codes that constitute the culture of this nation were hardly the expressive individualistic revolutionaries whom we associate with contemporary art. I have gathered some of their history so that we may understand the traditions that link their work to ours, and I will turn to the feminist art of Judy Chicago to show how women artists have used that understanding to transform the conditions and possibilities of their own work.

The artist is a worker, a parent. She pays rent, owes a letter to a friend in Denver, and yearns for ripe peaches in February. What I wish to explore here are the conditions and traditions of teaching and the degree to which they support practice that we would designate as aesthetic. I believe that to adopt the stance of the artist is to challenge the taken-for-granted values and culture that one shares with others. Because most of the people who teach our children in the public schools are women, we must ask whether there are particular conditions surrounding women's lives that will influence our capacity to take up and live out an aesthetic approach to our work in the classroom. I want to ascertain what it is that we are asking a teacher to do when we exhort her to see teaching as an art. I want to discover what is possible in a world of stencils, permission slips, and revelations that glimmer in pools of melting snow and mud.

THE SUBORDINATION OF ART TO THE CULT OF NATURE

It is the function of art to reorganize experience so it is perceived freshly. At the very least, the painting, the poem, or the play cleanses a familiar scene, washing away the film of habit and dust collected over time so that it is seen anew. When it is most radical, the work of art draws the viewer to it, engaging expectations, memories, recognitions, and simultaneously interrupts the viewer's customary response, contradicting expectations with new possibilities, violating memories, displacing recognition with estrangement.

The distinction between art and craft rests on this process of estrangement. For the object that is contained within the category of craft is destined for daily use and intended to enhance the common order, not to disrupt it. It is only with the passage of time that the works of craft achieve the function of cultural commentary, when the balance and economy that sustain daily life have changed sufficiently for the object whose form has expressed yesterday's social order to achieve the distance needed for critique. If teachers have often found themselves caught within the conventional confines of craft, artists have too.

Neil Harris's history of the American artist from colonial times to the Civil War reveals a culture dominated by craft rather than art, and we can find very little evidence of the independence and expressiveness that we associate with art in Harris's chronicle.[5] Colonials, Harris argues, associated art with the abuses of nobility, and they spurned the signs of vanity, luxury, and despotism associated with a greedy monarchy and church.[6] In Benjamin Franklin's autobiography we read Franklin's contention that all forms of government are artifice. Contemptuous of tradition, Franklin maintained that when the forms of government are imposed or fail to express the changing interests of the people, they must inevitably falter.[7] The suspicion of form that accompanied the birth of a national self-consciousness repudiated artifice in favor of nature.[8] If we agree that it is an essential property of art to challenge convention, then in a new country with few conventions, and in a nation consciously repudiating the conventional religious and class structures of European traditions, the American artist was hard-pressed to find a culture to counter or copy. Furthermore, aesthetic activity was seen as a waste of time in a new society dedicated to mobility, physical effort, and productivity.

Alienated from their European origins, "Americans," Harris maintains, "demanded of their art continual proofs of paternity," and it was the project to develop a national ethos and character that dominated the artists of the eighteenth and early nineteenth centuries;[9] for if artistic forms expressed variety, in portraits, historical renderings of the War of Independence, or landscapes, they rarely expressed dissent.[10] It was this fear of divisiveness that dominated the school controversies of the early 1800s as well. Although education in the colonies had been dominated by the church, it was Horace Mann's support for "neutralism," secular moral instruction, that prevailed in the common schools after the turn of the century. This movement to forge a common culture through the education of the young echoed architecture's readiness to provide a secular and common imagery for the new nation by adapting classical Greek designs to public buildings.

An avowed preference for nature over culture was accentuated when artists, teachers, and clergy joined together to condemn industrial and urban development. On canvas, in classrooms, and in churches they celebrated nature and grieved for our pastoral origins and lost innocence. Life in the growing manufacturing centers horrified both the religious conservative and the transcendentalist avant-garde, bringing about what Harris describes as an unlikely coalition that deplored what it considered to be the materialism, decadence, and disorder of city life. He cites excerpts from Emerson's "Thoughts on Art," where the transcendentalist praises nature as the visible expression of universal morality:

> The universal soul is *the* alone creator of the useful and the beautiful, the individual must be submitted to the universal mind. . . . [The power of nature] predominates over the human will in all works of even the fine arts. . . . Nature paints the best part of the picture; carves the best part of the statue; builds the best part of the house. [The artist who would be great] must disindividualize himself, and be a man of no party, and no manner, and no age . . . an organ through which the universal mind acts.[11]

Harris tells us that there were few paintings of American city life before the Civil War. Similarly, artists were summoned to provide an antidote to the disorder of cities by providing works that would tame the city mobs as the palaces and museums of Europe were thought to have cultivated and tranquilized the citizens of Florence, London, and Paris.[12] Sentimental, nationalistic, and supported both monetarily and intellectually, artists were promoted by the educated middle and upper classes to provide the imagery that would facilitate social control of urban workers.

THE SUBORDINATION OF TEACHING
TO THE CULT OF MOTHERHOOD

It was during this era of industrialization that women, displaced from homes that were no longer centers of economic productivity, sought employment in the common schools. Underpaid, constrained from marrying, poorly prepared to face the chaos and harsh discipline of the urban classroom or the isolation of the rural schoolhouse, young women poured into the common schools when their male counterparts turned away from teaching to positions in the new industrial economy and when the classroom, the mill, and domestic service were the only options available to a woman who wished employment. Although teaching provided one of the few ways that women could see themselves as participants in the world outside the home, the rationale for their presence in the classroom replicated the sentimental rhetoric of child nurturance that was being heaped on motherhood. Transformed from a producer of commodities to a consumer, bearing the children that prosperity invited, in homes bereft of fathers and sons drawn into the factories, mothers were trapped and isolated in child care. Their daughters who entered teaching to flee a suffocating domesticity were absorbed by the institutional paternalism that substituted the discipline of the state, of the school day, its language, rituals, and coercion, for the moral responsibility of the family. Women were not asked to create this moral leadership in either the home or the school, but they were expected to be the medium through which the laws, rules, language, and order of the father, the principal, the employer were communicated to the child. Their own passivity was to provide the model of obedience for the young to emulate. The self-abnegation and submission to universal principles of morality, decorum, and beauty constrained teachers, as they had artists, from developing a style of practice with which they were personally identified and for which they felt personally responsible.[13]

Although aesthetic sensibility, like child nurturance, had been rooted in the pastoral childhood of the nation as the line was drawn between those who produced the culture and those who received and rationalized it, the antinaturalism movement that developed in Europe after 1910 transformed the artist's relation to common perception. That development had been heralded by Constable in 1836: "Painting is a science, and should be pursued as an enquiry into the laws of nature. Why then, may not landscape be considered as a branch of natural philosophy, of which pictures are but experiments?"[14] This approach to art as research was taken up by the artists of the twentieth century who, supported by the insights of Marxism, psychoanalysis, anthropology, and phenomenology, grasped the degree to which the designation of any phenomenon as natural masked the social construction of perception. Impressionism, abstraction, dadaism, fauvism, cubism, and surrealism are some of its experiments.

Although artists escaped the cage of nature and made it over the wall to where it was legitimate to reveal the "ordinary as strange and in need of some explanation,"[15] teachers, who were by now predominantly women, remained ensnared by the supposedly "natural" imperatives that established parameters for their experience, perception, and expression.

The profound rupture created by the shift from farm to city, from nature to culture, was never mended, nor was it left behind or outgrown. It too became part of urban life, glimpsed in the growing schism between public and private, work and home, men and women, adults and children. Workingmen were on one side of the line; women, children, artists, and teachers on the other. This collective, historical process recapitulated the repressions that accompanied the development of male gender identity in its abrupt denial of its matrisexual origins and the ambivalence of female gender identity, still identified with Mother but wary of her. As we shall see, it was only the artists who were able to articulate the view of society that they developed from their side of the divide. Women and children, subordinated to the family and the school, were muted in the sentimental images of their vulnerability, and teachers have yet to announce which side of the line we are on.

DRAWING LINES

The dilemma facing teachers may presage the paradox that other women will confront as we participate more fully in the public world. Women dominate the ranks of teachers and have for many years. Yet, when we are summoned to adopt a form of practice that is aesthetic, we find that the workplace replicates those structures in domesticity and in female identity that constrain freedom and action.

First of all, the structure of the school replicates the patriarchal structure of the family. The women who maintain daily contact with children and nurture them are themselves trained, supervised, and evaluated by men. Now, we must recognize the degree to which women who teach are complicit in this distribution of power between the sexes in the education establishment. In other words, if women have fled from the isolation of domesticity to the company of classrooms, how come the school still feels like home? Why do teachers maintain the isolation of their kitchens in their classrooms, seeing each other surreptitiously, during breaks, as they might have broken up the domestic day with a long phone call or occasional bridge game? Consciousness raising, that conversation between women that called us to describe the arrangements of our lives, revealed more than the oppressive stipula-

tions of patriarchy to its participants. It also revealed our internaliza-
tions of that oppression in our fears of responsibility, of our own anger,
of isolation, and of being identified with other women. Now we hardly
expect the teacher who is an artist to be utterly invulnerable, exempt
from attack from without and qualms from within. She cannot challenge the school's sexism and her own doubts and ambivalence alone.
When our egos expand to incorporate what have been heretofore alien
impulses or fantasies into our repertoires of personal action, identity
defenses are challenged, and we feel threatened. Consciousness raising
provided support for women learning to see ourselves and our world in
new ways. What community provides support for teachers who would
be artists?

The failure of teachers to create such a community for ourselves may
come from our reluctance to acknowledge our commitment to our
work. Although many women teach to provide income for our families
and/or ourselves, it is also possible that the expected allegiance to home
and family that has framed women's work in the world has exaggerated
a subsistence motive in order to camouflage the illegitimate pleasure
that the woman who teaches finds in the work itself. Ostensibly secondary to maternal and conjugal responsibilities, teaching is relegated to a
secondary position when women deal with the conflicting demands of
home and family. The advanced study, travel, and internships that
could be tapped to enrich work deemed important are relinquished in
order to maintain the illusion that teaching is not directly identified
with one's own ego identity and aspirations.

In many ways the temporal structures of teaching resemble the
routines of domesticity. Fluid and ubiquitous, housework and children
have required women to accept patterns of work and time that have no
boundaries. Not surprisingly, it is women who compensate for the
highly rationalized and fragmented arrangements of school time and
space with our own labor and effort. For those who sustain the emotional and physical lives of others, there is no time out, no short week,
no sabbatical, no layoff. The incredibly time-consuming work of con-
sulting with students and of responding sensitively and helpfully to
their work is too often ignored when the teaching schedule is drawn up,
when class size is determined, when salaries are negotiated. Mindful
that these are other women's children we write to, criticize, and comfort, we are wary and minimize the power of our pedagogy lest it
offend. These are intimate communications; they rest on enduring

teacher/student relationships that involve trust. They recapitulate the mother/child intimacies of our own childhoods and our own parenting. And so, even though we secretly respect this maternal pedagogy of ours, it seems personal to us, not quite defensible in this public place, and we provide this nurturant labor without demanding the recompense it deserves. Chodorow and Dinnerstein have both argued that, because the woman is not only the primary parent of the infant but also the only person who sustains an intimate relation with the growing child, Mother becomes the only person whom the child desires when needy.[16] Even as adults, we maintain patterns of emotional dependency on women that involve both mothers and children in a symbiosis that each simultaneously requires and resents. Women are both the subjects and the objects of this relation. Over and over again, teachers turn down sabbaticals, in-service, and educational opportunities because they don't want to leave their classes, as if the development of the teacher and the development of those she teaches were inimical to each other.

Attempts to create hierarchies of teaching roles, reaching from novice through master teachers, express the impulse to provide a logic and a telos for teaching, to give it a story of professionalism because it appears to lack one of its own. Deprived of the opportunity to design the structures of their own lives, their own work, many women, mothers and teachers, live through other people's stories. Kim Chernin has argued that daughters who sympathize with the hurt and disappointment of their mothers' frustrated aspirations and diminished lives feel guilt when they choose other forms for their own experience.[17] If we accept the forms of our own lives, as given, how do we challenge or transform the questions at the end of the chapter, the organization of the textbook, the conventional territories and agendas of the disciplines? The maternal ethos of altruism, self-abnegation, and repetitive labor has denied the order and power of narrative to teachers, for to tell a story is to impose form on experience. Having relinquished our own beginnings, middles, and ends, our stories of teaching resemble soap operas whose narratives are also frequently interrupted, repetitive, and endless.

Judy Chicago tells us that when she assembled her first women's art class and challenged its members to talk seriously about their work and their ideas she was greeted with dead silence.[18] But expressive speech, Merleau-Ponty teaches us, "does not simply choose a sign for an already defined signification, as one goes to look for a hammer in order to drive a nail . . . or to put the matter another way we must uncover the silence that speech is mixed together with."[19] The actor who trains with Jerzy Grotowski also learns to harvest silence. Grotowski's instruction is a *via negativa*, not a tirade of instructions or a manual of codes but a series of exercises designed to create some space between the defenses that constitute our personalities, space that will provide the room for new forms of expression.[20] Freedom, like silence, runs deep, way below the babble of habitual speech. We need space and time to find it.[21]

I am joining Virginia Woolf and Tillie Olson, Hawthorne, Melville, Conrad, and Kafka when I call upon teachers to make a place for themselves where they can find the silence that will permit them to draw their experience and understanding into expression.[22] Now, the world is not silent; drenched in media, announcements, commercials, instructions, and discussions, neither the classroom nor the kitchen is the place to cook up a good lesson. This assertion does, I realize, extend the boundary that defines the aesthetic object or event to encircle aesthetic processes in general, suggesting that aesthetic experience is necessarily defined against the standard of daily experience, which it in some way contradicts or challenges. This is the opposition that John Dewey struggled to reconcile. In both his aesthetic and his educational writings, Dewey deplored the polarities that distort our experience, severing one piece from another and distributing aesthetic, technical, intellectual, and emotional varieties of experience to different categories of citizens.

His conviction that the "aesthetic is no intruder in experience from without, whether by way of idle luxury or transcendent ideality, but that it is the clarified and intensified development of traits that belong to every normally complete experience" roots the aesthetic object in common experience.[23] It is distinguished from the flow of daily experiences, the phone conversation, the walk to the corner store, only by the intensity, completeness, and unity of its elements and by a form that calls forth a level of perception that is, in itself, satisfying. I have no quarrel with Dewey's aim to recover the freedom and continuity of human experience from the institutions that had divided, catalogued, and sequestered it so that it could be distributed rather than claimed. But despite Dewey's attempt to piece together what man had pulled asunder, I am arguing that we women must construct a special place for ourselves if our work as teachers is to achieve the clarity, communication, and insight of aesthetic practice—if it is, in short, to be research and not merely representation.

THE STUDIO AND THE GALLERY

It is not immediately clear what kind of studio we require. The ambivalence that is strung between the teacher and the school is present as well between the female artist and the art establishment. If you are engaged in expressive work but find that the symbols and content of expression that dominate your field, as well as the condition and relations of its work, are alien to you, what do you do? This is the problem of women in educational theory who would talk about responsibility rather than accountability, who would talk about reproduction rather than production, about the relationship among eros, nurture, and schooling rather than the relationship of the school to the factory, the corporation, the professions, or the GNP.

Judy Chicago found many women artists caught in this dilemma, both the women who had retreated to studios in their attics or in mudrooms tucked behind their kitchens and those who had brought work into a public space:

> The alternatives represented by the woman's situation were dismal indeed, and they were alternatives that I had struggled with. Either be oneself as a woman in one's work and live outside the art community or be recognized as an artist at the price of hiding your womanliness. . . . I saw that the women who had opted for their personal subject matter had suffered the price of never seeing their work enter the world. The women like me whose work had become visible had sacrificed a part of their personalities to do so.[24]

Now, our "natural" history has shown us that despite paeans for the teacher's tenderness and sweetness, expressiveness has never been a quality of pedagogy encouraged in teachers. As we have seen in Chapter 2, Charters's exhaustive 1928 study of the attributes of teachers and characteristics of teaching repeats the familiar litany of self-control and denial of emotion articulated in 1795 by the Reverend John Bennett.

Even recent projects, ostensibly developed to bring more expressiveness into the classroom, such as the humanistic education initiatives of the late sixties, featured a Rogerian, client-centered, self-abnegating facilitation of another's expression rather than dialogue that just might be abrasive, challenging, revealing, and estranging for teacher and student alike. Although educational research of the last decade has come to acknowledge the degree to which the teacher mediates between the child and the curriculum, the response of curriculum developers, book publishers, and administrators to this perception of the potential power of the teacher has been to prescribe teacher/student interactions by providing scripts for their discourse. The move to acknowledge the influence of teachers and, simultaneously, to control it is evident in the scripts provided for teachers in the basal readers and by the scripts imposed in teacher-effectiveness courses and evaluation protocols.[25]

I want to argue that we need to fortify the aesthetic boundaries that define teaching. We need to re-create safe places, even in schools, where teachers can concentrate, can attend to their experience of children and of the world, and we need to create community spaces where the forms that express that experience are shared. The process of creating these spaces will be as important as the places themselves. And should we rely on the state or the affluent, we will find ourselves, like the nineteenth-century artist, co-opted by our patrons.

Furthermore, we must take care that in re-creating spaces that offer privacy we do not merely encourage the repetition of forms that have sequestered and hidden women's perceptions rather than revealed them. The teacher who sees basic skills as an impoverished, reductive approach to thought, who is nevertheless distributing dreary, time-consuming materials that keep each student quiet and busy—and are thus "individualized"—can go along with the prescribed curriculum and keep her job, try to change it and risk her job, or wait for a few moments to be alone with her class when she may have the time and the opportunity to undo the damage. Michael Apple, concerned about this "deskilling" of teachers, the substitution of standardized materials for teachers' creation of curricular forms, provides this teacher's response to the rationalized curriculum: "Kids are too young to travel between classrooms all the time. They need someone there that they can always go to, who's close to them. Anyway, subjects are less important than feelings."[26]

Apple appropriately warns us against the retreat into what has been traditionally considered the woman's sphere: the support of feelings. By identifying the perception of emotion with a form of solace rather than with action and communication, we replicate the patterns constituted by patriarchal relations in history and society and its divisions of public and private experience. We teachers hide the work we care about in our own classrooms just as artists stack it in their attics. "Behind the classroom door" used to be the phrase that stood for the domain where the teacher ran the show. The closing of the door, the drawing of the line: Now it begins. This is what matters. Now we are together. This is our space.

It has been the pattern of recent pedagogy to view that teacher, sequestered with children for long hours behind the classroom door, as an old-fashioned isolate. The call for accountability has required visibility. All hands on deck; progress measured across the grade, facilitated by specialists. The beat of Sesame Street goes on. Keep 'em busy. Keep 'em moving. Team planning, team teaching. Stating our objectives, meeting our goals. It is one giant fund drive. Let's get those scores over the top. The lure for teachers thus degraded is professionalism, a status attractive to women when it promises to defend our work from the intrusions of the state and from male dominance.[27]

It was the refusal, however, to replicate the patterns of dominance and subordination so essential to ranks within the professions as well as to relations of professionals to their clients that led Judy Chicago and her associates to form another community that would support and protect women's art. In *Through the Flower*, which relates her own development as an artist and the development of a women's art community in California, Chicago invokes Virginia Woolf, who, even in the thirties, saw straight through the privileges promised to the professions to the inequities and insensitivities that constituted those privileges:

> If people are highly successful in the professions they lose their senses. Sight goes. They have no time to look at pictures. Sound goes. They have no time to listen to music. Speech goes. They have no time for conversation. They lose their sense of proportion—the relations between one thing and another. Humanity goes. . . . What then remains of a human being who has lost sight, sound, and sense of proportion? Only a cripple in a cave.[28]

And so it is often the response of the teacher who would keep her senses alive to leave the "system" or, if she is able, to create some window of time or space within the school day. (Recently programs for the "gifted" have provided havens for those willing to support their aesthetic habit by dealing with those who peddle the myth of meritocracy.) Combining seniority with determination, with a reputation for eccentricity, and a little larceny, such a teacher makes her classroom a studio. It holds her books, her record of Dylan Thomas reading "A Child's Christmas in Wales," and an old record player that doesn't need to be ordered from AV three days in advance. It has places to keep what Didion calls "bits of the mind's string too short to use."[29] I mourn every ditto I ever threw away because there was no place to keep it: the notes for the unit we never did, the parody of *The Waste Land* that an eleventh-grade class wrote. I miss the collection of poems that I chose after sitting on the living room couch—Swedish modern it was in those days and not very comfortable—until two or three in the morning. I don't know when I would ever use a collection of poems about cats again, but its absence reminds me of the childhood charm bracelet that I lost in college or that huge stainless steel bowl we used to keep the Halloween candy in that also disappeared. Why do we cherish the places where artists have worked? Listen to Nancy Hale, as she rummaged through the studio that her mother, an artist, left when she died:

> These objects seem more ineffable than material, like voices. At their realest, they are objects of virtue, keys to release the life that trembles behind them in the void and that I otherwise would never have suspected was there. It is as if you whirled around very quickly and caught the furniture in the room up to something: or as if, by a trick you had at last been able to catch the uncatchable—the blind spot in your vision where anything can happen.[30]

The objects stand, sentinels guarding the silence that is the source of new forms.

In a 1930 Woolf journal entry: "I cannot yet write naturally in my new room, because the table is not the right height and I must stoop to warm my hands. Everything must be absolutely what I am used to. . . . I am stuck fast in that book."[31] Woolf was certain that women needed rooms of our own for work and decried the economic dependency that denied that privacy. The woman who has chosen to teach because this work also permits her to be home with her family particularly craves a space that bears her signature, holds her resources. Many teachers find such spaces by choosing particular portions of the curriculum (those often less monitored by supervisors) that can provide this ground.

The danger is that a room of one's own becomes a bunker. It becomes a place where we quietly sabotage the skills program without releasing the methods and meaning that we have devised so that they may attract attention, stir comment, ultimately influence textbook selection, state requirements, and the in-service program. Terrible vulnerability accompanies aesthetic practice. Where do we find the courage to reveal our work, the confidence to be as vulnerable as Judy Chicago?

> For a solid month before the opening, I suffered from depressions, anxiety attacks, even rashes. I felt that the openings of the building and the exhibition of my new work truly revealed my commitment, my ideas and my values, and I was afraid that they would be rejected.[32]

Or as vulnerable as Virginia Woolf?

> Friday, April 8th. 10 minutes to 11 a.m. And I ought to be writing Jacob's Room; and I can't, and instead I shall write down the main reason why I can't—this diary being a kindly blankfaced old confidante. Well, you see, I'm a failure as a writer. I'm out of fashion: old: shan't do any better: have no headpiece: the spring is everywhere: my book out (prematurely) and nipped, a damp firework. . . . Well, this question of praise and fame must be faced. . . . One wants, as Roger said very truly yesterday, to be kept up to the mark; that people should be interested and watch one's work. What depresses me is the thought that I have ceased to interest people—at the very moment when, by the help of the press, I thought I was becoming more myself. . . . As I write, there rises somewhere in my head that queer and very pleasant sense of something which I want to write; my own point of view. I wonder, though, whether this feeling that I write for half a dozen instead of 1500 will pervert this?—make me eccentric—no, I think not. But, as I said, one must face the despicable vanity which is at the root of all this niggling and haggling. I think the only prescription for me is to have a thousand interests—if one is damaged, to be able instantly to let my energy flow into Russian, or Greek, or the press, or the garden, or people, or some activity disconnected with my own writing.[33]

The privatization of teaching repeats the exile of domesticity that has split public from private life and drained each domain of its vitality. Woolf sought seclusion, was terrified of rejection, and flourished in the support of the Bloomsbury group so long as that companionship survived to sustain her. Chicago, who forced herself to leave her studio regularly to work with other women in an educational project, the Feminist Studio Workshop, did so, she tells us, because the female artist needed to learn not to succumb to isolation. The creative process is not just about bringing experience to form; it is also about expressing our thoughts and feelings about that experience to someone else and finding out what she thinks about it.

There is a dialectic of withdrawal and extension, isolation and community, assertion and submission to aesthetic practice that requires both the studio where the artist harvests silence and the gallery where she serves the fruit of her inquiry to others. Just as I would send the teacher to a room of her own where she can shed the preconceptions that blind her to the responses of her students, I would ask her to bring the forms that express her understanding of the child and the world to the children, to her sisters who are her colleagues, and to her sisters who are the mothers of the children. The distrust that divides the women who care for children grows in the dark like mold. The challenge for women who would be artists in their classrooms is to create the community that will encourage and receive their expression:

> When one goes from the order of events to the order of expression, one does not change the world; the same circumstances which were previously submitted to now become a signifying system. Hollowed out, worked from within, and finally freed from that weight upon us that makes them painful and wounding, they become transparent or even luminous, and capable of clarifying not only aspects of the world that resemble them, but others too.[34]

So the line that separates ultimately connects submission to mastery, event to sign, experience to curriculum, and self to other. All that we need to decide, each day, when we are ready and the light is right, is where and when to draw the line.[35]

5 My Face in Thine Eye, Thine in Mine Appeares: The Look in Parenting and Pedagogy

"My face in thine eye, thine in mine appeares."[1] With this double image John Donne portrayed the complete and perfect intersubjectivity of lovers. Contained within each other's look, they share one world, constituted in the utter reciprocity of their feeling and attention, sustained by a shared perception:

> Let sea-discoverers to new worlds have gone,
> Let Maps to other, worlds on worlds have showne,
> Let us possesse one world, each hath one, and is one.[2]

The poet condenses the ego, the other, and the world, drawing the sciences that organize our knowledge of this and other worlds back into the orbit of the lovers' gaze. As the poet places the world within the orbit of the lovers' looks, so may one explore the looks that pass between parent and child and teacher and student to discover the worlds they contain as well as the worlds they exclude.

By locating the world within the look, I am positing its intersubjective origins and status as an intentional object of consciousness of all who live and act within it. That is not to say that our minds create the world but that the world we know is the one we share with others. Conversely, our capacity to know others depends on this world we share for, as Merleau-Ponty has argued, we know others through their actions in the world:

> At first the child imitates not persons but conducts. . . . My consciousness is turned primarily toward the world, turned toward things, it is above all a relation to the world. The other's consciousness as well is chiefly a certain way of comporting himself toward the world. Thus it is in his conduct, in the manner in which the other deals with the world, that I will be able to discover his consciousness.[3]

We come to know another through the world and the world through another. Strasser describes the first moment of intentionality, of turning-to, as a primordial association of infant and mother. In his genesis of intentionality, turning to things is collapsed into the "you" as world, things, and mother are all sought by the life energy drawn to love, knowledge, and finally survival.[4]

There is style and form to the nurturance, the intimacy, the control, the expression, and the dialogue of both parenting and pedagogy. That is not to say that the forms of these two phases of care are isomorphic or that they exist in a cause-and-effect relationship. It is to say that each configuration influences the other and is in turn affected by the relations of reproduction and production.

The look provides an index to the complex relations that prevail in both parenting and pedagogy. The direct passage between persons, the look, has been celebrated by Confucius: "Look into a person's pupils; he cannot hide himself"; by Plato: "They set the face in front . . . and constructed light-bearing eyes and caused pure fire to flow through the eyes"; by da Vinci: "The eye sees many things without seizing hold of them, but suddenly turns thither the central beam which . . . seizes on the images and confines such as pleases it within the person the memory."[5]

The look, fusing nature and culture, both provides our information about the world and expresses our understanding of it. The look that Donne's lovers share is distinguished by its reciprocity. Mutually initiated, received, and held, its symmetry is such that it shuts out the world that surrounds it. This perfect and complete mutuality of lovers is an ideal of romantic love that is sometimes echoed in sentimentalized portraits of pedagogy and parenting. Nevertheless, we sentimentalize the powers, Ann Douglas tells us, that we have already surrendered.[6] As industrialization pushed women to the edges of the economy and exiled them to domesticity that substituted consumerism for productivity, educators extolled the maternal glance, praising its tenderness, modesty, self-abnegation, and moral clarity. As industrialization and urbanization prolonged childhood, requiring the exclusion of children from productive labor, the impotence of childhood was aggrandized as the innocent and pure look of truth was imputed to children.

Although I am not willing to adopt Sartre's phenomenology of the look that identifies the glance of the other as an inevitable and unavoidable assault on my freedom, I do share his recognition of its essential asymmetry.[7] The structure of the look is essentially dialogical. Like speech, the look can be given and received, returned or refused, but only in those fleeting moments of fusion, those instants in the lives of lovers, parents and children, teachers and students can the look contain the complete reciprocity of which the poet dreams. But would the poet linger in such an equilibrium for long? Balance is static, Grotowski's actors know, for only in asymmetry is there movement.[8] As the glance moves between parent and child, between teacher and student, it picks up pieces of the world and so enlarges our collective consciousness.

THE LOOK IN PARENTING

During the first day of life the eyes of the newborn are calm. The gaze of the nursing infant is disinterested, though strangely receptive to the inquiring gaze of the mother searching for signs of temperament or need. Perhaps it is the deep stillness of the infant's gaze that invites the mother's identification. In Chapter 1 I told of the day following the birth of my daughter, my first child, when my skin, suffused with the hormones that supported labor and delivery, felt and smelled like hers, when I reached for a mirror and was startled by my own reflection, for it was hers that I had expected to see there.

It is with some chagrin that I must admit that this infant whom I had become did not then know me. Her gaze was nonspecific though it often rested on my face. She existed in an egocentrism of a *one*, which Merleau-Ponty describes as "unaware of itself, liv[ing] as easily in others as it does in itself—but which being unaware of others in their own separateness as well, in truth is no more consciousness of them than of itself."[9] Merleau-Ponty calls this phase precommunication, in which somehow individuals are undifferentiated and experience a group life where the other's intentions play *across* my body while my intentions play across his.[10] The symbiotic relation of mother and child is expressed in their gaze of mutual misunderstanding. The infant's gaze embraces the mother in an all-inclusive identification that does not recognize her. The mother sees herself in a child who lacks a self. Yet this misunderstanding hardly deserves the embarrassment that follows a false assumption of familiarity, as when you call out across the street to someone whom you thought to be a friend but who turns toward you with the defensive hesitation of a stranger. The infant's inclusiveness, the mother's projection, even the hearty greeting to the utter stranger, bespeak the recognition of the transcendental ego. It is a profound recognition that slides below and through the layers of identity formed through time, choice, circumstance, eluding the defenses that Wilhelm Reich called character armor.[11]

The look that passes between the newborn infant and its mother violates common courtesy. Too empty on one side, too full on the other, it is the primordial look, the first intimacy. The truth of its fusion and confusion is, like the glance of Donne's lovers, an instant that is rarely replicated. The nursing infant sees her own face reflected in the mother's, and the mother, in turn, can see her image in the child's eye. Soon, for both mother and child, something, someone, intervenes. Yet there will be other moments as their histories are intertwined through time when they again exchange the look of generations that transfers and transforms the possibilities of personhood from one being to another.

R. L. Fantz reports that as early as forty-eight hours after birth infants show a preference for pattern, probably related to contour rather than shape or color.[12] A drawing of a face is preferred to one of concentric circles, and after two months solid objects are preferred to flat ones. In the early weeks of life an infant is able to focus clearly only on objects that are eight or nine inches from her eyes.[13] The face of a mother nursing her baby is ideally situated to be so perceived. Nevertheless, the baby seems not to acknowledge the appearance of the mother as quickly as she responds specifically to her voice and touch. A differential response to a mother's voice precedes the specific response to her face, a response that does not develop until the infant is fourteen weeks old.[14] By the fourth feeding the infant demonstrates the clinging, sucking behavior as she anticipates nursing as a response to the tactile stimulus of being held close to the mother's body and, as early as three weeks, will turn her head toward the mother at the sound of her voice.

I have offered a brief mention of some of the extensive research on neonatal development because it confirms my impression that for parent and child the look trails behind the touch and the sound as a sensory link between mother and child. Felt before it is seen, the infant's movements announce her reality to the woman who carries her in her womb.[15] The infant is first felt, cradled against the chest, supported by hands and arms. The crawling baby clings to the legs; the toddler is present at the fingertips of an outstretched hand. For the first three years of a child's life, parents and child move through a choreography of touch with constant physical contact as a theme that joins their movements through time and space and memory.

Just as the "you," as Strasser maintains, is older than the "I," so the touch is older than the look.[16] The child under six months does not have a specular image of her own body. Whatever information she may have of her body may come from its physical sensations, from its movement, from the degree to which its movements replicate the behavior of those around her. Still, the infant may not perceive those who come and go as distinct persons. Her cries when her mother or father leaves the room may bewail her own incompleteness rather than the particular absence. What Henri Wallon has called social syncretism, that delightful fusion between self and other that we call confusion, never fully disappears.[17] Its reappearances in adult life are tolerated in romance, in the parenting of our own children, in the experiencing of another's world through aesthetic and religious experience. It also provides the possibility of caring for other people's children, the most serious and promising commitment of pedagogy. We are ashamed of these perceptions when they are disclaimed by another, by the rebellious child or the distracted lover, the reluctant student, reminding us that our expectation is an atavism from our infancy.

I also offer these portraits of neonatal development because they reveal our own investments in these narratives of our origins. Daniel Stern, whose own work will be discussed presently, explains that researchers combine their data on what he calls the "observed infant" with their own understandings of lived social experience in order to infer what life is like for the infant: "the subjective life of the adult, as self-narrated, is the main source of inference about the infant's felt quality of social experience. A degree of circularity is unavoidable."[18] This hermeneutic of the infant text, reading the beginning through the end and the end through the beginning, is of particular interest to the questions about education and reproduction that we are asking here. If curriculum is the deliberate effort to contradict and compensate for one's original relation to the child, it is important to see how that original relation is construed. When the attachment of mother and child is depicted as empty, undifferentiated need, then paternal intervention is indeed warranted if ego development is to occur. Or is it that in order to justify paternal intervention a fantasied, regressive maternal attachment is constructed? Women must remember and articulate the experience of child nurture so that we can bring what we know from the complex, sustained, and exciting labor of child care into the intellectual structures of the disciplines and the methods of pedagogy. It becomes important to ascertain what role, if any, this knowledge derived from the experience of nurture has in contemporary theories of development and the self.

Jacques Lacan's sense of the etiology of the self is of interest to us, for it is he who has also theorized the relation of identity to knowing, linking language to the structuring of the ego and the process of becoming gendered. He works with a concept of identity that is founded upon an understanding of how one looks to others. When the infant first recognizes herself in a mirror, she receives information about herself that she never had before, information that she may never have received at all without the presence of a reflecting agent outside her own body. The one that the infant discovers in a mirror, in her mother's eye, is, Lacan maintains, a narcissistic identity that is alienated at the moment that it is claimed, for the visual image is mediated through the other.[19] Lacan assumes that, prior to this mirror or "Imaginary" phase, as he calls it, the child is amorphous, and he calls the libidinous infant *l'hommelette*, a "little man" or "omelette."[20] Elizabeth Wright's account of Lacan's mirror stage follows:

> Whereas before it experienced itself as a shapeless mass, it now gains a sense of wholeness, an ideal completeness, and this all without effort. This gratifying experience of a mirror-image is a metaphorical parallel of an unbroken union between inner and outer, a perfect control that assures immediate satisfaction for desire. . . . [Both the child's and the mother's desire] combine to keep the child's ego-concept in a profoundly illusory state. The absence of a gap for the child between a concept and its application is a proof of the concept's inadequacy; the ego-concept has never been tested in use. The gap appears with the initiation of the child into the order of language, what Lacan calls the "Symbolic Order." The structures of language are marked with societal imperatives—the Father's rules, laws and definitions, among which are those of "child" and "mother." Society's injunction that desire must wait, that it must formulate in the constricting word whatever demand it may speak, is what effects the split between conscious and unconscious, the repression that is the tax exacted by the use of language.[21]

This assumption of the formlessness of the infant and of the undifferentiated sense that he has of himself and the world prior to the mirror phase, which endows him with a sense, however spurious, of his distinct integrity, is contradicted by the recent research of Daniel Stern, who reports an emergent sense of self in the infant's early days, related to organized and organizing perceptions of his own body and of those with whom he interacts. No scrambled egg, Stern's infant does have some sense of self prior to language and reflection and never experiences self/other undifferentiation:

> During the period of from two to six months, infants consolidate the sense of a core self as a separate, cohesive, bounded physical unit with a sense of their own agency, affectivity, and continuity in time. There is no symbiotic-like phase. In fact, the subjective experiences with another can occur only after a sense of a core self and a core other exists. Union experiences are thus viewed as the successful result of actively organizing the experience of self-being-with-another, rather than as the product of a passive failure of the ability to differentiate self from other.[22]

The gaze that organizes this infant's world, clearly more coddled than scrambled, is active and communicating. Unlike the gaze of Lacan's babe, this infant doesn't cling, holding the mother in a narcissistic grip, but engages and withdraws, responds and refuses. The early maturity of the visual-motor system permits the infant to "exert major control over the initiation, maintenance, termination and avoidance of social contact with mother," thus helping to regulate the intensity and frequency of social stimulation.[23] As the infant focuses or averts his eyes, stares, becomes glassy-eyed, or stares past his caregiver, Stern holds that he is negotiating issues of autonomy or independence that we later recognize in early walking behavior, or the "terrible twos."

Furthermore, the mother, as well, is not frozen in the primal gaze for she is an active, initiating, and responding subject herself, engaged in a vibrant prelinguistic dialogue with her infant. Now Webster defines symbiosis as "the living together in more or less intimate association or even close union of two dissimilar organisms" and as "mutual cooperation between persons and groups in a society esp. when ecological interdependence is involved." Stern's repudiation of symbiosis suggests that he too has collapsed the word that signals the intimate and contingent relations of mother and child that link them through time and space into a sticky, viscous undifferentiation. Despite the exquisite attention that his research and his book bring to maternal nurture, in the attempt to establish the credibility of the infant's emergent self he falls into the old trap of overstating the distinction between mother and child. The middle is hard to sing.

This is the realm of the semiotic that Kristeva claims for female knowledge. Grounded in the body, engaged with the other in play, Kristeva's child, in Wright's words, "chuckles its way into selfhood" and retains this presymbolic capacity to celebrate disorder even after acquiring language and sexual identity.[24]

Secure in the awareness that was grounded in feeling, in the mimesis of touch, movement, and a sense of self that did not isolate one's self from others, the child confronts discontinuity between herself and others as well as the unsettling information that she is seen by others as she can never see herself. Although narcissistic character disorders described in individual pathology by Heinz Kohut and in cultural pathology by Christopher Lasch come to expression at this junction in development,[25] they are caused much earlier by a disruption in the parent/child attachment. Only when the passage to the world and others is facilitated through touch and feeling, the movement and melody of the primordial choreography of early attachment, can the child tolerate the threat of the look. Only when the child is secure in her attachment to the looker can the rupture in that attachment that the look signifies be borne. Otherwise, the child and, later, the adult she becomes must strive to subsume the look and the looker, to take to herself the source of herself, which is the image that the other has of her.

Lacan's genetic history of the look has contributed to our understanding of narcissism. The popular misunderstanding of narcissism as self-love, perpetuated by the myth of the Greek youth morbidly drawn to his own image, misconstrues the narcissist's preoccupation with the other's look as an expression of excessive self-esteem. On the contrary, it is the child whose early dependencies and attachment needs have been thwarted or disrupted who is drawn to her image, not as a projection of herself but as that part of herself that she gets from others.

Hide-and-seek games, and the refusal to be observed, all accompany the child's perception of the look. Her realization of her own separateness implies the autonomy of others, and as she plays out her anxiety about their appearance and disappearance in hide-and-seek and peekaboo games, she also experiments with the power to control the gaze of the other.

In an attempt to capture the look that has captured her, the child is drawn to the objects of the parents' world with which she shares the look that constitutes her identity. Now the look of the parents is actively sought. "Look, look," the child implores, begging the glance that will ratify her activity. Now the child follows the parent's gaze when it is not directed toward her and is thus drawn into the world of her parent's attention.

For the parents and the child, the touch, the voice, and the living space they share persist in tying them to each other like the crossed taut strings of a cat's cradle. Disapproval, encouragement, contact, and guidance are as likely to come through touch and sound as they are through sight. Home is mapped on coordinates of physical intimacy: the rhythm of feet on the stairs, the sound of breathing, the cough in the night. The jacket draped over the chair, the laughter, and the warm forehead are moments of a child's presence that displace the sight of her as the primordial sensation of the other. Carl Frankenstein's phrase, the "near one," captures both the proximity and the differentiation that the mother and infant enjoy. Significantly, this spatial metaphor for attachment defines closeness by the space between mother and child, acknowledging that their love "takes place" in a world.[26]

The child is lived before she is thought. The look that passes between mother and child is not their only passage to attachment or differentiation. And even if the look confers the illusions of individuality upon the child as Lacan argues it does, its antecedents, sound and touch, continue to testify to the ways that mother and child are and continue to be fused. The look that passes between mother and child does not constitute only the child's sense of self; it contributes to the mother's as well. Surrounded by a world she already cares about, and other people she cares for, the mother's identity may not be subsumed in that look as Lacan maintains the child's is. But, as Chodorow's work suggests, the mother's identification with her child is a significant one, recapitulating her own infantile attachments to her own mother and intertwining her own activity, development, and future with that of the infant she parents. To think the child is as difficult for the parent as it is for the child to think herself.[27] It is not that the parent doesn't construct an image for her child that records memories of and hopes for her but that the child's identity with all its imagery is perpetually undermined and corrected by the parent's grasp, however intuited and silent, of the latent possibilities within the child that circumstances have prohibited from achieving expression. Even though the look supersedes touch, as the child draws away from parents into the family that will be formed through her own touch, and just as rational secondary processes evolve to dominate the primary thought and sensual apodicity of infant experience, the parent/child relationship has the capacity to be the social relation where these archaic modes of relating to the world through others may be sustained and expressed.

Because the parent/child relationship has the capacity to endure, it undergoes transformations that release the child from the trap of the parent's look. Every look emanates from a certain perspective. The look requires distance. The nursing child, nine inches from her mother's face, is placed at a nearness that precludes the manipulation of distance: the nearness of attachment. But as movement and space enlarge the child's world, as the child's capacity to symbolize, to hold the world in her head through imagery, develops, the perspectives that she takes on the world and that the world takes on her grow more varied and complex. The world that could be claimed only by being grasped can now be pointed to. Desire, the search for the absent object, provokes the look that fills the eye with intentionality. The signals that the child learns to express her need are signs that evolve within the look of the other. There is no consequence in pointing to an object if no one is there to witness the gesture.[28] The capacity to symbolize, to associate signs with the world and abstraction with gratification, rests on the ratification of the other's look and ultimately upon her response.

And it is through signs or language that, Lacan maintains, the child masters the code that will release her from the look as she grasps the history and particularity of the perspective that shaped the look that shaped her. The reflection that transforms the child from the object of another's gaze into a subject requires understanding the image of oneself that is formed in the other's eye. Reflecting upon her own educational experience, Carolyn Proga wrote this narrative a few years ago when she was an undergraduate at William Smith College:

> Saturdays, when I was younger, were always fun. I appreciated them, and looked forward to them with great eagerness. I remember one Saturday morning, in particular, in the fall of my sixth year.
>
> My brother and I were very close. He is only a little more than a year older than me, so we were automatic companions for each other. He loved his "seniority"; a day didn't go by when I wasn't reminded of this by his saying, "I'm older, you know." On that Saturday, we were playing outside together. At the time, my mother had a big thing about matching outfits.

My two older sisters were dressed alike, as were Mark, my brother, and I. We were wearing similar blue jeans, T-shirts, and sweatshirt jackets, his red, mine blue. One of our favorite playthings was a silver and copper-colored, pedal-powered car. There was room for only one to provide the energy, but the open space behind that seat allowed plenty of room for someone else to catch a free ride. Mark was giving me lessons on how to steer the car, everything about how to get to where you wanted to go, from both forward and backward directions. I remember how I ran over his toes, quite a few times, and smack into him, once, when the brakes proved to be a bit tricky to set into action. (Later, when I was learning how to drive a real car, Mark refused to have anything to do with the lessons.) During the course of the morning, I remember looking up at our house and seeing my father at the window of one of the upstairs bedrooms. He held his movie camera, and was recording my brother's and my every movement.

I remember feeling very surprised. Perhaps that morning would have not remained so clear in my mind if seeing my father with a movie camera was a common thing. But it wasn't. He loved filming special occasions of my cousins or other more distant relatives, but almost never took movies of my sisters, my brother, and me. The times he did take films of us were always seldom, and, also, of completely everyday actions, like summer days when we would all play in the stream of water from the garden hose in the back yard, or the games of my brother and me that fall morning.

I learned that turning a steering wheel right when moving backward makes the front end swing left, that my brother's patience in instruction was really for his own benefit, for after that morning, he got far more free rides than me, and, from my dad, that maybe the special, unusual occasions of those people very close to you aren't always what's priceless to capture; to remember a few of the little things might be worth more.

After writing this narrative of educational experience, Carolyn deconstructs the look that turned time into memory, that froze play into meaning:

It seems so strange to remember how I felt when I saw my father at the upstairs window of our house, with his camera. My brother and I just didn't have as good of a time, after we realized that we were being watched and recorded. I wanted to show just how unusual the entire event was. Yet I couldn't do it very clearly.

I never like photographs; I always figured that if you needed a photograph of someone or something, to remember, then the person or event couldn't have been too important. John Berger, in his article, "Understanding a Photograph," talks about the possibilities as to why photographs (I think that films, movies, can really be considered close to the same thing) can seem so invading. The photographer chooses ". . . between photographing at x moment or at y moment" (p. 180). The subject doesn't have that much of a choice. And to see the picture, later, ". . . always and by its nature refers to what is not seen" (p. 180). When I see those home movies, I can remember the games; I can remember that little car so clearly, I can almost reach out and touch it. But I remember the feelings, toward my brother, toward my father, when I look at, and remember the situation, through my own mind's eye. No one else can feel that, when they see those movies.

I couldn't describe that feeling clearly at all. I made light of my "learning"; was it really so vital that I had learned how to steer that car? I think that it was more vivid, more painful, to realize that I didn't like my father watching so closely; invading. And to see those films now makes my remembrance too objective; how can I learn anything from that? ". . . nor can any such self-knowledge be properly characterized as objective knowledge" (Earle, *The Autobiographical Consciousness*, p. 9). It's aggravating—I don't like the feeling of confusion. "Know thyself," Earle stresses. But how can I, with someone—maybe even myself—looking over my shoulder?

This student, like so many of us, will carry this question throughout her life, reclaiming through language the perspective that objectifies her.

THE LOOK IN PEDAGOGY

The "look" in pedagogy, like the "look" in parenting, is also arranged in time and space. If the history of the parent's look is lodged in the biological moments in the history of the child's physical development, the history of the teacher's look is lodged in culture, in the social forms and institutions that exist at any given historical moment and through which society shapes the young. The moments of the parental look, from its initial misunderstanding to the shifting asymmetries of attachment, from its objectifications to the reclamation of subjectivity through mastery of sign and language, are also essential phases in the dialogue between teacher and student that we call pedagogy.

Within the intimacy of the family these moments are mediated through the material struggle to maintain life. The family is always preoccupied with material necessity. Procuring and preparing food, providing and maintaining shelter, sustaining each others' bodies are the work of the family. Martin Buber points to the apprenticeship relationship to exemplify a pedagogical relationship that is, like parenting, engaged with the material world.[29] Apprentice and master were engaged in a similarly purposeful yet barely rationalized relation where the work literally *at hand* defined the dimensions of their task. In contrast, the relation of the contemporary teacher to student has evolved into one which, though less clearly instrumental, has become more self-consciously intentional as the press of material necessity seeps out of schooling. Teachers and students manipulate signs and symbols. The medium through which we communicate is knowledge, the codes and methods of the academic disciplines, by now highly abstracted from the material necessity and politics that originally shaped them. Buber describes the purposeful character of contemporary pedagogy:

> The world, that is the whole environment, nature and society, "educates" the human being; it draws out his powers and makes him grasp and penetrate its objections. What we term education, conscious and willed, means *a selection by many of the effective world*: it means to give decisive effective power to a selection of the world which is concentrated and manifested in the educator. The relation in education is lifted out of the purposefully streaming by of all things, and is marked off as purpose. In this way, through the educator the world for the first time becomes the true subject of its effect.[30]

Buber goes on to consider the problem of intersubjectivity when purpose is gathered only into the eye of the teacher:

> If education means to let a selection of the world affect a person through the medium of another person, then the one through whom this takes place, rather, who makes it take place through himself, is caught in a strange paradox. What is otherwise found only as grace, inlaid in the folds of life—the influencing of the lives of others with one's own life—becomes here a function and a law. But since the educator has to such extent replaced the master, the danger has arisen that the new phenomenon, the will to educate, may degenerate into arbitrariness, and that the educator may carry out his selection and his influence from himself and his idea of the pupil, not from the pupil's own reality.[31]

The purposes that pulse through a family's labor—the blanket that is spread, the dish that is washed—or through the work of the apprentice and master—the glass that is blown, the bricks that are laid—mark their shared attachment to the world. The material, sensual presence of the world draws the one who teaches and the one who learns to each other as they approach it; the third term is the object of their intentionality and the basis for their intersubjectivity.

In object relations theory the third term appears both as the father, the one who forms the relational triangle releasing mother and child from a dyadic isolation, as in Chodorow's presentation, and as a transitional object invested with the child's ambivalent feelings for the mother, as in the work of Winnicott.[32] In Winnicott's work the "potential space" of play invites the child to express his conflicting and shifting desires for attachment and independence, as he, for instance, cuddles and abuses his teddy bear or his blanket. It is tempting to seize these constructs for curriculum, for we seek a middle place, and the third terms of each triangle appear to provide the middle terms of curriculum by offering bridges that span the distance between mother and child. Whereas Winnicott's transitional objects honor their relation, bringing them together when they are apart, Lacan's intervening father holds them apart, allowing the span that might mediate their relation to subsume it.

Lacan's version of the relational triangle collapses into a dyad. In his account, as we have seen, the symbolic overwhelms the imaginary, and even though the child continues to look for the mother in the forms of the father's culture, the gratification of that look is forever deferred. For the father, or "phallus" in Lacan's account, is merely the marker for that power we attribute to someone else, always imputed to another— the father, the word, the law, the state, the science, the deity—but never realized. This account makes the third term an unrepentant murderer, destroying the illusion of completion given in the dyadic romance of mother and child and never providing the compensation it promises. Lacan accomplishes both matricide and patricide, and because Lacan has effaced touch and sound, his domain of the "real," even though it contains the imaginary and the symbolic, loses the world and reduces culture to nostalgia. Our traditions of teaching literature described in Chapter 6, "On Teaching the Text," provide a curriculum that recapitulates the ritual of this double murder.

Winnicott's version could be appropriated to the same conclusion if we interpret the "transition" of the transitional object and the transitional space to be merely a developmental passage to the accommodations civilization requires. A curriculum model that adopted that schema would offer schooling as a mediating space that invites students to work out their passage from their families to the public world, tolerating their ambivalence, providing space and forms for its expression and finally its surrender. Wright recognizes this tendency in Richard Kuhns's application of Winnicott's work to art:

> Objects viewed from the standpoint of private sexual need remain fictional; reality belongs with the public object. Kuhns thus contradicts his attempt to keep ambivalence in the argument: tragedy becomes tamed to an experience which will enable spectators to refashion unreal inner needs in the mold of the real public and political system.[33]

The problem is that both agents of the third term in objects relations theories, the father and the transitional object, are transitional themselves.[34] Materialism and idealism assert their dualistic demands again. If, as Wright suggests, Winnicott's transitional play activity offers us objects as they *are* and allows us to fool with them until we have come to play with them as we *must*, then the materialist demand that we accept the world as it is before we have acted on it and allow *it* to act on *us* is fulfilled. If the father intervenes to destroy one illusion in the name of yet another, then the world he provides is a tragic fiction and we are wandering forever in idealism's maze. The constructivist epistemology alone allows the real to be situated in the middle space. There, what we know is the symbolic expression of our action in the world, and that action requires feeling as well as thought, touch and sound and movement as well as the look. It provides the possibility that in the action and reflection of teachers and students the world that we live and know will change.

Buber's vision of education that takes up the world requires that the third term be both method and content of education. Nevertheless, if touch and sound are the sensual passages between parent and child and world, those modes of contact are associated with an intimacy that we limit to erotic or familial relations or to some strenuous forms of labor. In contrast, the look dominates the classroom. As centralized and efficient urban schools draw large numbers of students together, intimacy diminishes. Touch is avoided, and sound is muted in the corridors of the nation's schools. And when touch and sound do appear, they come banging on the door, demanding to be let in, pounding with anger, flailing with violence. The grip of the visual and the primacy of spectacle are problems of contemporary life that we may turn to later, but first we need to examine the postures and perspectives that have led to the look that transfixes pedagogy.

The child's reality that Buber calls us to share is filled with her life in the family. We have noted the way in which the school has been pitted against the family in the development of the individual's gender identity and the society's collective cultural identity. The reasons for this antagonism are manifold. In this country they were tied to the impulse to forge a community and a national character from a populace drifting off into a distracting wilderness.[35] The "Olde Deluder Satan Law" threatened members of the Massachusetts Bay Colony with the intervention of the church if families failed to teach their children to read Scripture. In the late nineteenth century the ethnicity of immigrant families was consciously undermined by schools and social agencies eager to shape a conventional work force that could support the norms of collective labor.

In our culture and in preindustrial cultures as well, schooling has provided the context where the maternal influence over the child's development, so pervasive in the domestic setting where mothers have provided so much of the primary nurturance, is denied. The gender analysis of schooling has led us to examine the connections between parenting and pedagogy as we investigate the meaning of the educational enterprise for the men and women whose most compelling and significant human relationships are those they have shared with their own parents and their own children. In Chapter 1 I have argued that the function of curriculum is to wrest the relation of child and parent from the overdetermination of biology and history, each parent hoping to contradict the necessary form of its first relation to the child, the inferential nature of the father's paternity, the symbiotic nature of the mother's maternity. Chapter 2 followed the women who entered teaching in the nineteenth century from their homes as they walked to school, shedding the power and intimacy of the mother look, accompanied by touch and sound, for the master's stern glance deployed in the theater of the classroom.

Exchanging the fluid, active space of their homes for the confining chambers of the school/church, teachers promoted the Christian conception of grace earned through the denial of the body, activity, sensuality, physical labor, and politics. Grace came from an all-seeing but unseen deity; confession was delivered to an invisible confessor.[36] The pulpit that separated the pastor from his flock permitted the look to operate, but at a distance. Initiated by the church, with clerics as the first teachers, the *mise-en-scène* of pedagogy gave the look locus and direction, establishing firm distinctions between those who gave it and those who got it.

Foucault links the deployment of the look to the history of the concept of discipline manifested in the developing institutions of medicine, the military, the penal system, and schooling. In *Discipline and Punish* he argues that the eighteenth century substituted a subtle and pervasive coercion through the training and supervision of human behavior for the terrifying spectacles of punishment and the control of the other's body achieved through slavery or vassalage that had functioned as earlier forms of social control. No longer was discipline to be imposed only upon a particularly aberrant population; now it was diffused throughout the populace not as a corrective but as an essential theme constituting the education of the young:

> The historical moment of the disciplines was the moment when an art of the human body was born which was directed not only at the growth of its skills, nor at the intensification of its subjection, but at the formulation of a relation that in the mechanism itself makes it more obedient as it becomes more useful, and conversely. . . . In short, it dissociates power from the body; on the other hand, it turns it into an aptitude, a "capacity," which it seeks to increase; on the other, it reverses the course of energy, the power that might result from it, and turns into a relation of strict subjection.[37]

Whereas the look of parenting surpasses touch, totalizing it without obliterating it or the symbiosis it expresses, the look of pedagogy as it has evolved in schools repudiates touch. The teacher is untouchable, invulnerable. The gradual and orderly surrender of one's body is the project of the elementary school. It may only be reclaimed once it is habituated to the forms of athletics and dance. When Piaget posits a stage of motor operations as essential to cognition, educators are at a loss to recover the bodies that this phase of cognition requires. Stillness is the achievement of the science of *super-vision*, an arrangement of persons in collective units accessible to constant surveillance. By arranging students in rows, all eyes facing front, directly confronting the back of a fellow's head, meeting the gaze only of the teacher, the discipline of the contemporary classroom deploys the look as a strategy of domination. Foucault maintains that the prototype for the surveillance of the classroom is the panopticon, a prison designed by Jeremy Bentham that permitted a single warden to scrutinize many but permitted the many to see only the one, the warden,[38] and cites N. H. Julius's definition of the panoptic principle:

> "To render accessible to a multitude of men the inspection of a small number of objects": this was the problem to which the architecture of temples, theatres and circuses responded. With spectacle, there was a predominance of public life, the intensity of festivals, sensual proximity. In these rituals in which blood flowed, society found new vigor and formed for a moment a single great body. The modern age poses the opposite problem: "To procure for a small number, or even for a single individual, the instantaneous view of a great multitude."[39]

The look that constitutes identity in school is organized to undermine dialogue. The theater of the classroom manipulates what Lacan has called the "scopic drive," permitting students to be seen and to look, but never at what they desire to see."[40] Foucault points to the analysis and categorization of students into ranks and hierarchies and to the examination as procedures that prescribe what is to be seen. This look does not search for the student's reality, as Buber suggests, for it does not receive "the purposefully streaming by of all things" but only examines the student before it to note the resemblance between the child and the image established for its development. The exercise displaces the dialogue as school identity is formed, not through symbiosis and differentiation but by mimesis and convention. Peer culture reinforces this surveillance, punishing nonconformity with exile and ridicule. Mystified and disclaimed, the perspective of pedagogy is withheld from the student. Rather than finding language to name and appropriate the interests and history that have named him, the student too often sees the perspective behind the look as impersonal, inevitable, and determining. Lifted from history, motives, and politics, the look of the teacher is endorsed with an authority that disclaims history, motives, and politics.

As women entered the classrooms, prepared to adopt the stance, the gesture, the glare of discipline—don't raise your voice, I was told when I started, just stand there and look at them—we brought our own history and associations to the roles we were expected to play. In *Ways of Seeing*, John Berger distinguishes man the surveyor from woman the surveyed:

Men act and *women appear*. Men look at women. Women watch themselves being looked at. This determines not only most relations between
men and women but also the relation of women to themselves. The
surveyor of woman in herself is male: the surveyed female. Thus she turns
herself into an object—and most particularly an object of vision: a
sight.[41]

The power of the look to dominate is inscribed in the visual images of
women found in our great museums, tawdry porn theaters, and fashion
magazines. Static, inhibited from moving by binding clothing, high-
heeled shoes, ornate coiffures, or naked and supine, female subjectivity
is absorbed into flesh, arranged for the viewing pleasure of men. Berger
argues that these images designed for pleasure and lucre express the
gender politics of the men and women who look at these images as well
as the men and women who paint and pose for them. If we accept this
premise then we cannot assume that when the young female schoolteacher entered the classroom designed to deploy the look of the male
minister, she did not first and foremost experience herself as the object
rather than the subject of the look. I suspect that we may still be frozen
in the costumes, gestures, and theater that she devised to assert and
sustain her agency in the classroom.

Submitting to the school's fears of sexuality, especially female sexuality, fears that were clearly the projections of the men who designed
the spectacle so that they could look at others, we dressed for repression. Until the sixties, when students violated dress codes with flam-
boyant impunity, we were dowdy. (And we still take out the white
blouse with the little ruffles around the collar for Open School Night.)

Dreading the objectification of the look, prohibited from extending
touch, the female teacher turns to talk to assert her subjectivity. Although John Goodlad's findings that the majority of classroom discourse is dominated by teacher talk can be traced to the lecture traditions of Greek rhetoric and Christian liturgy, it is also possible that we
are sending out waves of words to ward off the look that surges toward
us in the stillness of the silent classroom.[42] If teacher talk dominates
classrooms in which we hear sound, in quiet classrooms teachers have
avoided the student's gaze by immersing him in the workbook or
"ditto" exercise that grasps the gaze, draws it down, and keeps it
anchored until the next assignment is handed out. Avoidance of the
gaze of male students may also explain the female teacher's tendency to
call on boys more frequently than girls. Studies indicate that boys

receive more direct teacher questions than girls, more praise and criticism, more help and attention to their work, and more receptivity to their ideas in classroom discussion.[43] Although engaging them in classroom discourse may be a form of control, it is also a way of interrupting their gaze by breaking it with the specificity and animation of speech.

Forbidden to look at each other, and now forbidden to look at the teacher, children become adept at surreptitious glances and clever about protecting themselves from being seen when they look. Learning and teaching become defined by what can be seen, and, as John Holt has argued, both teachers and some achieving students become adept at a theater of understanding that strikes the gestures of comprehension and conviction for the approval of the attentive viewer.[44]

An infant's response to the excessive ordering and shaping of her experience may suggest the curriculum histories of the blank and distracted looks that often mask the eyes of students. Stern reports the response of an infant he calls Molly to the controlling and intrusive agendas of her mother:

> She determined which toy Molly would play with, how Molly was to play with it ("Shake it up and down—don't roll it on the floor"), when Molly was done playing with it, and what to do next ("Oh, here is Dressy Bessy. Look!"). The mother overcontrolled the interaction to such an extent that it was often hard to trace the natural crescendo and decrescendo of Molly's own interest and excitement....
>
> Molly found an adaptation. She gradually became more compliant. Instead of actively avoiding or opposing these intrusions, she became one of those enigmatic gazers into space. She could stare through you, her eyes focused somewhere at infinity and her facial expressions opaque enough to be just uninterpretable, and at the same time remain in good contingent contact and by and large do what she was invited or told to do. Watching her over the months was like watching her self-regulation of excitement slip away.... When playing alone she did not recover it, remaining somewhat aloof from exciting engagements with things.[45]

Teachers are themselves evaluated by "being observed." Under the eye of the silent supervisor, often the male administrator, the teacher arranges herself, her classroom, her children for display. D. Jean Clandinin's recent study of two teachers is deliberately organized to liberate them from the objectifications of educational evaluation and research by describing the images they hold about their work. In order to avoid the look that dominates by seeing but not being seen, she refuses a privileged view, engages in the work of the classroom, and reveals her own perceptions as well as those of the teachers she describes.[46] Not only does this approach rectify the politics of supervision that has dominated teaching, it also makes it possible to address new aspects of the work of teaching if it releases teachers from the obligation of arranging themselves, their students, and their spaces for someone else's view. Marie Clay's research on reading instruction in New Zealand avoided the distortions of observation by having very successful reading teachers view videotapes of themselves teaching children how to read. It was from the teachers' views of their own behavior that the purpose and logic of their actions were drawn.[47]

In an attempt to disassociate themselves from an authority that disallows dialogue, many teachers have adopted the stance of humanistic psychology that would replace the look of domination with the mutuality of egalitarianism. Loath to dominate others or be objectified under the gaze of their students, they strive for reciprocity. Seeking a feminist pedagogy, Susan Friedman reports that, reluctant to identify with male authority, she turned to "facilitation," only to discover that she had muted the authority and energy that the nurturance and teaching of her students required.[48] Refusing the surveyed/surveyor oppositions of pedagogy, feminist teachers are sometimes tempted to repudiate their power, mistaking it for authority. Just as that abdication releases them from the tyranny of the look, it also relinquishes the power of pedagogy: the capacity to share the world that is the object of our scholarship, our concern, our passion, and our action with our students.

"My face in thine eye, thine in mine appeares." That mutuality, for all its romanticism, fails the pedagogical project in three respects. First, like the fascination of lovers, it is blind to the world, making the other's look the end rather than the means in the act of knowing. Second, this stance is dishonest, for it denies the asymmetry in the student/teacher relation. It disclaims the teacher's power, in the world and in the institution, and in so doing prohibits the student from deconstructing and appropriating the perspective of the teacher's look for his or her own vision. Third, the ideal of equality fosters an eroticism that ensnares both teacher and student in their reciprocal gaze. Buber imputes the same objectification to eroticism that he locates in the will to power.[49] Both agendas undermine the dialogue he calls education: the former by appropriating the other to one's own subjectivity, the latter by ignoring the subjectivity of the other it objectifies.

Parenting permits the ultimate reciprocity that pedagogy denies because it evolves in time. The history of the parent/child relation is one of exchanged glances. The child will walk many miles and make many visits to understand the look under which he has stood. Even the adult who has grown beyond the frame of his parents' look will pursue them, imploring them to see again and alter their perspective. Finally, as old age reverses the original relations of dependency, the adult who was once the child is now the overseer within whose gaze the aged parent still sees his former power and possibility.

Denied duration, pedagogy precludes such reciprocity. Denied duration, pedagogy precludes the long dialogue through which the child reappropriates that which he gave up in order to be a person in his parents' eyes.[50]

The teachers look out to the world and through the world to the student. It is this detour through the world that we call curriculum, the third thing. It is what engages us, just as making dinner engages the family or making goblets engaged the goldsmith Marcone and his apprentice Cellini. The look of pedagogy is the sideways glance that watches the student out of the corner of the eye. It is not easy to act like a teacher in the theater of contemporary schools. It requires seeing others and being seen, without being reduced to our images.

Finally, the world we work with, the curriculum, is itself an archive of the look as it is a collection and ordering for representation of the signs of our collective experience. It is the teacher who responds to the curriculum as a living sign beckoning us to the world that moves beneath it and curls up against its edges. Or it is the teacher who presents curriculum as a prohibition. NO TRESPASSING, a sign that denies access, enforces distance, and walls off the world. When curriculum is alive, it invites the student to reappropriate it as she reclaims her identity from its origin in her parents' look, grasping and dislodging and reclaiming its perspective. When the curriculum is a dead sign, all of us, teachers and students, stumble under its empty stare.

6 On Teaching the Text: Trapped in Transference; or, Gypped Again

I did not start reading *Teaching the Text* so that I could write about feminist pedagogy.[1] In fact, the project offered respite from the politics of knowledge, I thought, as Jo Anne Pagano and I planned the symposium where we, Max Van Manen, and William Pinar would each respond to the teaching lectures of twelve members of the English faculty of Cambridge University. One would read a text that is teaching a text, as a teacher I assumed; and I stepped into the text expecting to receive and return the gracious, if not complicit, glance of collegiality. I met, instead, a polite but distracted stare, and within it I became a student once again, mesmerized in the look that did not look at me. What follows is the process that brought me from my seat in the back of the room to the points of view enjoyed and suffered by my British colleagues. To understand their perspectives is not necessarily to share them, and in the space between their practice and my perception of it, perhaps this other pedagogy will appear.

AS I BEGIN TO WRITE my response to *Teaching the Text* I am as displeased with myself, its reader, as I am irritated by its writers. The text has placed me in a position that I had hoped to have escaped long ago. It is like being seated once more in the dining room of the grand-aunt who used to be so disapproving when you stole a glance at yourself in her mirrored wall or slurped your soup. Or it is like reentering the restaurant where you used to meet for lunch all during that humid summer as he waited for the right day to tell you he was leaving. My aunt is long dead, and my tentative friend has probably spent thirty more summers in sticky restaurants waiting for the right moment to split. And still I cannot enter those places without becoming the peeking, slurping child, the nonchalant, dread-filled girlfriend.

I am reminded of a play by Witold Gombrowicz, *The Marriage*, where the situation and a careless gesture catapult the players into roles that they had not expected to play.[2] After reading *Teaching the Text*, I find myself petulant, defensive, and petty, and these are not the responses that I had expected or would have chosen. I have long been an admirer of Frank Kermode, one of the contributors to this collection. I even watch for the ad he runs in the *New York Review of Books* offering to sublet his London flat and spend some time imagining what it would be like to live among his books, to find his thoughts where they have slipped down between the sofa cushions, or sip them from his coffee cups.

I am afraid that I have found Kermode's ad somewhat more inviting than this text. The editors provide an elegantly negligent hospitality. You're welcome to breakfast; take whatever you'd like out of the fridge. They merely wish "to reflect the reality of teaching in a university English department."[3] And so they have placed before us a sample of their teaching lectures to demonstrate how literary theory is revealed in the practice of their teaching. With some modesty and with no attempt to anticipate or to manipulate our responses, they stand before us—Kermode, and Christopher Prendergast, Lisa Jardine, Tony Tanner, Raymond Williams, et al.—as they have stood before their students, leaning on the podium perhaps, maybe pacing now and then. In the theater of their pedagogy, I become a student again: "In this lecture I want to investigate some of the terms in which Milton's language has been discussed in the twentieth century."[4]

That is how Colin MacCabe starts out. And again I am slipping into one of the rows of the small theater in Millbank Hall, always just late enough to miss the first few words of Professor Rosenberg's Milton lecture, copying the first few words from the notebook of the person in the next seat. And so it is again as a student, a sulky twenty-year-old, that I must read these lectures and hope that as I take notes and rage again at the mystification, the obliqueness, the distance, I will catch a glance, a gesture, that will beckon me closer.

It was at Barnard College, after I boarded the IRT pursuing the text across the East River, that I attended such lectures in courses labeled Chaucer, Milton, and Shakespeare. I had no idea what studying the text was about then, but I wrote papers about it, trying to get it right. Most often, I got a B−, which meant, "You seem to have done the reading and are trying to get it right."

On Morningside Heights I thought I had met the humanities in person when Mark Van Doren came to speak to English majors at the Friday afternoon tea in the college parlor. He told us that the truth of Shakespeare was not hidden in cracks between the lines or in deep underground streams that ran beneath the text but that it was visible, completely articulated, and fully drawn—there in the text itself. That afternoon in the college parlor, holding my gold-rimmed coffee cup, sinking into the rosiness of the five o'clock sky, the ruby orientals, and Van Doren's pink cheeks, flushed with revelation, I was grateful for this clear enunciation of truth. It was so clear that I couldn't figure out why I hadn't thought of it myself. Now that I had his thought of it, of course, I had absolutely no idea what to do with it. But I remember it to this day, and I suspect that he may have actually told us what to do with it and I missed or misunderstood the directions. To this day the pronouncement is still remembered with awe and guilt, even though I now see that Van Doren wasn't talking to us at all but to the psychoanalytic critics who were certainly not seated there among us in that college parlor on that Friday afternoon.

During those years my favorite author was Henry James, and it was just as I was composing these remarks and reminiscences that I understood my undergraduate affinity for his tentative Americans abroad, stumbling around in another world, trying to get it right, and finding out the real truth always when it was too late to do anything about it.

Now, there is some justification for feeling displaced in this text about teaching texts. The texts themselves are familiar, save for a few, but the course that surrounds them is not. There is hardly any acknowledgment of context. Few of these teachers provide a clue to the course that frames each lecture. We do not know whether this is one of a series of lectures on one author or book. We do not know whether the course is organized by method or genre or era. And we certainly have no idea what we, the students, are supposed to do in it. Once again, it is like coming in late to the lecture, but there is no one to tell us what we missed.

Teaching the Text makes me angry. I feel gypped. Not ripped off— nobody has grabbed my incredulity and run off with it—just gypped, like paying a cover charge when the act never shows up. Except for a colloquialism here or there, the texts do not seem markedly different from critical essays. In many cases the only indication that these are teaching lectures is the abrupt introduction of their subjects, suggesting to the reader that some statement of purpose, of selection, of intent, has been negotiated in another time and place. Late to the lecture again. I am so uninspired that as I write "I've been gypped" in the margin, I spell gypped "jipped" and then, wondering whether I have ever had occasion to write the word before, go to the dictionary to look it up. Both Webster's and the OED agree that gyp is short for gypsy, making my version insufficiently ethnic. But the OED also identifies gyps as the servants who used to wait on students at Cambridge. "An idle, useful set of hangers on the college, who procure the ale, pence &c. by running errands, and doing little services for their masters." There is this citation from a 1767 poem: "No more the jolly Jips . . . carol out their songs." (And here it *is* spelled "Jips.") Then there is this later reference from the writings of H. K. White in 1805: "My bed-maker, whom we call a gyp, from a Greek word signifying a vulture, runs away with everything he can lay his hands on." Toward the turn of the century we hear Wilkins and Vivian referring to "the spiritual destitution of the bedmakers and the gypes."[5] Clearly, this is an honored tradition that our distinguished Cambridge colleagues are observing as they offer their students less than they have bargained for. Convicted by the OED no less!

Now the crime as I see it is that the students are sitting there, taking notes, trying to learn how to read, and these teachers are not about to tell them. This is not to say that the teachers have no method to their madness but that it is not made explicit to the students seated before them. Two exceptions to this charge may be found in the lectures of Barrell and Williams.[6] Their approaches require students to see how the meaning of the text changes as they reorganize it by varying the prosody of a poem or the rhetorical conventions of the dramatic monologues. Barrell even leaves some space in his lecture for students to do something, to read the poem, to say what their reading suggests. The students in these classes can hardly leave the lecture muttering that they do not know what is going on. Nevertheless, reading these events, I am impatient. The code is given, explained, applied. it is everything I ever asked for, what Rosenberg and Van Doren never even intimated; yet, this focus on method, particularly in Williams's case, has the effect of subordinating the work to the code that the readers bring to it. It feels technical.

Here in the instrumentalism of the code-defining pedagogy, I can find my diploma, my exit visa from my seat in the lecture hall, the aisle seat, nine rows back. For it is my own students' reliance on instrumentalism that I rage against in this work we call teacher preparation. Their requests for method come in all forms: slavish imitation of standard models, endless repetition of the exercises presented in the teachers' manuals, impersonations of their professors' gestures, movements, intonations that border on caricature. Demands for method come from those whose actions are not organized around their own intentionality. And though I do not repudiate the reflexive review of the path once taken that may reveal another approach to yet another face of the mountain, all the marking and mapping and routing are but the obsessive preoccupations of an eagle scout looking for the badge instead of the mountain. So if it is my desire for method that identifies me as a student and brings back my own undergraduate mystification, humiliation, and uncertainty, it is my students' desire for method that shifts my identification to the other side of the podium and sends me back to the text for another reading.

This shift from student to teacher, from listener to speaker, from audience to actor, from child to parent, is not merely a developmental modulation. It is not a function of years or experience or a genetic unfolding of anything that I can see or name. Nevertheless, it is what I think reading and teaching are both about. In fact, I am arguing that the classroom and the text are the material through which this shift manifests itself. The shift is the dynamic movement within the form we call pedagogy.

Once again I am drawn to Susanne Langer's assertion that the "virtual," as distinct from the actual, is the subject matter of aesthetic meaning.[7] I turn back to an essay that I wrote in 1975, "Toward a Poor Curriculum," when I first started to think about Langer's analysis of art in relation to curriculum:

> Just as the artist's canvas holds virtual, not actual space, the composer's score, virtual not actual time, the curriculum provides virtual not actual experience, embodied in the academic disciplines. As such it is a field of symbols, abstract in the sciences, particular in the arts, for contact with the world.[8]

Now, for Langer an art form's presentation of the virtual is not merely a symbolic mirror of the material and action of existence. The virtual draws our attention to the organization of experience, the tensions, polarities, forces that are at play in every perception, act, form. So it is that music makes time itself perceptible by giving form and expression to its elements of duration, interruption, extension, repetition, and painting makes space visible by giving form and expression to its elements of presence and distance, continuity and separation, enclosure and expansion. It will always be easier to think of music and painting as art forms than it will be to think of teaching as an art form. This distinction is lodged in the material status of the art object and our tendency to isolate it from our existential worlds, an honorific isolation that has attenuated the power of the knowledge of art in our everyday lives, even as it has intensified its capacity to provide a critique of instrumental epistemologies. Because the class will never be as separate from the buzzing confusion as the painting or the symphony, the relation of its virtual sense to its actuality will never be easy to assess. Nevertheless, I wish to show that the issue of method and the shift that I have described earlier are essential elements in the virtual transference that is teaching and reading.

In psychoanalysis, transference refers to the process wherein the feelings and attitudes once attached to persons involved in the traumatic events in the analysand's history are displaced onto the analyst. The processes of therapy require the analysis of the transference so that these feelings and attitudes may function as markers, indicating the path back to the original relations that have been repressed. Transference takes place, Lacan argues, always in relation to the one who "knows," and knowing here means the one who appears to have control of the symbolic process.[9] Rather than seeing transference as the particular process that takes place between a neurotic patient and his psychoanalyst, Lacan identifies the process of becoming a self that everyone experiences as traumatic, a mistaken identity, and recognizes our relationship to the symbolic order and to anyone who signifies its power as transference. So this is the transference, then, that we bring from our infantile introduction to the symbolic order to our teachers. We expect them to know and, in that knowing, to confer knowledge and power on us. When we ask for their method we are struggling to wriggle out of the transference, our dependence on them, at the very time that we perpetuate that dependence as we assume that they "know." In effect we are asking for the links that form the chain of their intentionality without wondering or worrying whether we want to put this particular chain around our necks. In the preface to *Teaching the Text* the editors disclaim method as distinct from theory and refuse to isolate either aspect of teaching from the forms they assume in a particular pedagogical process.

> It is a particular feature of English "literary" criticism [they tell us], as opposed to continental modes of criticism, that it has rarely concerned itself with "pure" theory. The strength of English criticism lies in its practice; its potential weakness, in unreflected practice. It is thus neither surprising nor uncharacteristic that a commitment to theory among English critics reflects itself in practice, and that the emphasis is on approach—which is approach to—rather than on pure methodology and theorising.[10]

Now, I find this passage curiously and deliberately vague. It situates English literary critics between two audiences, one generally named and the other merely suggested, like a shadow or a passing breeze. The adversary is named: continental critics. But the other audience, the readers and students of English criticism, remains nameless, present only as the receiver and ultimate witness of the approach. This veiled address is not merely an expression of the collective coyness of this group of Cambridge scholars. Terry Eagleton's portrayal of the history and present politics of English literary criticism suggests that there is a tradition that claims criticism as its ritual and prohibits us from seeing it as a quirk peculiar to this group of colleagues.[11]

His analysis does help us to hear their resistance to continental criticism's "pure theory" as a refusal to relinquish the religious function of literature, whose forms, ceremonies, and language provide expression for a way of being in the world that is English—a reluctance, so to speak, to rattle their own chains.

Eagleton depicts English critics as intellectual immigration officers:

> their job is to stand at Dover as the new-fangled ideas are unloaded from Paris, examine them for the bits and pieces which seem more or less reconcilable with traditional critical techniques, wave these goods genially on and keep out of the country the rather more explosive items of equipment (Marxism, feminism, Freudianism) which have arrived with them.[12]

Now, what Marxism, feminism, and Freudianism make explicit is the relation of form to power. Each discourse is an exposé that identifies the manifest forms of ego identity, gender, production, art as cover-ups, crafted to conceal powers that are their negations. If the British emphasis on practice is designed to perpetuate their intentionalities without questioning them, the French interest is to deconstruct those intentionalities without practicing them. Each orientation gives up the world and, with the world, the student. What we share with students is the human project, which no one can escape, of transforming the stuff that surrounds us into a world we share through the action of our intentionality. If the British are fascinated with the object of their thought, the text, and the French with reflection on the structure of that thought, neither seems particularly concerned with the experience of the student, who is invited in each case to be the witness of approach, in short, the voyeur. When we observe the classroom from their perspectives, the interpretation of texts becomes theater and the relation of knowledge to power is played out in space and time. Well, if that is what our Cambridge teachers are about, it is clear why they would be a bit tentative about declaring it, draping this hegemonic mission in mysterious allusions to approach. Eagleton cannot tell us what their intentions are, finally, in respect to the audience of readers and students; that, finally, is what I am trying to find on the other side of my response to this telling of their readings called teaching.

Lacan has extended Freudianism into an analysis of the relations of sexuality, language, knowledge, and power.[13] Lacan's account of ego identity is a history of the look, a transaction between mother and child, that is present in the blocking, stage directions, and action that we call the theater of the classroom. In Lacan's account of ego identity, the child achieves a sense of self-image at the price of an enduring alienation. The child's self-image is granted by the presence and the look of the mother. In Lacan's tragic history this look that constitutes the ego is not only alien, it is misunderstood. The child misunderstands the mother's desire, thinking that her look encloses them in self-sufficient dyad. Rose presents Lacan's account of the great mistake—"The mother is refused to the child in so far as a prohibition falls on the child's desire to be what the mother desires"—and quotes Lacan:

> What we meet as an accident in the child's development is linked to the fact that the child does not find himself or herself alone in front of the mother, and that the phallus forbids the child the satisfaction of his or her own desire, which is the desire to be the exclusive desire of the mother.[14]

This phantom that comes between mother and child is, in Lacan's account, the *phallus*, not the actual father but a term constructed to designate the paternal order imagined to satisfy the mother's desire and the symbolic order of power that promises more than it can ever deliver.[15] Because ego identity is so contingent, the child purchases it at the price of alienation of self. It finds a self in a look that is directed beyond him toward the symbolic order. We gain a self by losing a self, and all subsequent relations with the other are in some way implicated in an attempt to get the self back, to reclaim what was once ours but was returned to us bonded to language, culture, gender, and patriarchy. The desire for the other is from then on always articulated by demand expressed in the symbolic orders of our culture. Language brings us to the other, but it also comes from the other to us. The language of the other is the basis of the self, and the desire for the other is always a desire to appropriate that power and to undo the alienation that is the basis of ego identity. Lacan maintains that all of us, male and female alike, are castrated. He argues that we enter the symbolic order in an action of desire that can never be fully gratified. This symbolic inscription returns the need to the subject in a symbolic form that can only partially contain the desire from which it has sprung. As we can only ask for just part of what we want, all symbolic activity is motivated and outstripped by desire. Now we have arrived back in the classroom, facing front, eyes on the instructor. What funds our attention is hope. We expect to grow into a self within his look. But we always suspect that he is actually looking not at us but at another whom we do not know but who is finally more powerful and compelling than we.

In Chapter 5 I challenged the specular, dyadic, and patriarchal aspects of this narrative for excluding the mimetic, maternal, and semiotic identifications that, established in preoedipal experience, are more, as Stern's work testifies, much more, than "imaginary." Nevertheless, I grant that the politics, theater, and object relations of academia do indeed resemble Lacan's scheme. His error has been to project the male compensation for the inferential nature of paternity back onto the relation of mother and child, reducing their interaction to confusion and their dialogue of touch, sound, and sight to the look. If, as I have argued in Chapter 1, a phase of our reproductive projects has been the repudiation of the constraints in our original relations to our progeny, then Lacan's narrative of our origins should be read as a reasonable rendering of the father's contradiction of his original relation to the child as it is expressed in the pedagogy of the academy.

When I identify reading and teaching as art forms that express virtual transference, I am saying that teaching the text expresses the relations of identity to language and knowledge. As a reader of these teaching lectures, I was at first a student. My transference was a familiar one: anger at the social, symbolic, institutional power of the parent/teacher. This kind of reading is not unusual. Initially, I read as a child, frustrated by my impotence, raging at the parent for withholding the secret of how to grow up, raging at the parent for not seeing me. And in my raging I hear the voice of my own children, and that echo shifts me to the other side of the transference. I am now ready to read as a colleague.

To read as a colleague requires what Jane Gallop describes as a recognition of the mother's desire.[16] In "The Monster in the Mirror: The Feminist Critic's Psychoanalysis," Gallop attempts to shift the motive of differentiation from daughter to mother, pointing out that we regularly assign the motive of differentiation to the child and the motive of symbiosis to the mother. The interpretive enterprise she suggests—to the extent that it requires a distance from the text and the relations it encodes—has traditionally attached itself to the child (*enfant terrible?*) or at least to the male who, in the Chodorow schema, has taken up differentiation from his mother as the project of his own gender identity.[17]

Instead, she invites us to follow the gaze of the parent. Now when we follow the gaze of the Cambridge lecturers we find it fastened not on the children seated before them but on the phallic order in which the identity of the parent has been constituted, and castrated. If this text displays an *approach*, as its editors suggest, it also displays an avoidance. As each lecture approaches a text, it also petitions the phantom in an attempt to wrest phallic authority from a conventional or established reading. Can we expect a teacher who is reading like a child to teach like a parent?

At first the sense of opposition that frames many of these discourses seems to be one of disabusing the students of their misunderstandings. Of course, this is the tone that I remember. Always vaguely guilty of the misreading that the lecture castigated, I would sit there, wondering why I hadn't been warned away from it. Why did they let me arrange a motor tour of the bayou country without telling me that the only interesting places to see could only be reached by boat? The lecture proceeded from the assumption that the ingenuous reading that I had brought to it was misguided or inadequate, although, of course, it was never *my* reading that was discussed or that of the girl next to me, the one who was always on time. Our readings were assumed to be conflated with another one, and it was this other one that held my teacher in thrall. It was this phantom reader that he saw when he looked at us, and it was this phantom's interpretations that he accused us of sharing. *Teaching the Text* is dedicated to an army of these phantoms, and the most passionate lectures are battles waged against them. What we observe in each instance is the attempt of the lecturer to wrench the text away from the parent, the law, from phallic authority. A few of these teachers make this project to rescue the reading from the phantom, and thus reclaim the power to constitute their own egos, explicit.

Hear Stephen Heath rescue Dorothy Richardson and Stephen Heath from D. H. Lawrence:

> What is "narcissism" for the critics is necessary journey for writer and reader, oneself coming from being.[18]

Hear Tony Tanner rescue *Jane Eyre* and Tony Tanner from the readings of Matthew Arnold and others who saw in it only "rebellion and rage":

> If you can say "I am" then you can also say, "You are"—self-apprehension leads to proper recognition of the other. Learning to articulate and define and hold on to her own identity, Jane Eyre is also able accurately to identify others. In this way she is able to resist being absorbed into false selves which other people wish to make of her for their own selfish means.[19]

Hear Anita Kermode rescue Emerson and Anita Kermode from the refusal of the American *literati*, Pound, Stevens, Stein, Whitman, to acknowledge Emerson's struggle to create himself:

> But the power to displace the fountain of literature by a fountain of revelation—that is to say, by a radically "new" description of reality— this power can only be felt to proceed from a strongly individual voice, one which does speak in its own proper person (even if this is an invented person). And such a voice must sound strong enough, individual enough, to persuade us that it is independent of the "fountain of literature" just when it is most profoundly alluding to, referring itself to, that fountain.[20]

And hear Frank Kermode rescue *Troilus and Cressida* and Frank Kermode from everybody:

> And we should not imagine that a text of this degree of complexity can have or be a message. All attempts to simplify it by reducing it to some particular genre—satire, comedy, tragical satire—have failed.[21]

What you are hearing is the courage and failure of pedagogy. Each of these reader/teachers flings himself against the phantom, against the phallus. The lectures express their vulnerability as they throw language like a rope across the chasm in themselves that language has created. But they are throwing the rope to the phantom, not to the students who sit there, trying to catch it, trying to save the teacher and themselves. I do suspect that the "great teachers" are the ones who, in spite of themselves, perform their child's passion for the student who is moved by it, who grasps it mimetically, gesturally, and grasps a sense of the human project that lies beneath the distracted stare.

I am grateful to the gyps. They have not hidden themselves behind the structures and abstractions of what they call continental theory. For the first time I understand that when they are ripping me off they themselves are struggling to recover their losses. Must we perpetuate this economy? Must we observe the golden rule of pedagogy and withhold from others what has been withheld from us? And if teaching the text calls on us to struggle for the ownership of meaning with our own parents, wouldn't it be decent to confess that they are the ones we see when we lean across the podium to teach the twenty-year-olds who are our students?

If we think of teaching as an art, then we have a responsibility to be the critic as well as the artist, parent as well as child. If teaching reveals our own transferences and our struggles to reclaim the look within which we came to form, that display only partially addresses the aesthetic possibilities of our pedagogy. Besides indicating art's disclosure of the "virtual," Langer also has reminded us that art is the expression of *knowledge* about feeling, not just the raw expression of that feeling itself.[22] That is how she discriminates between the crying baby and Bach. To teach as an art would require us to study the transferences we bring to the world we know, to build our pedagogies not only around our feeling for what we know but also around our knowledge of why and how we have come to feel the way we do about what we teach. Then, perhaps, teaching the text may lead us to devise new forms for knowing that will not compel our students to recite the history and future of our desire.

7 Bodyreading

At first glance reading appears to reside within the dominion of the look. Grasped by the look, the words of the text require
"image-ination" before they can assume coherence. Trapped in the
dualisms of individualism and idealism, we become convinced that
whatever we see in our "mind's eye" is a private vision, split off from
what others know and feel, split off from the synesthesia that integrates
all our perceptions, split off from the body, the other, the world. The
"body-subject" was Merleau-Ponty's term for human consciousness.[1]
He invented it to rescue thought from its exile to the vast, inaccessible
reaches of idealism. And despite the great complexity of his analyses, to
read his work is to feel ourselves come home, to gather up our politics,
our psychology, our history, our literature, and our science and to carry
them like this week's groceries, over the snowbank that blocks the
driveway, up the stairs, through the storm door, and into the house—to
the place where we live.

In "bodyreading" I borrow this body-subject to run some errands, to
bring what we know to where we live, to bring reading home again. To
bring what we know to where we live has not always been the project of
curriculum, for schooling, as we have seen, has functioned to repudiate
the body, the place where it lives, and the people who care for it. Our
current concern about the distance between what we know and how we
live is mirrored in our fear that our children do not read. It is a serious
concern. It is the fear that what we know, the symbolic inscriptions of
our collective experience in the world, moves away from them like an
ice floe and leaves them stranded, separated from the past and, we fear,
from the future as well. We have seen the impulses to grasp that which
seems to be escaping us expressed in the reactionary back-to-basics
drills and in the school reports that encourage us to extend, tighten, and
enforce all sorts of requirements. I think the new concerns about

reading acknowledge, at least tacitly, the many ways in which reading is contingent, tangled up with the world from which texts and readers come. The act of reading requires what Paul Ricoeur calls both sense and reference, both what we know and how we live.[2] The sense is the *what* of the text. The reference is *what it is about*. Ricoeur establishes these categories to undermine idealism, that confusion which Sartre describes as taking the word for the world. In *Interpretation Theory*, Ricoeur maintains that "language is not a world of its own. It is not even a world. But because we are in the world, because we are affected by situations, and because we orient ourselves comprehensively in those situations, we have something to say, we have experience to bring to language."[3]

Ricoeur's work is drawn from an enterprise that we call hermeneutics. This word, which refers to the various methods that we employ to draw meaning from texts, comes from the name of the messenger of the Greek gods, Hermes. Both in literature and in cult, Hermes was identified as a protector of cattle and sheep, a point that may not seem to be immediately significant; yet, as I shall try to demonstrate, it is essential to this argument. Representations of Hermes show him either in flight—hence his winged feet—or in a more pastoral moment, carrying a shepherd's staff, a sheep slung over his shoulder. Whereas hermeneutics was originally grounded in philology, as interpreters of the Bible endeavored to justify their interpretations of text through recourse to historical and comparative linguistics, contemporary hermeneutics provides what Susan Suleiman calls "the self-conscious moment of all criticism, when criticism turns to reflect on its own intentions, assumptions, and positions."[4] I have created the persona of the body reader to bring to reading what Merleau-Ponty's figure of the body-subject brings to epistemology, the sense that reading is an act that is oriented toward what the subject can do in the world. Bodyreading is strung between the poles of our actual situation, crowded as it is with our own intentions, assumptions, and positions, and the possibilities that texts point to. Contemporary feminist theories of the text and programs of literary criticism such as poststructuralism or deconstruction have also pitted themselves against the idealism that imputes a meaning to the word, the sentence, the text, that is distinct from the actual and possible world of their readers. Their analyses reveal the ways that reading throbs with the conflicts that shape our mortal condition: the dialectics of birth and death, of private and public meaning, of gender, of class.

Reading instruction in the public schools is not exempt from these concerns. These are human concerns, and reading is a most human activity. It would be a gesture of shallow arrogance to suggest that we can resolve these issues. What I hope to suggest are ways of working with teachers and students that honor them, ways that permit the sorrow and celebration that Yeats seeks in the poetry of the mortal condition: "Soul clap its hands and sing, and louder sing, for every tatter in its mortal dress."[5]

Decentered, lost in thought, locked into the courtesies and protocols of our very formal operations, we forget that the symbolic systems of language, number, art, and culture are part of our lived worlds. Even though Saussure has convinced us that language is not the echo of nature, we need not think that the arbitrary character of the signifier is proof that we live locked into a linguistic fiction.[6] Merleau-Ponty maintains that "words, vowels, and phonemes are so many ways of 'singing' the world, and that their function is to represent things not, as the naive onomatopoeic theory had it, by reason of an objective resemblance, but because they extract, and literally express, their emotional essence."[7] I have argued that curriculum, like language, is a moving form; conceived as an aspiration, the object and hope of our intentionality, it comes to form and slips, at the moment of its actualization, into the ground of our action. It becomes part of our situation.[8] And of course it is this fluidity that Ricoeur and Merleau-Ponty are trying to recover for language. It is more difficult to grasp the protean nature of the word once it has become the text. "So long lives this, and this gives life to thee."[9] I will not take time now to recount the history that has bonded text to class and caste, made it the emblem of authority, the sign of immortality, and a rebuke to the lively imagination. Literacy has traveled a long and winding path from reading entrails to answering multiple-choice reading comprehension questions on the SAT, although on second thought both enterprises may be seen as attempts to control the future by making the correct interpretation. One wonders whether the priest ever looked up and muttered, "None of the above."

I recognize that there is a certain sadness that clings to the notion of bodyreading. The very need to present it seems to come from a sense that it expresses a continuity and integration that we have lost—that it describes a place where we once were, a way of being that we can only remember. Psychoanalytic theories of language reinforce this sense as they establish desire as the precondition of symbol formation. They predicate the presence of the word on the absence of pleasure. To think, to speak, to read, to write is to celebrate the presence of an absence. It follows then that all our assertions become suspect, like television commercials that push the very features their products lack. Perhaps I do produce the body reader to recover what is lost. The body reader denies our terror of being lost in the world. It denies the sad intuition that the world as we have named it and now manipulate it is no longer a world that will sustain our bodies or those of our children. It repeats that tendency to impute to the past the ideal we wish for the future. Our lives are full of such histories: Marx's species community, Freud's infantile symbiosis. Perhaps a body reader is such a fantasy and Lacan is right when he suggests that the word is a sign of our alienation, that language is the expression of desire that is predicated on loss.

But this melancholy sense of language sings our sadness, and it is our responsibility as educators not to be caught in an understanding of symbol systems that reduces them to elegies for lost worlds. Language can lead us somewhere else, to the place where we live, to the world, and to the world as it might be, and bodyreading may be seen not as a nostalgic fantasy, but as a practical necessity, the exploration of a world where we can live. When we consult the etymology of the word "read," we find that "read" is lodged in the very guts of the word "ruminate," which means "to think things over." Nevertheless, the word "ruminate" is not associated with a group of animals noted for their erudition. Ruminants are cattle, also sheep (enter Hermes), goats, antelope, giraffe, and deer.

> The skeletal and muscular systems of the ruminant together form a perfectly constructed running mechanism; their digestive system is also elaborately planned so that they may hastily snatch a meal in some favorable grazing ground and store the food temporarily in a special compartment of the stomach until they have found a refuge where they can masticate and digest it at leisure.[10]

The ruminant does not give up the world in order to think about it. On the hoof it stores the world that it consumes in multiple stomachs until it has found a place of safety to bring back what has been swallowed in haste for a good chew. Actually, the ruminant's stomach has four compartments, and it is the very last compartment that has gastric glands in its walls for secretion of digestive juices. It is this fourth stomach that is called the read. The OED offers us a citation from 1450 where the *reid* not only is associated with the stomach of a cow but is used to signify the stomach of a human as well: 1450 Holland Howla, He cry'd "Allace . . . revyn is my reid. I am ungraciously gorrit, halthe guttis and gall." Some of us have had a similar response to what we take as being misread. The OED also tells us that "The original senses of the Teutonic verb, *reden*, are those of taking or giving counsel, taking care or charge of a thing, having or exercising control over something else." (Can we then assume that the Angles, the Saxons, and the Jutes were more interested in comprehension strategies than in decoding?) "The sense of considering or explaining something obscure or mysterious is also common to various languages," the OED tells us, and it is this sense of mystery that I hope to recover for our work with children and texts when I maintain that we have not lost our stomach for reading.[11]

The anatomy of mystery that lodges explanation in the stomach of the cow suggests that reading was and may still be a ritual of divination, for ritual, in the words of Meyer Fortes, prehends the occult and makes it patent.[12] It seeks what is hidden, internal, unseen in our experience. The reader pores over the text, like the priest reading the entrails, seeking signs of how to live. Nevertheless, unlike our ancient predecessors, we are plagued by our intolerance for ambiguity. Embarrassed that we cannot make the task clear and simple, we misrepresent it to children, suggesting that meaning is hidden in the folds of the topic sentence or the story structure. That is the positivism that characterizes most of the language arts curriculum as well as reading in the content areas. Its simplistic certainties are balanced by the solipsism of what we call recreational reading where we surrender to prose, cherishing reading experiences that envelop us in fantasies that confirm our individuality, drawn from unrealized selves that no one else could ever know. This tendency to locate meaning either in the words, sentences, and structures of texts or in the secret thoughts of the reader tells us that both community and curriculum are defunct, an impression that has been confirmed in the narratives of educational experiences written by students who have studied philosophy of education with me. Some of those students are practicing teachers, some teachers in training. Rarely are experiences related to reading as part of the school curriculum presented as educational.

When reading presents itself under the category of educational experience it is usually presented as a process that creates privacy, substituting self-satisfaction for a relation that originally required another, usually a mother.

Even before I can consciously remember I know that I was read to every night of my early childhood. I loved to be read to. At ages three and four, my brother and I would each pick out a book for my mother to read us. John always picked "Boy" books such as the Little Tug Boat and the Little Engine that Could. I picked fairy tales and Peter Pan, and Winnie the Pooh. We would both get ready for bed and go into John's room and listen to his story, which I always loved almost as much as my own. Then, although he is two years older than I, he would go to sleep and my mother would read my story in my room. . . . I loved the stories so much that I would memorize them and tell/read them to the amazed cleaning lady the next morning turning the pages at the appropriate times.

Finally, I was old enough to go to the first grade. I knew the alphabet already and soon I learned all kinds of amazing things about vowels and consonant blends. Then it seemed one day that I just suddenly knew how to read. It was the most incredible gift. I could do for myself the thing my mother had always had to do for me. I remember reading ahead in my first Dick and Jane reader, amazed at my own ability to find out what would happen next. I read an entire book before dinner that I received on Christmas morning. I read almost all the books in my age's section of the children's room at the library. I had the most construction paper balloons on the wall for summer reading books.

The novelty of reading has worn off to a certain extent. However, I still find myself engrossed in novel after novel, upset and dazed when I am forced back into the real world outside my book. I still read every night before I go to bed; it is force of habit, I guess.[13]

The narratives evoke reading as a form of comfort and safety—reading in bed, surrounded by pillows and quilts, reading surreptitiously by the light of the flashlight, giving oneself to the text as one dare not surrender oneself to the world. Rarely do the readers in these tales offer an account of their reading experience to anyone else. It is a private pleasure. "We read," Stanley Elkin says,

to die, . . . it has something to do with being alone, shutting the world out, doing books like beads, a mantra, the flu. Some perfect, hermetic concentration sealed as canned goods or pharmaceuticals. . . . Not so much a way of forgetting ourselves as of engaging the totality of our attentions, as racing car drivers or mountain climbers engage them, as surgeons and chess masters do.[14]

Elkin celebrates reading as retreat. His reader is immersed and inaccessible, his intentionality safe from the look, the word, the act of another. It is Elkin's sense of retreat that usually prevails in these accounts, for it is rare to find a reading narrative that presents this kind of negotiation:

> Later in France. A summer day. I remember a sleeveless dress. The poster was big with red, black, and white colors. It showed two hands holding each other tightly, and the caption read as follows: "Workers, unite against poverty for freedom and justice!" Very impressed, I stood in front of it. With all the wisdom of my eight years I thought it was great. I did not really know why; I just liked it. My aunt, by that time, had caught up with me. "Isn't it beautiful?" I asked her, still contemplating the poster. "What?" "The poster," I answered, wondering how she could have missed it. She grabbed my hand, pulled me away, and told me with a harsh voice, "Never do you understand, never read posters like this one. They tell lies. They are bad. They are communist."[15]

Often, when schooling is the location of the reading narrative, meaning falls into one of the two forms presented in these stories. Either it is an individual's fantasy, sensual, ideal, offering visions of power and control to the reader that are uncontested, or meaning is imposed, negating the reader's interpretation of the text and substituting a rebuke for negotiation. In *With Respect to Readers*, Walter Slatoff decries this dualism:

> Most aestheticians and critics . . . speak as though there were only two sorts of readers: the absolutely particular individual human being with all his prejudices, idiosyncrasies, personal history, knowledge, needs and anxieties, who experiences the work of art in solely "personal" terms, and the ideal or universal reader whose response is impersonal and aesthetic. Most actual readers except for the most naive, I think, transform themselves as they read into beings somewhere between these extremes. They learn, that is, to set aside many of the particular conditions, concerns and idiosyncrasies which help to define them in every day affairs.[16]

It is this process of gauging the context for meaning that helps us to constitute the understandings that make us members of what Stanley Fish calls interpretive communities.[17] Discriminating the idiosyncratic from the general is delicate business. It is the basis of the prediction that Frank Smith defines as the prior elimination of unlikely alternatives.[18] But what reading is about, very much like writing, is bridging the gap between private and public worlds. Its purpose is not to reduce mystery to what is obvious, patent, or to confirm solipsism but to provide a passage between the images, impulses, and glimpses of meaning that constitute being in the world and our encoded representations of that world. If we were to transpose the terms of hermeneutics into ego psychology, translating what we consider to be idiosyncratic, on the one hand, and general, on the other, into the terms "internal" and "external" nonego, respectively, we would have to acknowledge that, like ego identity, meaning is the provisional achievement of a dynamic and somewhat risky process. If reading is a passage between the public and the private world, the journey is fraught with danger. To give oneself up to the text is to relinquish the world in order to have the world; it is a birth and a death. And so it should not surprise us to find a child wary of reading, reluctant to follow that line across the page without knowing where it leads. Permit me to read to you. I promise that we won't go too far, just far enough to share Galway Kinnell's childhood discoveries of the mysteries of birth and death and culture. Once again, it is a ruminant that leads us into the light as well as the darkness:

> Freedom, New Hampshire
>
> We came to visit the cow
> Dying of fever,
> Towle said it was already
> Shoveled under, in a secret
> Burial place in the woods
> Weeks, we never
>
> Found where. Other
> Children other summers
> Must have found the place
> And asked, Why is it
> Green here? The rich
> Guess a grave, maybe,
> The poor think a pit
>
> For dung, like the one
> We shoveled in in the fall
> That came up green
> The next year, and that,
> For all that shows, may as well
> Have been the grave
> Of a cow or something.

2

We found a cowskull once; we thought it was
From one of the asses in the Bible, for the sun
Shone into the holes through which it had seen
Earth as an endless belt carrying gravel, had heard
Its truculence cursed, had learned how sweat
Stinks, and had brayed—shone into the holes
With solemn and majestic light, as if some
Skull somewhere could be Baalbek or the Parthenon.

That night passing Towle's Barn
We saw lights. Towle had lassoed a calf
By its hind legs, and he tugged against the grip
Of the darkness. The cow stood by chewing millet.
Derry and I took hold, too, and hauled
It was sopping with darkness when it came free.
It was a bullcalf. The cow mopped it awhile,
And we walked around it with a lantern.

And it was sunburned, somehow, and beautiful.
It took a dug as the first business
And sneezed and drank at the milk of light.
When we got it balanced on its legs, it went wobbling
Toward the night. Walking home in darkness
We saw the July moon looking on Freedom, New Hampshire,
We smelled the fall in the air, it was the summer,
We thought, Oh this is but the summer!

3

Once I saw the moon
Drift into the sky like a bright
Pregnancy pared
From a goddess doomed
To keep slender to be beautiful—
Cut loose, and drifting up there
To happen by itself—
And waning, in lost labor;

As we lost our labor
Too—afternoons
When we sat on the gate
By the pasture, under the Ledge,
Buzzing and skirling on toilet-
papered combs tunes

To the rumble-seated cars
Taking the Ossipee Road

On Sundays; for
Though dusk would come upon us
Where we sat, and though we had
Skirled out our hearts in the music,
Yet the dandruffed
Harps we skirled it on
Had done not much better than
Flies, which buzzed, when quick

We trapped them in our hands,
Which went silent when we
Crushed them, which we bore
Downhill to the meadowlark's
Nest full of throats
Which Derry charmed and combed
With an Arabian air, while I
Chucked crushed flies into

Innards I could not see,
For the night had fallen
And the crickets shrilled on all sides
In waves, as if the grassleaves
Shrieked by hillsides
As they grew, and the stars
Made small flashes in the sky,
Like mica flashing in rocks

On the chokecherried Ledge
Where bees I stepped on once
Hit us from behind like a shotgun,
And where we could see
Windowpanes in Freedom flash
And Loon Lake and Winnipesaukee
Flash in the sun
And the blue world flashing.

The fingerprints of our eyeballs would zigzag
On the sky; the clouds that came drifting up
Our fingernails would drift into the thin air;
In bed at night there was music if you listened,
Of an old surf breaking far away in the blood.

Children who come by chance on grass green for a man
Can guess cow, dung, man, anything they want,

To them it is the same. To us who knew him as he was
After the Beginning and before the end, it is green
For a name called out of the confusions of the earth—

Winnipesaukee coined like a moon, a bullcalf
Dragged from the darkness where it breaks up again,
Larks which long since have crashed for good in the grass
To which we fled the flies, buzzing ourselves like flies,
While the crickets shrilled beyond us, in July . . .

The mind may sort it out and give it names—
When a man dies he dies trying to say without slurring
The abruptly decaying sounds. It is true
That only flesh dies, and spirit flowers without stop
For men, cows, dung, and all dead things; and it is good, yes—

But an incarnation is in particular flesh
And the dust that is swirled into a shape
And crumbles and is swirled again had but one shape
That was this man. When he is dead the grass
Heals what he suffered, but he remains dead,
And the few who loved him know this until they die.

                    For my brother, 1925–1957[19]

Well, I think this is a poem about reading. And if the last few pages have
succeeded, schema theory maintains that you now share the assumptions, associations, vocabulary, and expectations that confirm this interpretation.[20] Together we appropriate this text with impunity; we use
it to make sense of the work we have to do. As the poem continues, it
becomes clear that what concerns the poet is not the way that the
corpse of the cow, or its sun-drenched, time-filled skull, or its damp,
milky calf encode birth, death, and the passage of time called civilization. What concerns the poet is the death of his brother Derry, who
along with the speaker constitutes the *we* of the tale, the *we* who search
for the buried cow, the *we* who find the cowskull, the *we* who see the
Parthenon in it, the *we* who attend the birth of the calf. And Derry is not
a mere witness to these moments, for the world and its symbols evolve
within human relationships. It is Derry's presence that makes such a
reading possible. Every text, every symbol, every word, is a passage
between one consciousness and another. And not just any other consciousness will do. As the poet recovers the singularity of Derry's life
and of his love for him, we are reminded that all the forms of culture
that we revere also evolved within the relation of people particular to
each other and to the world they share.

In almost every story of reading that my students tell, someone else is there in some way to witness the symbolic act, to receive or repudiate the reader's interpretation. Even when reading is a refuge from society, from friends, from parents, they are there, hovering on the other side of the door. Just as the capacity to have a world is mediated by other people for the body-subject, the capacity to read a world is mediated by other people for the body reader.

Now it becomes clear to us why the "great debate" about reading instruction in the primary grades has been waged with such passion ever since Icklesamer published a primer in 1527 in Germany entitled *The Shortest Way to Reading* that proposed introducing children to speech sounds associated with well-known words before teaching them letters as the basic unit of instruction.[21] The issue about whether phonics or sight words provide the best foundation for beginning readers is now generally conceded to be a nonissue, as it is now recognized that the complexity and richness of the reading process are hospitable to multiple instructional approaches. What is interesting to note at this point is that in this controversy we find not only a history of ideas about cognition but a history of the human relationships that each form and unit of instruction implied. The feminist studies of the ways that language and text are manipulated to buttress patriarchal privilege have led us once again to look at the human relationships within which symbolic competence develops.

The debate over whether to privilege sight or sound in reading instruction becomes pertinent to our understandings of the epistemologies and cognitive styles associated with male and female gender identities. Despite the drill sequences and the repetitious and highly organized character of phonics, the mimesis and recitation of sounds that it requires are reminiscent of the echolalia that constitutes the babble of infants and early speech. This is the preoedipal discourse of mother and child, highly inflected, immediately echoed—the original language, the mother tongue, sounds that communicate intimacy without denotative meaning. A differential response to a mother's voice precedes the specific response to her face, a response that does not develop until later. Girls, permitted to sustain the original identifications with their mothers, need not repress sound and touch as significant ways of being attached to the world. For males, on the other hand, gender identity requires a repudiation of preoedipal experience. To be male is to be, in effect, not Mom, and that early identification as well as the sensual modalities that dominated it are repressed so that an identification with a father whose presence and relation depend more on sight than on sound or touch can be achieved.[22] Surrendering the detail, the intimacy and texture that touch and sound provide, sight provides us with a view and privileges the structural relations of abstract and rational thought that accompany literacy. These speculations drawn from object relations theory and phenomenology suggest that coming to know the world may differ for boys and girls, orienting them to epistemologies at particular stages of their development that are gender-specific. Such theories are less useful in predicting who will read well when than they are in reminding us that symbolic competence is generated within intense human relationships and that our understanding of the relation of gender to language acquisition cannot be limited to sexual stereotypes and the sexual politics of the classroom but must also address the evolution of language in the mediation of desire and the constitution of the ego.

Touch and the voice are the sensual passages between parent and child. Because these modes of contact are associated with the intimacy of familial or erotic relations, they are barred from the classroom where sensuality in any form is anathema. Even if early reading instruction maintains the singsong chant of children's voices, that maternal modality soon gives way to silence. Recitation is replaced by workbooks, and the look dominates the classroom. Now, it does sound as if I am taking the phonics side in this dispute as I invoke echolalia and the maternal voice as the foundation of linguistic competence. And I want to make it clear that I am quite convinced that Frank Smith is right when he maintains that phonics works only when you have a rough idea of what the word is that you are trying to read and some sense about how it sounds when you say it.[23] Smith has some difficulty accounting for the success of phonics, given his conviction that it is merely epiphenomenal to the process that attaches meaning to print and that its complexity and artifice estrange those children whom we later call dyslexic from texts. What Smith needs to acknowledge is the ceremony that surrounds phonics. The physical activity is stimulating. The turn to phonics in many systems has been accompanied by the move to decrease the teacher/pupil ratio by hiring aides to work with children. In *Divinity and Experience*, Godfrey Lienhardt observes that the rituals of the Dinka require that all ceremonial utterances of the priest be repeated by everyone in attendance at the ritual.[24] Prayers and incantations have no efficacy if muttered in private. Performative utterances rely on social confirmation to be compelling. (And that's probably why I run around telling everyone I know that I am starting a new diet when I decide to try to start a new diet.) And so, if, as Merleau-Ponty maintains, speech sings the world, phonics provides a choral grasp of meaning that brings a social and emotional resonance to the meaning of texts.

Now, I acknowledge that a goal in the development of reading skill is to release us from the physical marking and iteration of sound. And even Julia Kristeva, who invokes the sensuality and intimacy of echolalia to assert the epistemological claims of the first language, the mother tongue, warns feminists not to sink into its rhythms and secrets, not to forsake the public and political sign for the private, familial sound.[25] Like the ruminants, we must learn to swallow print without chewing it. The problem is that when we stop to think it over we lose our sense of where the thought came from, and confusing the contents of long-term memory with memory itself, we fall into insidious idealism. If cattle treated grass the way we treat text, they would soon starve to death, thinking that they are the producers of their own cuds. The problem is that in the silence of the secondary classroom, too often, nothing is happening, no grazing, no galloping, no chewing, no mooing, no nothing. Even babble is preferable to that kind of silence.

The body reader who is still alive and well in many elementary classrooms where language experience, directed reading/thinking activities, and phonics provide a rich and varied sensory and interpersonal ground for learning soon gives way to the reader who discriminates the private self from the public text. Meaning is either in here or out there. When it is in here, it is identified with feeling, sensuality, and imagination that cannot be communicated and cannot be negotiated into any statement that deserves or attains the status of knowledge. When it is out there, it belongs to the text and to the teacher, and understanding means that the reader stands under the text, under the gaze of the teacher, and learns to anticipate and repeat the interpretation that is an index of comprehension.

The world, Merleau-Ponty has told us, is the answer to the body's question.[26] What we discover is what we can look for. "One's own body is the third term, always tacitly understood, in the figure-background structure, and every figure stands out against the double horizon of external and bodily space."[27] The body that makes it possible for us to have a world does not assemble a motley group of objects around it that it crowns with the title of objectivity. The world we have is the world that rises to meet our intentionality; it coheres around our needs, wishes, possibilities, real and imagined. The coherence of the text, like that of the world, is the possible and actual ground of our action. Meaning is something we make out of what we find when we look at texts. It is not in the text. Now, this is hardly news, but I am sorry to tell you that the myth of the meaningful text still flourishes in the secondary classroom. Abandoned by cognitive theories, by episte-mology, by aesthetic and literary theory, the secondary school curriculum stands alone, proclaiming the authority of the text. Using single textbooks, sometimes supplemented with library readings or handouts, the students are sent to read unburdened by motives, interest, questions, tasks, rationales, or expectations. If there is such a thing as a pure read, the textbooks of the secondary curriculum get it. All the baggage that I have just listed appears after the fact, when it appears at all, usually in some evaluation format.

We can see an example of this approach in Harold Herber's text, *Teaching Reading in Content Areas*, a book that is widely used by reading specialists. Herbert identifies three levels of comprehension: the literal, the interpretive and the applied. Herber presents these levels as a sequence:

> First, the reader examines the words of the author and determines what is being said, what information is being presented. Second, the reader looks for relationships among statements within the materials, and from these intrinsic relationships derives various meanings. . . . Third, the reader takes the product of the literal—what the author has said—and the interpretive—what the author meant by what he said—and applies it to other knowledge that she already possesses, thereby deepening the understanding.[28]

The absurdity of this sequence would be matched only if I took out flour, sugar and butter, milk, eggs, vanilla, cardamon, and baking powder, mixed them all in a bowl, observed the blend, noting its texture and flavor, applied this information to my previous experience, and hypothesized that I might be making either a cake, a pudding, an omelette, or a quiche, a blintz, a crepe, or a pancake. As Frank Smith has noted, only in schools are we so stupid. Only in schools does the text become a spectacle, and we the dazed spectators, eyes glazed, sit in mute reception, waiting for something to appear. No, television has not ruined reading. Reading in school has trained us for television.

Let me stop this tirade, or at least turn its energy to something more useful. First, we must ask how the very women and men who bake cakes, drive cars, and maybe even write poetry come to banish intentionality from human action when they teach children to read. That question leads us to the history of reading in the culture of schooling and to an understanding of the status of the text as a guarantor of patriarchy. In Chapter 2 I explored the situations of the young women who taught in the common schools following industrialization to discover what induced them to deny their own experiences of childhood, of nurturance, and of desire as they complied with the ethos and epistemologies of schooling. Their experiences of reading, given the school's repudiation of sensuality, fantasy, and emotion, must have been literally unspeakable.

Because schooling is a complex, ceremonial, and ritual form, it is important to study the status of texts in the exchange systems, totem systems of the classroom. For we have displaced school bodies with school texts. I do not ask my students, "Do you understand me?" Instead I ask them to understand my reading of the text. We pass texts between us. We touch the text instead of each other and make our marks on it rather than on each other. The text is material, it has texture, it is woven; we pull and tug at it, it winds around us, we are tangled up in it.

We need to work with teachers to investigate our understandings and experience of reading. Writing projects have shown us that the process of composition is very different from the ways that it has been conceived and taught in the school curriculum. Writing does not record preaccomplished thought; the act of writing constitutes thought. The Bay Area Writing Project and its spin-offs in the National Writing Project are aimed at engaging teachers in writing so that together they may participate in the activities that bring thought to expression and name those processes.[29] Reading seminars for teachers drawn from various disciplines may provide us with the opportunity to reclaim reading as intentional activity.

It is no accident that the analysis of writing comes to mind when we think about reading. Attention to the moments of composition has revealed the contingencies, elisions, contradictions, and explosions that constitute the text. Think of the repugnance one often feels for a text that is recently completed. There, clinging to all the lines, are shreds of the ideas that never quite made it to expression, fragments of the negative example, the other possibility, that the sentence, the chapter, the ideology, the deadline, the habit, the defense mechanism just could not admit. Only time and forgetfulness smooth these rough edges so that we no longer remember what has been left behind, and then the text that has seemed so partial, merely provisional, prevarication, becomes THE TEXT, clear, complete, necessary, and sufficient. Some of the reader response research done in Indiana by David Bleich and Eugene Kintgen confirms my own impression from engaging students in that process we call "close reading" of texts.[30] We see that both writing and reading require what Ernst Kris has named regression in the service of the ego.[31] The interpretation of theoretical texts and dense prose often calls on students to draw from their own store of associations, and very free ones at that, in order to construct the world that the word can live in.

The clarity and apparent independence of the complete text are illusions that contemporary literary criticism has assailed. It does seem unfair and unkind to keep children playing in the shadow of the authority of the text, while the grown-ups dismantle it and revel in the newfound light. Whereas structuralists had seen the oppositions in a text as functioning to maintain its shape and integrity, deconstructionists celebrate the discovery of contradictions that undermine the authority of the text. They study the sense of the text to discover its multiple and conflicting references. Here is Eagleton's portrayal of the "writable" text, a text filled with what Barthes has called double signs, signs that reveal that they are merely provisional, material, historical signifiers that can barely contain the meanings that leak from their seams, boil over their rims, cascade over their banks into a new channel.

> The "writable" text, usually a modernist one, has no determinate meaning, no settled signifieds, but is plural and diffuse, an inexhaustible tissue or galaxy of signifiers, a seamless weave of codes and fragments of codes, through which the critic may cut his own errant path. There are no beginnings and no ends, no sequences which cannot be reversed, no hierarchy of textual "levels" to tell you what is more or less significant. All literary texts are woven out of other texts, not in the conventional sense that they bear the traces of "influence" but in the more radical sense that every word, phrase or segment is a reworking of other writings which

precede or surround the individual work. There is no such thing as literary "originality," no such thing as the "first" literary work: all literature is intertextual. A specific piece of writing thus has no clearly defined boundaries: it spills over constantly into the works clustered around it, generating a hundred different perspectives which dwindle to a vanishing point. The work cannot be sprung shut, rendered determinate, by an appeal to the author, for the "death of the author" is a slogan that modern criticism is now confidently able to proclaim.[32]

Well, hallelujah. Dingdong, the witch is dead, dissolved in the spillage of those liquid texts. Barthes's playfulness, his nihilism, may be the most extreme, antic spirit to undo the text. Because most of us are more didactic than he, we cannot quite accept the telos of a vanishing point and rush to grab hold of meaning before it disappears around the bend of signification. (Our experience also suggests that vanishing points provide a teleology that has a poor track record with most school boards.) Nevertheless, his assassination of the text is a coup d'état that can return the text to teachers and students, once again material, malleable, to be fashioned by them into what it is they need. Intertextuality invites us to use multiple texts, splicing them, interweaving them with each other, with our commentaries, with our questions. This is the promise of word processing, not some video version of the questions at the end of the chapter but the presentation of text that can disappear at the touch of the delete button. There are no sacred texts. Let the cursor unravel the binding of the text as readers erase what they do not believe, or add whatever it is that the author left out. Why not invite them to weave their questions, responses, and arguments into the texts themselves and so acknowledge the wisdom of graffiti?

The deconstructionist approach of Derrida is less jocular. He works, as Eagleton says, to embarrass the text, to show where the text, in spite of itself, slips up, says what it does not mean, means what it does not say. The work is more serious, and more abstruse. Supported by the theory of Lacan and the critiques of the French feminists, deconstructionism exposes meaning as an alias, a false identity constructed to disguise the plurality of meanings that is the text. But this openness to meaning does not collapse into an absence of meaning. It allows meaning to be provisional, lively, fluttering. It allows interpretation to be an act that transforms the text, the world, and their interpreters as well. Barthes has returned the pleasure of reading to us, its sensuality, its power. Over and over again he shows us how the passages that lead us into and out of texts are also forms of intentionality that we bring to the world around us:

> To be with the one I love and to think of something else: this is how I have my best ideas, how I best invent what is necessary to my work. Likewise for the text, it produces in me, the best pleasure if it manages to make itself heard indirectly; if, reading it, I am led to look up often, to listen to something else. I am not necessarily *captivated* by the text of pleasure; it can be an act that is slight, complex, tenuous, almost scatterbrained: a sudden movement of the head like a bird who understands nothing of what we hear, who hears what we do not understand.[33]

Barthes's own texts show us that the glimpses of our world that our reading of another world provides need not slip from consciousness because they are not in themselves complete or elaborate literary forms. His texts about reading resymbolize his experience, gathering up not only the sense and reference of the text but the sense and reference of his own intentionality as well and winding them into a new spool.

Less outrageous than Barthes, less destructive than Derrida, are the reader response theorists. Response theorists who have been very influenced by Piaget's epistemology contend that meaning does not reside in the text, or in the schemes of the reader, but that it symbolizes the reader's experience of the text. Although these theorists offer us some information about the processes of individual readers, reader response founders in the classroom where even Stanley Fish, who has placed meaning in the response of the reader to the text, falters and accedes to interpretive communities who can, according to their own consensual light, privilege some interpretations as being better than others. Norman Holland's identity themes provide a psychoanalytic frame for reader responses that portrays them as unconscious ego adaptations revealing readers' identity themes, thus conflating the reality principal with the text. Bleich solicits the writing of response statements, documents that record readers' associations and interpretations. He does not reduce these documents to case histories or diagnoses, but he does have difficulty when he talks about the contribution of response statements to the negotiation of meaning. It is not clear what is being negotiated and what the protocol for that negotiation is.[34]

It is an easy task to find the flaws in each of the reader response schemes for the identification of meaning. Each of these critics has been kind enough to attack the rationales and claims of the others.[35] Their

disputes reveal that, despite these theorists' apparent readiness to return meaning to readers, those meanings and the ways they are articulated and negotiated are still claimed as the property of the critics.
Sensing each other's attachment to this capital, they accuse each other
of being Indian givers and delight in finding the deeds that insure that
the property will revert to its original owner—the critic, of course,
hidden under the mattress of every reader response theory. But their
property squabbles need not undermine our sense that the text is a new
territory for our explorations with students. And their work is very
important to us because it acknowledges the classroom as an interpretive community and makes its protocols and curriculum absolutely
essential to this process we call reading.

If we can just wrest meaning from the grip of knowledge and return it
to art, we will be able to give students something to do with texts.
Activity-based curricula that are bonded to social, political, and physical action cannot contain the possibilities of meaning. The world is too
unwieldy, the classroom too constricting. Exhausted, confusing the
reference of the text with tomorrow, those teachers who have sensed
the glory of engagement too often are disappointed and retreat to the
cynical postures of critical thinking, adversarial, analytic attacks on
meaning, where students are endlessly playing the seconds in their
teacher/critic duels.

Because art forms express knowledge about feeling, they provide a
bridge between public and private readings. Because aesthetic activity
requires the making of things, comprehension is made palpable and
accessible to the perception and response of other readers. Every time a
text is drawn into performance, it is the reading of the text and never
the text itself that is performed. We need to cultivate the irreverence of
theater director Jerzy Grotowski if we are to recover the mystery that
our ancestors associated with reading:

> For both actor and producer the author's text is a sort of scalpel, enabling
> us to open ourselves, to transcend ourselves, to find what is hidden in us
> all. In the theatre, if you like, the text has the same function as the myth
> had for the poet of ancient times. The author of Prometheus found in the
> Prometheus myth both an act of defiance and a springboard, perhaps even
> the source of his own creation. . . . For me, a creator of theatre, the
> important thing is not the words but what we do with these words, what
> gives life to the inanimate words of the text, what transforms them into
> The Word.[36]

Meaning is continually deferred. Like Io, ranging over the earth, pursued by the gadfly of Hera, meaning never rests in the Word but in our ceaseless rumination and resymbolizations. Ricoeur is clear that the reference of the text, what the text is about, can never be identified as either the author's or the reader's situation. "The sense of the text is not behind the text, but in front of it. It is not something hidden, but something disclosed. What has to be understood is not the initial situation of discourse, but what points to a possible world."[37]

Theater is the enactment of possible worlds. It is performed in a middle space owned by neither author nor reader. Constructed from their experience and dreams, this liminal space cannot be reduced to the specifications of either the author's or the reader's world. It is a space for negotiation. It is the middle place of the curriculum. Theater places action in this middle time and space. Literally, the action takes place. Something happens, and what theater displays is the comprehension of the body reader. Performance simultaneously confirms and undermines the text. The body of the actor, like the body of the text, stumbles into ambiguity, insinuating more than words can say with gesture, movement, intonation. Mimesis tumbles into transformation, and meaning, taken from the text, rescued from the underworld of negotiation, becomes the very ground of action.

Susanne Langer sees this as the function of theater; neither show biz nor ritual, theater's function is "to delimit the world where virtual action takes place."[38] And this, I suggest to you, is what curriculum can bring to reading. Not only does it bring purpose to the reading process by providing a ground for intentionality, it also provides another stage where the possible worlds that the text points to can be identified and experienced as good places for grazing.

Part Three

8 Redeeming Daughters

The wolf also shall dwell with the lamb, and
the leopard shall lie down with the kid; and the
calf and the young lion and the fatling together,
and a little child shall lead them.[1]

The child redeemer makes his debut in this passage of Old
Testament prophecy. But even then, when, from our vantage point, the
world was new, it required reordering for this little child, this coura-
geous innocent, to prevail. So the verse both assumes and transforms a
world divided between nature and culture as it brings wild predators
and domesticated animals together in peace. The division that splits
our consciousness, the schism between the public and private world,
rests on this even deeper fault: the radical division of ordered civil life
from the threatening and chaotic domain of nature. Additional verses
appear to repair this wound in human consciousness and thus establish
the smooth, unrippled world that provides the ground for the child's
power:

And the cow and the bear shall feed; their young ones shall lie down
together: and the lion shall eat straw like the ox.
    And the suckling child shall play on the hole of the asp, and the weaned
child shall put his hand on the cockatrice' den.
    They shall not hurt nor destroy in all my holy mountain: for the earth
shall be full of the knowledge of the Lord, as the waters cover the sea.[2]

As the oppositions are resolved, the prophecy sustains the new order
by extending it through the child's maturation and into succeeding
generations. This unity is identified as divine knowledge, fluid, encom-
passing the old division in a soothing bath of amniotic peace.

The vision of the child leading and healing a troubled world has
never left us. We meet it regularly in our assumption that by educating

our children we are preparing "tomorrow's leaders," an epithet that obligates the next generation to redeem us and the world. Isaiah's understanding that the child can only be as innocent as the world that welcomes him is lost to us as we burden our children with an impossible task.

The education of the child redeemer has brought forth curricula devised to transform the child into Plato's philosopher-king, Cheever's Puritan saint, and Horace Mann's industrious American, intensifying human energy into steady beams of coherent light that are intended to maintain their frequency and direction through space and time. The curricula of Plato, Cheever, and Mann were devised not only to produce particular persons but to replicate them and, in so doing, to conserve and strengthen their influence on society as well. The laser (an acronym for light amplification by stimulated emission of radiation) rests on a similar principle. Bombarding an excited atom with photons of a particular frequency stimulates that atom to emit another photon of the same frequency, creating a chain reaction that produces a sudden burst of coherent radiation. Nevertheless, the light of the Republic, of the City upon the Hill, and of the American metropolis has dwindled, for, unlike atoms, the energy and direction of human activity cannot be externally manipulated and maintained.

The history of curriculum devised with these manipulative intentions is understandably a history of failure, a chronicle of energy lost, of direction diffused. The direction of human activity is not, as Maurice Natanson reminds us, imposed by others but is grounded in human consciousness.

> the image of Man which is projected is that of a being whose presence in the world is a unitary reality in which self and object are integrally grounded in consciousness, understood as a directional force sustaining the entire range of perceptual life. Individual and action, self and situation, person and world are then bound to each other not only in their implications for each other but in their fundamental structure.[3]

Whereas Natanson asserts the primacy of human consciousness as the ground where person and world, knower and known, are constituted, curriculum still speaks to us in terms of intended learning outcomes, process/product paradigms, and behavior modifications. It still strives to change children without reordering the world we give them. We live in a world where asps are still venomous; and even though the cockatrice, the deadly serpent of Old Testament mythology, has given way to the deadly missiles of modern technology, the light that radiates from their malevolent glance also kills.

The expectation that the child would reform the world has saturated the Judeo-Christian tradition. But whereas the Crucifixion marks the world's failure to receive Christ and thus speaks the religious tradition's acknowledgment of the world's responsibility for the child, education has come to focus on the child at the exclusion of the world, extending an altruism that Paulo Freire has so aptly named "malefic generosity."[4] Philippe Aries's study of the social processes that led to the association of childhood with innocence and isolation reveals a process of parturition that separated the child not only from the womb but from the world as well.[5] He identifies the churchmen, lawyers, and scholars who actively promoted educational institutions exclusively for the young as those who were critical of the license and anarchy of medieval society. Their criticism of that society's growing urban centers was projected onto its children, who were to be treated no longer as adults in miniature but as a special class born to bear the burden of their parents' lost innocence. The innocent babe in his chronicle is the scion of a guilty and ambivalent patriarchy manipulating its young in order to sustain its own power, control, and privilege. Ironically, the attempt to protect children from the corruption of the adult world meant withholding from the very persons appointed to save society the social skills and knowledge the task demanded. Aries's history of the culture of childhood demonstrates its contrived innocence and impotence, traditions extended into the youth culture of this century and its interminable adolescence.

James Axtell's study of education in colonial New England echoes the patterns of infantilization we find in Aries.[6] Whereas the sons of the lower and middle classes enjoyed adult responsibilities and status as farmers, apprentices, and craftsmen, upper-class youths attending the colonies' nascent colleges were subjected to humiliating rituals that emphasized their inadequacy and dependency.[7] Those who were to become the clergymen, magistrates, and legislators, those who would interpret the national culture for others, were the first benighted recipients of the American adolescence. In Axtell's account, as in that of Aries, the very children who, by virtue of their sex or class, may be expected to become the adults who will wield power are the ones whom education must make submissive and compliant. The child redeemer has become the adorable symbol of society's self-deception, a means of foisting the mission of our own liberation upon those least able to effect it.

If colonial education bent its child redeemers to the world their fathers made, the national literature of the new Republic provided a fictive escape from that world for the sons, and for the fathers themselves. Bernard Wishy portrays the child redeemer as an innocent figure who emerged from the rubble of the Civil War to save Americans from the pluralism of urban industrial life. He points to Huck Finn as the child redeemer par excellence, menaced by civilization, fighting to resist its evil lures by escaping to the river.[8]

But the great enemy of the child redeemer is time. By the time that the child, "trailing clouds of glory" as in Wordsworth's "Ode," is sufficiently powerful to be an active, influential participant in society, he is an adult.[9] His daily existence has been saturated with the temporal order, the spatial configurations, social relations, means of production, and patterns of communication of the society in which he lives. He fears asps and dreams of cockatrices. Huck knows that well. Even though Pap's death frees him from paternal power, Aunt Sally's care threatens an insidious socialization that Huck must escape: "I reckon I got to light out for the territory ahead of the rest, because Aunt Sally she's going to adopt me and sivilize me, and I can't stand it. I been there before."[10]

What the child redeemer has relinquished is his preconceptual contact with "that world which precedes knowledge, [that world] of which knowledge always speaks, and in relation to which every scientific schematization is an abstract and derivative sign language, as is geography in relation to the countryside in which we have learnt beforehand what a forest, a prairie or a river is."[11] The child has achieved the knowledge of object constancy only by relinquishing the shifting figure/ground structure of his original vision. The child has relinquished the prepredicative intimacy with nature and other persons that he enjoyed in infancy and early childhood. Transformed by his knowledge, derived from acting in the world that surrounds him, the child's bones and breath and beliefs belong both to him and to that world we would have him save.

Those of us who share our lives with children know that neither the image of the corrupt child born in original sin nor the image of the innocent babe describes the wily, winsome, wise, wild, and whiny creatures who are our kids. Nevertheless, our relations with these very real, very complex and contradictory creatures are influenced by the semiotic history of childhood. The images of the child that decorate procreation are marginal to it, an embroidered border that circles the cloth of care yet defines its boundary, suggesting its function and role in domestic culture. Though surrounded by images of childhood, the intimacy of family life is drawn into touch and sound and movement in the shared spaces of our homes, and the image must compete with these other more compelling and immediate expressions of the child's presence. Schools, on the other hand, requiring order and stillness, replacing touch with the exchange of performance for grades, are dominated by the images of adulthood and childhood and organize their curricula to mark the developmental space between them. The child redeemer is thriving in that space, where we expect him to absolve us from racism, poverty, drugs, and pollution. His education brings him from sentimental kindergartens and authoritarian classrooms to sun-dappled commencements where we exhort him to make the world a better place.

The use of the male pronoun in the foregoing passage does not express a conditioned sexism that conflates human agency or subjectivity with maleness. The pronouns are tailored to these particular historical subjects, the child redeemers, constructed by their fathers as alter egos to redeem them from their own transgressions. Perhaps we need to turn to the unsung sisters of these cherubic boys for redemption. But in order to discover how our daughters redeem us, we must forsake the innocent child, free of knowledge and guile, for the one who lies. "A child should always say what's true / And speak when he is spoken to," chides Robert Louis Stevenson.[12] Both the act and its admonishment testify to the contrivance that is the innocence of childhood.

Learning the truth is tricky business. Distinguishing the consensual agreements that constitute knowledge from one's own notions about the world is not always easy for adults and is often much more difficult for children, who may not know that there is a general agreement we call truth about many matters. Nevertheless, Sissela Bok distinguishes lying from ignorance with this definition of a lie: "an intentionally deceptive message in the form of a statement."[13] It is important to note that, whereas the child redeemer's innocence and moral superiority rest on his presumed disassociation from the world, it is this very separation that constitutes the offense of the lying child. And in the autobiographical accounts that follow where we find mothers, grandmothers, and aunts accusing their female children of lying, maternal rage does not pause to discriminate ignorance from deceit. Whether the distance comes from ignorance or from the deliberate resistance to another's will, the lie represents a chosen separation, a willful withdrawal from the adult world of the mother.

In *Daughter of Earth*, Agnes Smedley recalls the beatings she received from her mother for lying.

> My mother continued to say that I lied. But I did not know it. I was never clear. What was truth and what was fancy I could not know. To me, the wind in the tree tops really carried stories on its back; the red bird that came to our cherry tree really told me things; the fat, velvety flowers down in the forest laughed and I answered; the little calf in the field held long conversations with me.
>
> But at last I learned to know what a lie was; to induce my mother to stop beating me I would lie—I would say, yes, I had lied and was sorry, and then she would whip me for having withheld the admission so long. As time went on, to avoid a whipping, I learned to tell her only the things I thought she wanted to hear.[14]

Agnes Smedley never learned that lesson well enough to suit some. In the brief biography that Paul Lauter provides as an afterword to the Feminist Press edition of this autobiographical novel, we find an extraordinary woman. Raised in bitter poverty and committed to social action, she lived in Berlin in the 1920s, working to develop a state birth control clinic, traveling frequently to the Soviet Union, and working for the Indian freedom movement. In the late twenties and early thirties she went to China as a correspondent for the *Frankfurter Zeitung* and wrote the story of the Chinese Revolution in books that captured the struggles of the Chinese people who became her friends. She returned to the United States in the forties to discover that her stories of China and its revolutionary visions were once again read as lies by a country locked into the "Red scare." "The red bird that came to our cherry tree really told me things." Childhood's apostasy is repeated in adulthood as news of another world is understood as a repudiation of the mother country.

In Zora Neale Hurston's autobiography, *Dust Tracks on the Road*, lying is the passage that links the cultures of child and adult, white and black. A black woman born in the rural South, Hurston became an anthropologist dedicated to inscribing and interpreting black culture for white readers. Robert Hemenway cites this passage to show how Hurston uses her own life story to explain the idioms of her culture to white readers: "We held two lying contests, story-telling contests to you, and Big Sweet passed on who rated the prizes." And it is interesting to see that the border of storytelling and lying is crossed again in her reminiscences of childhood.

> When I began to make up stories I cannot say. Just from one fancy to another, adding more and more detail until they seemed real. People seldom see themselves changing. . . .
>
> I came in from play one day and told my mother how a bird had talked to me with a tail so long that while he sat up in the top of the pine tree his tail was dragging the ground. It was a soft beautiful bird tail, all blue and pink and red and green. In fact I climbed up the bird's tail and sat up the tree and had a long talk with the bird. He knew my name, but I didn't know how he knew it. In fact, the bird had come a long way just to sit and talk with me.
>
> Another time, I dashed into the kitchen and told Mama how the lake had talked with me, and invited me to walk all over it. I told the lake I was afraid of getting drowned, but the lake assured me it wouldn't think of drowning *me* like that. No, indeed! Come right on and have a walk. Well, I stepped out on the lake and walked all over it. It didn't even wet my feet. I could see all the fish and things swimming around under me, and they all said hello, but none of them bothered me. Wasn't that nice?
>
> My mother said that it was. My grandmother glared at me like open-faced hell and snorted.
>
> "Luthee!" (She lisped.) "You hear dat young 'un stand up here and lie like dat? And you ain't doing nothing to break her of it? Grab her! Wring her coat tails over her head and wear out a handful of peach hickories on her back-side! Stomp her guts out! Ruin her!"
>
> "Oh, she's just playing," Mama said indulgently.
>
> "Playing! Why dat lil' heifer is lying just as fast as a horse can trot. Stop her! Wear her back-side out. I bet if I lay my hands on her she'll stop it. I vominates a lying tongue."
>
> Mama never tried to break me. She'd listen sometimes, and sometimes she wouldn't. But she never seemed displeased. . . .
>
> I knew that I did not have to pay too much attention to the old lady and so I didn't. Furthermore, how was she going to tell what I was doing inside? I could keep my inventions to myself, which was what I did most of the time.[15]

Negotiating the status of her stories with her mother and grandmother may have provided Zora Neale Hurston with the appreciation

for perspective and relativism that informed her anthropological enterprise. It may also have provided the epistemological and social mobility
that took her from Eatonville to Barnard College and ultimately back
to an unmarked grave in a snake-infested field in rural Florida.[16]

Smedley and Hurston found secret wells within themselves where
they could hide their worlds from the maternal legislation that declared
them forbidden territories. These recalcitrant daughters and their
worlds terrify the mother and grandmother who dare not cross their
borders. And it is not only the confinement of culture, history, and
poverty that we find in the maternal refusal to play in a daughter's
magic garden. The refusal also signifies a defense against the lure those
places hold for the mothers themselves. Again, the object relations
theory provided by Chodorow may provide an explanation for this
maternal intolerance.[17] Less distinguished from our daughters than
from our sons, we find in our daughters' fantasies and fusions with the
object world our own lost connections to our own mothers. Women
retain greater access than men not only to our infantile attachments to
our mothers but also to the whole experience of infancy itself because,
unlike our brothers, the gender identity of women does not require the
repression of our earliest identification with our primary caretaker, our
mother. The harsh attack on the daughter's lie announces the mother's
struggle to forget the intimacy, the fusion, and lost possibilities of her
own preoedipal experience. The accusing mother and grandmother
repudiate the world of talking birds because their songs are too familiar
and threaten the defenses that these women have developed to tolerate
loneliness and to live in a world that divides culture from nature,
domesticity from mystery, private from public.[18]

These two accounts provide a glimpse of the lies that intimacy
demands, for its truth reminds us of what we have surrendered to the
gendered ego identities that circumscribe our worlds. Now, if it is this
experience of maternal intimacy that inspires a strict and bitter censor,
can we expect a broader tolerance from a woman who cares for
children raised by another woman, children the caretaker does not
really know? If it is a repressed sameness that provokes the furious
mother, the aunt who adopted Mary McCarthy is described in *Memories of a Catholic Girlhood* as attacking *difference* itself in her attempt
to deny the distinct boundaries that have formed around her niece's
experience. The sadistic regimen described here aspires to expunge an
intimacy the sadist cannot know but can imagine.[19] Perhaps it is the

frustrated desire to be the one the children have loved that makes any sign of private reservation a reservoir for the unloved caregiver's fantasies.

Aunt Margaret strove purposefully toward a corporate goal. Like most heads of institutions, she longed for the eyes of Argus. To the best of her ability, she saw to it that nothing was hidden from her. Even her health measures had this purpose. The aperients we were continually dosed with guaranteed that our daily processes were open to her inspection, and the monthly medical checkup assured her, by means of stethoscope and searchlight and tongue depressor, that nothing was happening inside us to which she was not privy. Our letters to Seattle were written under her eye, and she scrutinized our homework sharply, though her arithmetic, spelling, and grammar were all very imperfect. We prayed under supervision, for a prescribed list of people. . . . From the standpoint of efficiency, our lives, in order to be open, had to be empty; the books we might perhaps read, the toys we might play with figured in my aunt's mind, no doubt, as what the housewife calls "dust catchers"—around these distractions, dirt might accumulate. The inmost folds of consciousness, like the belly button, were regarded by her as unsanitary. Thus, in her spiritual outlook, my aunt was an early functionalist.

Like all systems, my aunt's was, of course, imperfect. Forbidden to read, we told stories, and if we were kept apart, we told them to ourselves in bed. We made romances out of our schoolbooks, even out of the dictionary, and read digests of novels in the *Book of Knowledge* at school.[20]

Even Wordsworth, who celebrated the innocence of childhood in "Intimations of Immortality from Recollections of Early Childhood," acknowledges the system from which it is derived: "Not in entire forgetfullness, / And not in utter nakedness, / But trailing clouds of glory do we come / From God who is our home."[21] Neither innocence nor deceit is a property of the child but is rather a property of the relation within which the child is nurtured. If innocence is the exclusion from the world demanded by the fathers, lying is the exclusion from the world demanded by the mothers. A gentler exile, I prefer lying to the radical suspension of relation and action that innocence implies. And as Kristeva argues, if the lies of the daughter encode the closeness to nature, to the other, that girls retain from their preoedipal experience, then those fibs and stories speak another way of knowing and being in the world, one that runs under the symbols of conventional knowledge and discourse, constituting what Kristeva calls the semiotic strata of signification.[22] For if we can listen to their birds and swim in their lakes we will recapture a glimpse of the possibilities our histories have denied.

I do not pretend that all those lies are as pleasant and pastoral as the ones recounted here. The ones that are most painful to hear are those that speak of a radical difference, a way of being, even of wishing, that I am afraid to remember or imagine. Nevertheless, it is the argument of this text that it is not the son's innocence but the daughter's lies that offer us redeeming knowledge. In showing us the world as they would have it, they reveal the world that we fled because we were not brave enough to pitch our tents and raise our flags there. Their lies can become our knowledge. Because the classroom is *not* the kitchen, because the teacher is *not* the mother, the child's fantasies can flower in the fictive ground of the curriculum. School is not the real world, and so it shares the property that Marianne Moore attributes to poetry: "imaginary gardens with real toads in them."[23]

The curriculum can conserve the divisions that cut up the world into little territories where we are all marooned, or it can entertain another geography. It is the teacher who stands guarding the territory where these secret gardens can grow, who can grasp these visions and grant them the legitimacy of knowledge. And if we hope that our children will transform our world, we had better heed Scripture and transform theirs. That is how it was for Smedley and Hurston and for McCarthy. They each remember teachers who lifted the maternal injunction and let them speak. Well, you say, they were writers. Yes, liars whose tales and stories were not buried in nostalgia or paranoia but encoded as literature and science. Writers are liars who get published.

But it is not easy for the women who teach children to encourage mendacity. First of all, the schools were designed to seclude innocent sons, not to publish lying daughters. Then, we are all daughters ourselves and must come to terms with our own altered accounts. We are, or we are not, mothers, and if we are not to reenact our own ambivalence about differentiation from our own daughters or sink into jealous interrogations of other women's daughters, we need to find out how to teach those who are and are not like us. Because knowledge encodes the human relations that are its source and ground, it is pointless to design a tolerant curriculum without examining the relations that create and sustain it. Even language experience or arts curricula that seem to invite the fantasies and memories of students challenge the teacher to come to terms with her own versions of truth and with the designations she reserves for those accounts that contradict the current wisdom. Let us remember that we are all Eve's children as well as Adam's.

9 Other People's Children

Like the *paidagogos*, the Greek slave who used to escort his young charge on the walk from home to school, we too pass the children from our kitchens, still sleep-creased and milk-moustached, through the doors of the public institution. We pass them from domesticity to public politics, from reproduction to production, from private life to public life. With our language we speak school talk, both familiar and strange to other people's children. We catch them and wind them up in our weave of words. As a teacher, a teacher of teachers, a parent, and a woman, I seek a process to transform this passage to another world into a middle place, neither here nor there, grasping both ends of the passage and pulling them together into a knot that refuses their oppositions, dualisms, exclusions, and sacrifices.

Ethics and the common culture provide the procedural form and cultural content for our current concepts of schooling. And if ethics and the common culture could gather together the concern and attention that we devote to our own children and extend this nurture to other people's children, then we might indeed find in the school the model for a just society that Dewey envisioned. But instead of extending the subtle, flexible responsive language that we have with our own children, curriculum devised by boards of regents, state education departments, superintendents, book publishers, even departmental committees, rarely rests on a thorough or even a casual acquaintance with the children for whom it is intended. They are other people's children, and so it makes perfect sense that to guide our decisions we shall rely on the rules we use to tell us how to treat people we don't know. "Other people's children" is a category that contains most of the children we don't know, save our own, our nieces and nephews perhaps, the kid from next door who was always in the house. Other people's children belong to other people, to single parents, urban poor, suburban scared, to the moral majority, to the eastern establishment. They are the abstract community guided by ethics that are equally abstract. The rules fit the curriculum, but the curriculum does not fit anybody.

MY CHILDREN

Rather than articulating a notion of care that extends the love we give our own to others, ethics shapes relations designed to repudiate the time and space and specificity that nurture requires. Nevertheless, because the first "me" is immersed in a syncretic relation with the other, it is not affiliation but differentiation that requires justification, and so ethics is compensatory. It provides not a basis for affiliation with strangers but a mode of reconciliation for those who once knew each other and are now estranged. The rational, logical, linguistic order of ethics reconstitutes attempts to establish relations between disparate creatures whose very humanity was originally predicated upon their mutual identification.

Both identity and community originate in mimesis. It is not the mere correspondence of form that is the basis for identification but the appreciation of shared intentions and responses expressed in the gestures and actions of the body. It is through the hands, the flushed face, the gasp, and the squint that we express our dreams and fears, that we understand what animates the lives around us. The semiotics of gesture, the language of the body, provides a rich lexicon that defies translation into linguistic correlatives. The clarity and specificity of the word dissolve into the fluidity and transience of the gesture. Tethered to specific contexts, gestures, as any anthropologist and as parents who have learned to read their child's shrug can tell us, provide compelling testimony for those who share configurations of space and time that we would designate as intimate. Schoeman associates this fluidity of expression with the love that flows through families:

> We share ourselves with those with whom we are intimate and are aware that they do the same with us. Traditional moral boundaries which give rigid shape to the self are transparent to this kind of sharing. This makes for nonabstract moral relationships in which talk about rights of others is to a certain extent irrelevant. It is worth mentioning that the etymology of "intimate" relates it to a verb meaning "to bring within" and that the primary meanings of "intimate" focus on this character of being innermost for a person.[1]

The transparent self that Schoeman describes is the achievement of intimacy. As adults we experience this amazing loss of boundaries rarely, although we may search for this fluidity in friendship, in love, in spiritual communion. The protean potentiality that was the unbounded promise of our infancies has with each year congealed into form; maternal symbiosis yields to ego differentiation, bisexuality to gender, babbling to a particular language, play to work. It is the parent who observes this process of coming to form and who remembers those forms that the inevitable crystallization of personality has precluded. So it is the parent who insists on the mass murderer's basic goodness, on the conformist's creativity, on the ne'er-do-well's ambition. It is not mere sentimentality that motivates the parents' contradiction of their child's salient attributes but their memory of those moments that never fell into sequence, of movements that never became habits, murmurs that never became words. And the tears at graduations, weddings, all those ceremonies that mark the child's mastery of and commitment to particular forms of being, are not merely the parents' maudlin expression of their own impending isolation but their grieving for the possibilities that each developmental crystallization denies.

The history of the self is difficult to reclaim. It is pulled out of obscurity by aesthetic processes when what Marcuse has called "a rebellious subjectivity" breaks through the ideological design of everyday life to bring the intuitions and impulses repressed in the process of development to form.[2] What the adult reclaims of his own unrealized possibilities through love of another, through religious experience, or through aesthetic or psychoanalytic processes are those latent aspects of the child's personality that parents implicitly retain as part of their understanding of the child's identity. The parent can also testify to the genetic history of the child's self, the forms that persisted despite their discouragement, the forms that evolved through resistance, avoidance, as well as through mimesis and adoration. The intimacy that bonds parent and child is a prism that can contain their changing forms, sustaining their identities not through physical resemblance or through a repetition of similar acts but through the memory and presence of shared, if never realized, possibilities. As an enduring structure whose continuity relies upon the reciprocal transformations of all its participants, the family provides the possibility of freedom without chaos, individuation without isolation. The intimacy that distinguishes the parent/child relationship is signified by the duration of the relation as well as by the capacity for recognition that acknowledges and sustains possible as well as actual expressions of identity.

Now, I am not trying to argue that families are free from ideology, that family relations are not often oppressive and abusive. There are unwanted children and neglecting parents. But I am arguing that continuity is a necessary condition for freedom, and in our society it is only within the parent/child relation that we find relations of sufficient duration to extend and experience that freedom. Traditionally, we have tended to associate family ties with the most static and limiting features of identity: class, ethnicity, religion. But those emblems do not function as signs of identity for persons within families. For the outsider, the family is Catholic. For the insider, there are shades and transformations of Catholicism as it is practiced, understood, embraced, resented, repudiated, reclaimed by each member. At any given time, for one member of the family it is a pose, for another a hope, for another a habit. And it is the same for class, the same for ethnicity.

In contrast to this grammar of intimacy, Schoeman observes that the language of rights "typically helps us to sharpen our appreciation of the moral boundaries which separate people, emphasizing the appropriateness of seeing other persons as autonomous and independent."[3] Ethics traditionally falls into this service of limiting relations, defining the boundaries of persons and protecting them from the unwarranted intrusions of others.

THEIR CHILDREN

The object of ethical discourse is the discovery of those principles that can guide the moral conduct of persons who do not know each other. After all, we rarely talk about the mother's treatment of a child as ethical, and a friend's behavior is unethical only when she allows her feelings and loyalties to influence a choice that is supposedly divorced from considerations of emotion and affiliation. Ethics has come to signify rules for relations between persons who are not bonded in feeling. The absence of feeling is implicit in the theme of constraint that runs through ethical discourse. This denial is explicit in the dictum of eros-bound promulgated by the Greeks as the highest good, extended in the restrictions of the Ten Commandments, and implicit in the libertarian designation of rights as being those acts that may be practiced by individuals free from the censure and intervention of others.

Both the historical traditions of schooling and the traditions of ethical discourse have despised the family, defining the standards for public conduct and political action in terms explicitly designed to oppose the relations, expectations, promise, and constraints of intimacy. They have consistently portrayed the public domain as the ground for freedom and depicted the family as cloying, restricting, and limiting.

In her study of political theory, *Public Man, Private Woman*, Jean Elshtain suggests that the exclusion of women and children from political discourse is to be understood not as accidental but rather as essential to political action as it has evolved within the traditions of Western political theory: "Politics," she argues, "is in part an elaborate defense against the tug of the private, against the lure of the familial, against the evocations of female power."[4] She reminds us that both Plato and Aristotle systematically denigrated the *oikos*, or household, and set up the *polis* in explicit contradiction to it. It was the polis, not the oikos, that was to be the context for those relationships and actions categorized as ethical. Distressed by the disorder of Athenian politics, Plato envisioned another world, not that, however, of the household where women, children, and slaves labored to sustain daily life but the world of the symposium, an all-male forum for discourse and pedagogy.[5] The home, where one eats and sleeps and makes love that makes children, is disqualified as a context for ethical behavior. The moral life will be defined in the polis or symposium where, if eros-bound slips its bonds, it will yield indiscretion rather than progeny. Elshtain reminds us that even the woman admitted to the ranks of the Guardians in Plato's ideal city qualifies on the condition that she display a nature commensurate with her function. Leadership is predicated on disassociation, the exercise of an impartial and abstract virtue. Woman may rule so long as she rules and lives as a man. She must repudiate the privacy of the family, mate according to the dictates of a system of eugenics, nurse any child but her own, and relinquish her child to a public nursery.[6] The family unit of particular persons bonded together over time through multiple and lasting forms of sexual attachment and infant nurturance is a threat to the unity of the ideal state, which must promote a vision of a disembodied, eternal, impersonal good. In the ahistorical and extra-linguistic forms of Plato's Republic, Elshtain points out, human bodies, human families, and human discourse present annoying obstacles to the creation of a "thorough-going rationalist mericratic order that would require, namely, the application to and assessment of all human beings on a single set of formal and abstract criteria."[7]

Acknowledging that Augustine, Luther, and Rousseau view women and families as providing a context where the acknowledgment of feeling is valued above the postures of public discourse, Elshtain identifies the schism between the public and the private that remains within their thought. The private realm is glorified when their political theory addresses the weaknesses of public life, but the acknowledgment remains sentimental when theory offers neither language, institutions, nor political processes that can bring the understanding of human needs and hopes from private into public life. Elshtain points out that even Marx, who understood and articulated the interpenetration of familial and economic public structures, offers resolutions that are drained of politics, for his species being suggests an abstract, unmotivated, eternally generic creature, divested not only of the oppressive state and its economic burdens but of all identity and intention as well.[8] The "species being" recapitulates the myth of the formless, undifferentiated, preoedipal infant, disqualifying the mother/child relation as a model for society at the very moment that it valorizes it as our ideal.

Lest we imagine that the terror of the flesh and the lure of the abstract are peculiar to Greek misogyny or Hegelian idealism, the curriculum of our neighborhood school will testify that the fascination of the ideal and contempt for the familiar are still with us. We sustain a fear of the family, of particular interests, as if we were colonists terrified by the wilderness or as if we were manufacturers trying to integrate a heterogeneous blend of farmers and immigrants into an industrial work force. The beast against whom the stockades of nation and industry were built has long since fled; yet we stay, milling around in the enclosure, even when our beast is not chaos but order, not fragmentation but deadly consistency, not the unknown but the known.

And here is the place where the hope of families joins the aspiration so cleverly distorted by the myth of meritocracy. For curriculum, as I have argued at the outset of this discourse, is our way of contradicting the orders of biology and culture.[9] Curriculum is our attempt to claim and realize self-determination by constructing worlds for our children that repudiate the constraints that we understand to have limited us. We associate all our yearning for affiliation with weakness and with family. We project that needy side of ourselves onto the women who once witnessed and answered to it and aggrandize the values, language, and conventions of the public world as a defense against the intimacy we miss so deeply. The history of political thought stresses this repudiation of the essential connections within which our humanity evolves: The male repudiates those feelings and actions that he associates with femininity in order to achieve maleness; the female repudiates her mother in order to participate in the public world. Politics repudiates the family. Ethics repudiates the experience of the body, of particular persons, and of intimacy as it strives to construct a logical argument to support autonomy and differentiation.

So, associating class and caste with inherited wealth and rank, American schooling has endeavored to loosen the grip of family and thus to provide equality of opportunity to its children. But denial never works. What is repressed, Merleau-Ponty maintains, lingers under the gaze.[10] Surely, we have seen evidence of this irony in the ethnocentrism of schoolteachers who, despising their own ethnicity, strive to expunge the ethnicity and familial attachments of their students, demanding a mimesis of their own manners, language, and carriage. So it was that, growing up in Flatbush, I and other Jewish children were taught to imitate the speech and gestures of our Irish teachers in order to be "American."

If the rules of the so-called public world have evolved in an explicit repudiation of family life, schooling in this culture, as in many others, has provided the training necessary to make this leap from intimacy to anonymity. The processes and principles of curriculum decision making perpetuate the myth that the familial context is limiting and the public context is liberating. The search for curriculum ethics perpetuates the project to draw boundaries that will demarcate areas of influence protecting the child, the teacher, the parent, the state from each other's influence. The goal of the common good that has supported what is taught in this nation's schools has extended the classical concept of *educos*, meaning "to lead out of," into the classrooms of a democratic nation. Identifying the family, the clan, the neighborhood, the region as stultifying, ethics of curriculum decision making has always appealed to those values that have the weakest ties to constituencies, the most anonymous advocates. The exclusion of parents from curriculum deliberations has been justified by the suspicion of private interests and of their capacity to drain the substance and energy from the project to create and sustain a common culture. The vision of a common culture is always the vision of another world: the next one of the Scriptures, the old one of the classics, the idealized one of the new nation. Originally conceived to free us from particular evils, an oppressive established church, a terrifying wilderness, turbulent industrialization and urbanization, the common culture has always implied a repudiation of the present culture. What is common is never how we live or what we share. What is common is the ideal, the dream that manages to elude all of us. Midgley chides us for trampling our specific experience and commitments in our pursuit of a generic idealization:

> We can think of our culture as a prison or a dead weight—or as our skin, or as the part of the world where we happen to be. Aspiring to be free from any culture is in one way like trying to be skinless. (Our skin does indeed come between us and the world—but it is what makes it possible for us to touch it.) In another way it is like trying to be nowhere. And of course restriction to a single place is a restriction; it stops us from being elsewhere. But being in any other particular place would do the same. All elsewheres are potential, which is a miserable shadowy thing to be compared with the splendid nowness of being actually here. Some people do feel that the proper thing would be to bring children up without a culture till they came to years of discretion, and then let them choose. But children who are held apart from life, or rushed from one set of people to another, do not become exceptionally capable of choosing. You can choose only between given alternatives, and to grasp any alternative you need years of acclimatization and practice in choosing from one particular set, in seeing what choices amount to. And you need to learn to hold onto something. *All this is not a misfortune.* A culture is a way of awakening our faculties. Any culture does this to some extent. People proficient in one culture can usually make some sense of another. There is no prison. We can always walk on if we want to enough. What we cannot do is something which is no loss—namely, be nobody and nowhere.[11]

When September rolls around and all the little "nobodies" get on the yellow buses to go "nowhere," we induct them into the "common culture." It is within the rationalization of the common culture that the content and decision-making processes of the curriculum have been combined to exclude the influence of the family from the classroom. What the common culture usually embraces is any culture other than the one lived by the children in that classroom. Because the common culture is always anywhere other than this world, its curriculum rarely speaks to a world children know, a world accessible to their understanding and action. It is a curriculum that controls through mystification, encouraging placid passivity. In *Pedagogy of the Oppressed*, Paulo Freire shows us how the interests of the oppressor are rationalized and promoted by a curriculum that pretends neutrality while it advances the ways of knowing, the forms of language and relation that enhance the privilege of those with power.[12] Power wears many masks, and if in some countries it appears as the Church or the Party, or even the People, here it is the Common Culture that does the trick. Situating the curriculum in a specific culture provokes the discourse that requires argument, specificity, imagination, and judgment and entails reflection that challenges whatever is parochial and complacent. Because it is labeled as neutral and is packaged and distributed as such, a standard rationale for the common culture is its accessibility. Ironically, it is this very posture of the curriculum's impartiality and neutrality that has contributed to the school's capacity to sort, stratify, categorize, and identify the children of the nation. It has supported the myth of the meritocracy that convinces parents and children that they have warranted the decisions they receive.

In order for curriculum to provide the moral, epistemological, and social situations that allow persons to come to form, it must provide the ground for their action rather than their acquiescence. It must be submitted to their reform, be accessible to their response.[13] Curriculum decisions can only be provisional and contingent and open to revision by the constituency to which they apply. Curriculum is a moving form. That is why we have trouble capturing it, fixing it in language, lodging it in our matrix. Whether we talk about it as history, as syllabi, as classroom discourse, as intended learning outcomes, or as experience, we are trying to grasp a moving form, to catch it at the moment that it slides from being the figure, the object and goal of action, and collapses into the ground for action. Through its movement curriculum intertwines the ideal and actual. Its epistemologies are translated into physical space and time where they determine where children sit, what they touch, whether they feel the heat of the sun. Curriculum, considered apart from its appropriation and transformation by students, curriculum defined as design, a structure of knowledge, an intended learning outcome, or a learning environment, is merely a static form. We cannot rationalize the surrender of educational experience to these phrases by imagining them to be deposits in the stream of educational theory that the current will somehow circumvent. They clog. They occlude. In their pretentious attempt to signify the encounter of the student and the curriculum, they obliterate all that is personal in favor of whatever is general, all that is actual in deference to what is hypothetical, all that is moving in deference to all that is still. I suggest that the application of ethics to curriculum decision making merely adds more debris to the stream, muddying the waters with traditions of deliberation and definitions of freedom that ignore the motives, purposes, indeed, the very existences of children and their families.

The interface between the school and the family is packed with pseudonyms for the child. Although the teacher may develop and maintain a subtle understanding of a child, that tentative, complex, dynamic impression is flattened into a print-out of evaluations that freeze the child into codes and into terse objectifications.[14] Paul is inattentive, Helen too social. Gloria is so bright, Kristin so helpful. The work of Aaron Cicourel and of ethnomethodologists who have followed his lead suggests that it is the very ability to understand and manipulate this naming process that determines school success.[15] But their insights have surely not discouraged the proliferation of the name game, which has, in the guise of individuation of instruction and under the pretense of sensitivity to differences, bestowed new names, such as "learning disabled," "gifted," and "disadvantaged," upon hundreds of thousands of children.

How in the name of humanism can a school defend an evaluation report that tells parents that in view of his or her capacities their child is doing very well? Not only has the school seen fit to describe the child's present activity without reference to the context in which it is taking place, it presumes to make that evaluation contingent on its assessment of the child's essential being. Past, present, and future are rolled into that IQ test or that reading score. Is there life after SRA?

Few of us would excuse our own children from their futures with the grace and understanding we extend to other people's children. Other people's children are abstract. They are reading scores, FTEs, last year's graduating class, last week's body count. A curriculum designed for my child is a conversation that leaves space for her responses, that is transformed by her questions. It needn't replicate her language or mine, but it must be made accessible to our interpretation and translation. Curriculum decision making requires our participation, the active, responsive, interpreting activity of parents and children.

Curriculum issues contain significant choices concerning the daily lives of children. But these choices emerge in the daily transactions of the classroom, and they cannot be prescribed by securing agreement to a set of standing principles. The development of curriculum requires multiple interpretations. One interprets a discipline, a text, the understandings, motives, and interests of particular students, and the constraints and possibilities of the situation they share. Parents and students need to participate in that interpretive process, for the consequences of those deliberations will determine how class time and space are organized. They will determine who speaks and who is silent. They will determine which choices teachers make for children, which they make for themselves, which they make for each other. They will determine how knowledge is defined and classified, who gives it, who gets it, and who gets away with it.

Although parents must organize politically if they are to influence school decisions, the degree of parent presence in schools that this essay is inviting goes beyond what we called in the sixties local control. The community or parent groups that surfaced in the sixties were formed in an adversarial political context, which, though it advocated participation and change, promoted macho politics and power brokering and shunted the child to the sidelines. The kind of participation that I am advocating would not preclude political action, but its purposes and focus would be considerably more specific. We need to bring the adults who are the advocates of particular children, namely, their own, into the daily life of classrooms. Their presence would interrupt the march to the common culture without necessarily shifting the whole parade to another destination. The struggle for local control persisted in conflating schooling and the legitimation of a particular identity, wresting control of the school away from the bureaucracy so that it could be shaped to the needs of dominant neighborhood ethnic groups. Although this acknowledgment of a school's constituency diminishes the hegemony of the common culture, it still does nothing to make the school a place where difference is expressed and received as a legitimate aspect of everyone's identity.

We have become infected with a sociologist's imagination, and we disclaim our own experience of our own identities if we believe that individuals experience themselves as professionals, blue-collar workers, bourgeoisie. Those descriptions are still photographs taken at one moment from a certain distance. They are moments so swollen with sociological import that they have burst the heuristic limits of their proper function and have leaked into our understanding of the specificity, complexity, and possibility that sustain our interest in our daily lives. All those hours spent in classrooms can hardly be collapsed into an equation that indicates whether the child has maintained or surpassed the socioeconomic status of his parents. But all those hours spent in classrooms constitute the content and consequences of curriculum decisions, as well as the moments, whispers, and memories of the child's day, and that time and space have become territories where parents dare not trespass. ALL VISITORS PLEASE REPORT TO THE OFFICE.

In the novel *Something Happened*, Joseph Heller portrays the desperation of Bob Slocum, a father who feels unable to influence the quality of his child's experience as well as his own. Slocum's boy does not want to go to school on the days he has gym. He's afraid of the teacher, Forgione, and so is his family. Slocum wants both to celebrate his kid's resistance and to have him conform. Anxious to the end, Slocum asks Forgione to reassure him that he won't punish the boy for the father's intervention:

"And you're not going to get even, are you? Take it out on him because I came here to ask?"

"No, of course not," Forgione exclaims indignantly, "why would I want to do that?" (Because you're human, I think.) "What kind of a man do you think I am?"

"Cro-Magnon," I reply crisply.

(But that, of course, I say to myself. Outside myself, I laugh softly in a pretense of congeniality . . .)

"Ha, ha, Forgione," is what I do say, to indicate to Forgione that my question was not intended to be taken seriously. "I do. I really do, Mr. Forgione."

"What?"

"Appreciate it. I'm glad you understand."

"That's okay, Mr. Slocum. I'd do that to help any kid."

"Thank you, Mr. Forgione. I feel much better now."

I put my hand out eagerly to shake his, and find that I feel much worse when I depart from him.

I went there braced for battle, prepared to take on all comers if necessary. I have won my point too easily, and go away feeling I have lost. I am depressed. Good God! I catch myself wondering as I commute into the city by train to my office again. What in the world have I done to my poor little boy now? I find myself furious with my wife for having prodded me to go there. Suppose Forgione is intent upon revenge?

Well, Forgione isn't. Forgione, "bless his noble heart, turns out fine," to the surprise of Slocum who confesses:

> I am more tense about gym than my boy at breakfast this morning. My coffee is flavored with the bitter taste of bile. Forgione is an executioner, masked in dire, enigmatic intentions, and I ponder all day long in my office over what kinds of criminal atrocities are being committed against my boy behind the brick walls, closed doors, and blind windows of that penitential institution of a school. . . . I am crazy; no wonder my boy tends to be fearful.[16]

This is the terror that fuels that resistance of the Creationists, that motivates parental assaults on libraries. These are not value conflicts. Value conflicts take place within individuals who have to make choices between competing goods. These are custody cases.

Fundamentalist attacks on the course of study may lead us to think that only the common culture stands between our children and a primitive sectarianism. Nevertheless, if we would keep the school syllabus and texts safe from the censure of parents, then we must provide some process where the perspectives those parents hold are introduced, considered, and discussed in the curriculum. I do not think we should substitute creationism for evolution in those communities who favor a religious rather than a scientific explanation of natural history. But I also do not think we should teach evolution to children who are taught to believe in creationism at home without acknowledging and addressing the conflict that they and their families experience as they negotiate these opposing belief systems. I suspect that some of the support for the fundamentalist campaign to impose its particular convictions on the curriculum comes from parents who feel estranged from what goes on in their children's classrooms, as well as from what goes on in their children. There is a sad irony to their aggression as they promote categorical religious dogma to express their own specificity and adopt atavisms of ancient thought to decorate their shield because they are, among other things, symbols of resistance to the common culture. Their sense of alienation provides fuel for those who are using the curriculum to pursue their own political aggrandizement and social influence.

We may teach the same text in Brooklyn and in Biloxi but if we rely on the teacher's guide and the questions at the back of the chapter to constitute how we talk to the children in these two very different communities, we should not be surprised when the parents' committee comes knocking on the classroom door with a court order. No text, no matter how clear its explanation of natural selection, can determine what that principle of evolution means to its readers. Curriculum is not books, but what we do with books. It is the defensive abstraction of classroom discourse and the estrangement of parents from schools that provoke parents to attack texts. These are battles for the child's name being waged by parents who feel as alienated from the products of their reproduction in the domain of private labor, the family, as they are from the products of their production in the domain of public labor, the job. Admittedly, the alienation of the workplace may contribute to the parent's need to claim and control his child, and that is why it may be mothers who, if they are not as immersed in the instrumental reason of the workplace as the fathers, should be the first emissaries from the world of the family to the world of the school.

OUR CHILDREN

Arguing that women's moral judgments are drawn from commitments to relatedness and care and to the specific contexts within which these concerns are attached to real people, Carol Gilligan offers a rationale that would designate women to be the agents who might rescue the classroom from the common culture and the rule of ethics.[17] In *Caring*, Nel Noddings articulates the feminist sense of the "good" that Gilligan has observed by naming the properties of an ethic predicated on connection and intimacy rather than separation and estrangement. The one who cares

> is *present* in her acts of caring. Even in physical absence, acts at a distance bear the signs of presence: engrossment in the other, regard, desire for the other's well-being. Caring is largely reactive and responsive. Perhaps it is even better characterized as receptive. The one-caring is sufficiently engrossed in the other to listen to him and to take pleasure or pain in what he recounts. Whatever she does for the cared-for is embedded in a relationship that reveals itself as engrossment and in an attitude that warms and comforts the cared-for.[18]

Noddings's concept of care substitutes relation for rules. But her emphasis on "engrossment," "presence," and "receptivity" reminds us that the relation in this feminist ethic is not abstract. It is not a state of being or a moral stance, but, like curriculum, it moves; it is an event. Noddings's insistence that we understand an ethic of care as situated in concrete relations simultaneously reveals to us why mothers can extend that care to their own children and why they can deny it to others. This ethic is rooted in *space*, requiring proximity and encounter, and *time*, requiring response and duration. It is part of history, and so are we. Our capacity to care for each other's children is entangled in our own reproductive projects, in the meaning of "school" in the histories of both mothers and teachers, and in our relationships to each other. In Chapter 2 I explored some of the tensions that estrange mothers and teachers. A mother may resent the teacher who leads her child away from her kitchen to an office, a factory, a world where she does not feel welcome. A mother may resent the teacher who wins her child's love or names her child's world. A teacher may project her ambivalence about her role in socialization onto the mother of her student, portraying her as clinging and regressive in order to rationalize her own and the school's intrusion. We have all been, after all, some woman's child, and we may also be some child's mother. When we teach other women's children, we do not forget those affiliations, and we worry about them. Unfortunately, the worry, which is realistic and needs to be negotiated between teachers and mothers, announces itself more often as an accusation than as a mutual problem.

Meeting with a young woman, a student teacher, who had just returned from working with a class of elementary school children, I remember hearing the accusation take form. She was proud and vibrant as she told me about the serious talk that she and the students had shared. Toward the end of her description she rationalized what must have seemed to her as an intrusion into the realm of the family: "You know," she said, "these kids' mothers never talk to them about things like this—they're too busy with other things." "How do you know that?" I asked, sad but not surprised to hear the denigration of parents become part of what this young woman was learning as she learned to be a teacher. Well, she didn't know it at all, but she believed it, and she believed it because it excused her from the anxiety that she had trespassed on the nurturant ground of another woman. Her sense of that privileged relation and of her justified yet guilty transgression was not merely a response to the way the school and the home are zoned in the cultural space of our society. It was also a response to her communication with her own mother, whom she loved deeply but would not confide in, fearing that her stories would offend her mother's religious commitments. And I know about that because she did confide in me, her teacher. I, of course, did not mention the story of my student to my own children because I did not want my adolescent daughters to feel displaced by this student's willingness to tell their mother what she would not tell her own.

We must make peace with the women who teach our children and acknowledge our solidarity with the mothers of other people's children if we are going to reclaim the classroom as a place where we nurture children. If, as Mary Midgley so persuasively argues in *Beast and Man*, the precondition for all forms of altruism is the care of the young, then we need to obliterate the territoriality that confines your children and mine, separating me from yours and mine from you. Our children's common interests escape our understanding because I do not know, nor do I nurture, your children. The very processes of identification and commitment that enable us to care for our own children with attention and sensitivity must not provide the barriers that prevent us from extending concern to other people's children.

The presence of parents in classrooms is essential if teachers and parents are going to trust one another, but it is also essential if parents are going to develop that concern for each other's child necessary to undermine the categorical and competitive character of schooling. When I have typed the story that your child reads or have tied his shoe or found his scarf, when you have told my child a story of your own or have helped her catch the bus, other people's children become our children. This kind of contact is a wide embrace that, allowed duration, contains the implicit as well as the explicit, possibility as well as achievement. It promises to extend a new tolerance not only to other people's children but to other people as well. For as we share the care of a child with her parents we engage in a mimetic and empathic relation with them as well as with the child, gaining access to their hope as well as to their habits of nurture. It is not enough to know other people's children. We must know, share a world with, the other people who love that child, wildly or tentatively, desperately, ambivalently, or tenderly.

It is, as Pagano has argued so beautifully in "The Claim of Philia," affiliation rather than eros or agape that will bind us into an educating community.[19] It is the sibling relation, bonded by reproduction extended through production, that affiliation offers us. It invites us to abandon our battle for our parents' resources and regard and to contribute our own vitality to our common future. For though philia, like the ethic of care that Noddings has portrayed, eschews abstraction, it does not, according to Pagano, ratify an "individualistic, privatized subjectivity."[20] It is attached not to property but to relation. If we see our children as our possessions, then to share them is to deplete our holdings. But if we understand ourselves to be in relation to them, then their relations to others support and sustain their capacity to receive and respond to our love.

As Pagano warns us away from the totalizing discourse of the fathers and the privatized claims of the mothers, we wander toward the middle ground of the knowledge we shared with our brothers and our sisters and with the kids we played with after school. And if school taught us to compete with each other, defining our interests as if they were discrete and separable, going back to school with our children will give us the opportunity to bring the "claim of philia" from the schoolyard into the classroom where it belongs.

MY FATHER ALWAYS claimed that if Lyndon Johnson had fathered sons instead of daughters, we never would have lost 56,371 men in Vietnam. Over the years I have taken pride in my father's pacifism and comfort in the protection that he extended to us, his own children, though I may have doubted the probability of his prediction. One morning the television news presents an interview with Clarence Long, congressman from Maryland, the only current member of Congress who is the father of a son wounded in Vietnam. He demands that we withdraw all military advisors from El Salvador, and I wonder how many fathers' sons must die before we stop killing other people's children. Even though we utter numerical testimonies to our good resolve—"The War to End All Wars," 116,516, 6,000,000, "Never Again" (only 56,371 in Southeast Asia)—the history of Western civilization marks time in the body counts of the fathers.

And the mothers, where are they? I, for one, have never been able to applaud when the car, draped in a banner that identifies its silver-haired occupants as the gold star mothers of sons slain in the wars of this century, passes in the Memorial Day parade. It is they, even more than the goose-stepping majorettes twirling wooden rifles and bayonets, who infuriate me because they smile, because they accede. I know that it is unfair to hold these women responsible for the decisions they did not make or for the unspeakable losses they have endured, so I keep silent when the silver-haired bereaved ride by, waving and smiling, and worry about what I will do when they draft my son.

My son, my daughters. Separated from extended kin, transient, mobile, dodging ICBMs and dreading SDI, we clutch the children closer. It takes the distance and affection of a doting aunt to show us how the exclusive attachment to our own progeny threatens their very survival. In *The Years*, written on the eve of World War II, Virginia Woolf gave us this glimpse of our parental possessiveness:

> Oh Lord, North said to himself, she's as bad as they are. She was glazed; insincere. They were talking about her children now.
>
> "Yes. That's the baby," she was saying, pointing to a boy who was dancing with a girl.
>
> "And your daughter, Maggie?" Milly asked, looking round.
>
> North fidgeted. This is the conspiracy, he said to himself; this is the steam roller that smooths, obliterates, rounds into identity; rolls into balls. He listened. Jimmy was in Uganda; Lily was in Leicestershire; my boy—my girl . . . they were saying. But they're not interested in other people's children, he observed. Only in their own; their own property; their own flesh and blood, which they would protect with the unsheathed claws of the primeval swamp, he thought, looking at Milly's fat little paws, even Maggie, even she. For she too was talking about my boy, my girl. How then can we be civilised, he asked himself?[21]

In schools we become civilized by denying attachment. We pretend the Slocums, Maggies, and Millies don't exist. We pretend they aren't waiting for the school bus, smoothing Jimmy's hair, touching Lily's cheek. Like Woolf's despairing bachelor, North, we consign primitive feeling, passionate commitments, to domesticity, and then we construct a public space purged of such contaminants. But attachment and difference never disappear just because we declare them invisible. They always seep back in. Schools have never been neutral places. For centuries schools have been places where some people's children learn to be subordinate to other people's children. But the same guise of neutrality that permits the meritocracy to flourish also can function to rationalize the most arbitrary and violent self-interest. It is the kind of dehumanized thinking that finds its ultimate terror in an Adolf Eichmann, who reported that he held no personal antagonism for the Jewish people but was merely effecting the solution to a "political" problem.

Survival is not a matter of principles. It is an ecology of space, clean air and water, food, shelter, and care. If women are more sensible about survival, it is because we have been entrusted with the care of other people's bodies, the young and the old. It is the opportunity to care for other people's children that schools can offer us, and that invitation will have to be offered and accepted if the "other" can be rescued from the abstractions that certify murder.

10 The Empty House:
Furnishing Education
with Feminist Theory

> You have won rooms of your own in the house hitherto exclusively owned by men. You are able, though not without great labor and effort, to pay the rent. You are earning your five hundred pounds a year. But this freedom is only a beginning; the room is your own, but it is still bare. It has to be furnished; it has to be decorated; it has to be shared. How are you going to furnish it, how are you going to decorate it? With whom are you going to share it, and upon what terms? These, I think are questions of the utmost importance and interest. For the first time in history you are able to ask them; for the first time you are able to decide for yourselves what the answers should be. Willingly would I stay and discuss those questions and answers—but not tonight. My time is up; and I must cease.[1]

I wish she had stayed. For as the title of this chapter suggests, I am not sure that this room of ours is any cozier than it was on the day Virginia Woolf walked out of it and left it to us to furnish. So I rattle around in it—picking things up and putting them down, rearranging the few chairs, wishing she were here and that it was still her place and that I could dwell in it. Now, you may think that this is an infantile response to the invitation to articulate a feminist theory for research in education. Why should I, a forty-six-year-old woman, who writes, teaches, publishes, parents, and keeps house in this year of 1987, look back to this Victorian child, this Bloomsbury bohemian who walked away from this world less than two years after I entered it? "We think back through our mothers, if we are women," she tells us in *A Room of One's Own*, so it is thinking back I intend to do. I would think forward if I could; I have never quite developed the knack for that. If I had, I think I could write novels. Instead, I write what some call theory.

The word "theory," Jürgen Habermas tells us, has religious origins.[2] The *theoros* was a representative sent from his Greek city to observe sacred festivals in other cities. Through *theoria*, "looking on," he abandoned himself to those events, to their version of the cosmic order, and strove to imitate its ordered relationships and proportions in his own self-formation. Theory was the perception and expression of the order that bonded society to nature, for once the natural laws of the heavens were observed and understood through theory, they would be replicated in the development and comportment of the individual and in the order and harmony of the polis. Feminist theory also contemplates the order of things, and we know that like the Greek philosophers our consciousness is tuned to its harmonies, our bodies bent to its proportions. Yet this is a mimesis we struggle to understand so that we may repudiate it and, in so doing, reclaim our minds and bodies from the entrapment in this so-called natural order of things. We are suspicious when nature is invoked to certify our commitments by denying that we are the source of our acts and choices. Nature displaces the source and responsibility for choice from us to an origin that is prior and imperious. Now, as Mary O'Brien has argued in *The Politics of Reproduction*, the Greek *theoros* and the political philosophers who followed him, jealous of the procreative powers of woman, claimed the creation of culture for themselves.[3] If they collapsed the memory of their own infancy and mother love into the terror and authority of nature, they also made it by definition unknowable. Repudiating preoedipal experience as the source of their own human identities, as well as the shape and history of culture, they claimed a second nature for men and relegated women to the inchoate mysteries of flesh and earth. When women think back through our mothers we look past the natural order expressed in physics, astronomy, biology, our second nature, to the first nature that male identity and male science have repressed.

The research on gender inequality in education, it follows, has attempted to ascertain the process and extent of feminine access to second nature. The study of difference has been the study of male and female performance on tests, of the cognitive styles and preferences of males and females, of the socialization processes relegated to each sex, and of the distinctions in public influence and social status that accrue to each sex. Construed in terms of male dominance, privilege has been articulated in terms of income, participation in professions and management, political office, and media. Theory functions in these studies to account for the subordinate position of women in schools, in the disciplines, in society. Is it biology? Is it the socialization of classrooms or families? Employing the methods of the social sciences, this research attempts to generate information about the constitution of second nature by using an epistemology and mode of inquiry that is an expression of second nature itself. We attempt to generate knowledge about difference using the ways of knowing that, in themselves, create, express, and perpetuate difference.

All the cognitive operations that we call knowing, all the methods of the disciplines, their collections of concepts, truths, assumptions, hypotheses, express relations between subject and object, knower and known, person and world. The relations of these terms "subject" and "object" in epistemology, consciousness on the one hand and all that is other to consciousness on the other, are preceded by the subject/object relations within which human consciousness comes to form, the relation of the infant to the person or persons who constitute his world. Becoming a subject means becoming a subject for someone. Once again, "The you is always older than the I."[4]

In *The Reproduction of Mothering,* Chodorow, as we have seen, makes the argument that because women are the primary nurturers of both male and female infants, the process of becoming gendered subjects is different for males and females.[5] A mother-raised male, the argument goes, achieves a sense that he is male by repressing his earliest experience when his own sense of being was fused with that of his mother. Being male is, in effect, being not like Mom, and in that denial is the disjunction from infancy, from the mother, and from one's original connection to the world that haunts male subjectivity. The subject/object relations that characterize the epistemologies of Western science mirror this denial of connection to the world. Statistical significance rests on the assumption that there is no relationship between variables and predictably notes difference as its goal, dismissing similarities as anomolous when they appear in the data.[6]

Reinforcing this sense of separation that comes from the radical repression of preoedipal experience is the inferential nature of paternity, an ambiguity that provokes the father to claim connection, to assert it as a defensive reaction to the conviction that he is detached from both his own mother/self and his own child/self, detached from both the past and the future. Masculine epistemologies are compensations for the inferential nature of paternity as they reduce preoedipal subject/object mutuality to postoedipal cause and effect, employing idealistic or materialistic rationales to compensate as well for the repressed identification that the boy has experienced with this primary object, his mother. Chodorow's work has shown us how masculine identification processes stress differentiation from other, the denial of affective relations and categorical, universalistic components of the masculine role, denying relation where female identification processes acknowledge it. So this is the second nature we keep auditioning for, trying to get on teams of technologists who can't remember that they are part of the world they are changing, into groups of professionals who claim that care and ethics can be derived from relations with another that are predicated on privilege and uneven distributions of wealth and power.

We, women who educate, are the ones who lead the children from first to second nature. *Educere*, "to lead out," to take the child by the hand to the bus stop, to the school, to the disciplines, to discipline. When we take them to school we take them to our father's house. Our own children must leave us at the door. Like the female guardian in Plato's *Republic* who can nurse any child providing it is not her own, we may linger with other people's children for a while. As second nature draws them in, it leaves us out. Where else would we take them?

Like the young female writer whom Virginia Woolf is describing in the excerpt from the speech, "Professions for Women," we women who would teach as women find ourselves in a bare room that is not empty. We can clean out the male curriculum, banking education, the process/product paradigm, the myth of objectivity. We can give the old furniture away to Goodwill or domesticate it, turning old school desks into planters and telephone tables. We can silence the clanging lockers, period bells, "now-hear-this" loudspeakers. We can make it a demilitarized zone. But still we are not in an empty space. Nor was the young writer. She is, Woolf tells us, at war with a spirit called the Angel in the House:

> She was intensely sympathetic. She was immensely charming. She was utterly unselfish. She excelled in the difficult arts of family life. She sacrificed herself daily. If there was a chicken, she took the leg; if there was a draught she sat in it—in short she was so constituted that she never had a mind or a wish of her own, but preferred to sympathize always with the minds and wishes of others. Above all—I need not say it—she was pure. Her purity was supposed to be her chief beauty—her blushes, her great grace.[7]

Where does this angel come from? Does she come with the house or with the young woman? What the young woman discovers is that there are no empty houses, only those houses our mothers left us. And the phantoms can't be so easily routed, for they travel within us. The difference that Woolf resolves to understand is not the difference between but the difference within, what Julia Kristeva has called the "demassification of difference."[8] Rejecting the signification of difference that has served as the emblem of the tribe, bonding *us* against *them* and rationalizing at the same time the violence *we* do to *them*, Kristeva insists that we abstain from conceptualizing liberation in terms that define our freedom by discriminating it from the privilege enjoyed and abused by "the other." She calls for

an apparent de-dramatization of the "fight to the death" between rival groups and thus between the sexes. And this not in the name of some reconciliation—feminism has at least had the merit of showing what is irreducible and even deadly in the social contract—but in order that the struggle, the implacable difference, the violence be conceived in the very place where it operates with the maximum intransigence, in other words, in personal and sexual identity itself, so as to make it disintegrate at its very nucleus.[9]

In 1927, four years before Woolf delivered "Professions for Women" to the London/National Society for Women's Service, she wrote *To the Lighthouse*. It was her project to think back through her mother, to find the difference within and then the form without that would bring a glimpse of first nature into the world of adult men and women. Mrs. Ramsay, Mrs. Ramsay, is the presence she provides, alternately received, resisted, and yearned for by Lily Briscoe, an artist who visits the Ramsay home before and after Mrs. Ramsay's death. Lily is not Mrs. Ramsay's daughter, nor am I Virginia's. Virginia thought back through Julia Stephen through Mrs. Ramsay, and I think back through Frances Rotter through Virginia. The task of thinking back through our mothers is not aimed at becoming them. Julia Stephen, Virginia's mother, was an antifeminist conservative, who signed Mrs. Humphrey Ward's antisuffragist petition. Jane Marcus sees Woolf's work as "public acts of expiation, songs of sisterhood, to atone for her mother's inability to accept feminism."[10] But this act of differentiation is not merely reaction formation; the task of thinking back through our

mothers is not aimed at repudiating them. In a recent article in Hester
Eisenstein's and Alice Jardine's wonderful collection, *The Future of
Difference*, Nancy Chodorow reminds us that differentiation does not
require difference: "In fact, assimilating difference to differentiation is
defensive and reactive, a reaction to not feeling separate enough."[11]
"To be or not to be" is not the question. Hear Lily Briscoe search for the
question as she studies her relation to Mrs. Ramsay:

> she was unquestionably the loveliest of people (bowed over her book); the
> best perhaps; but also, different too from the perfect shape which one saw
> there. But why different, and how different? What was the spirit in her, the
> essential thing, by which, had you found a crumpled glove in the corner of
> a sofa, you would have known it, from its twisted finger hers indisputa-
> bly? She was like a bird for speed, an arrow for directness. She was wilful;
> she was commanding. . . . She opened bedroom windows. She shut doors.
> (So she tried to start the tune of Mrs. Ramsay in her head.)[12]

Lily resists the tune. She resists Mrs. Ramsay's conviction that they
all must marry, that an unmarried woman had missed the best of life.

> Yet, as the night wore on, and white lights parted the curtains, and even
> now and then some bird chirped in the garden, gathering a desperate
> courage she would urge her own exemption from the universal law; plead
> for it; she liked to be alone; she liked to be herself; she was not made for
> that; and so have to meet a serious stare from eyes of unparalleled depth,
> and confront Mrs. Ramsay's simple certainty (and she was childlike now)
> that her dear Lily, her little Brisk, was a fool. Then, she remembered, she
> had laid her head on Mrs. Ramsay's lap and laughed and laughed and
> laughed, laughed almost hysterically at the thought of Mrs. Ramsay
> presiding with immutable calm over destinies which she completely failed
> to understand. There she sat, simple, serious. She had recovered her sense
> of her now—this was the glove's twisted finger. But into what sanctuary
> had one penetrated? . . .
> Was it wisdom? Was it knowledge? Was it, once more, the deceptiveness
> of beauty, so that all one's perceptions, half way to truth, were tangled in a
> golden mesh? or did she lock up within her some secret which certainly
> Lily Briscoe believed people must have for the world to go on at all? Every
> one could not be as helter skelter, hand to mouth as she was. But if they
> knew, could they tell one what they knew? Sitting on the floor with her
> arms round Mrs. Ramsay's knees, close as she could get, smiling to think
> that Mrs. Ramsay would never know the reason of that pressure, she
> imagined how in the chambers of the mind and heart of the woman who
> was, physically, touching her, were stood, like the treasures in the tombs

of kings, tablets bearing sacred inscriptions, which if one could spell them out, would teach one everything, but they would never be offered openly, never made public. What art was there, known to love or cunning, by which one pressed through into those secret chambers? What device for becoming, like waters poured into one jar, inextricably the same, one with the object one adored? Could the body achieve, or the mind, subtly mingling in the intricate passages of the brain? or the heart? Could loving, as people called it, make her and Mrs. Ramsay one? for it was not knowledge but unity that she desired, not inscriptions on tablets, nothing that could be written in any language known to men, but intimacy itself, which is knowledge, she had thought, leaning her head on Mrs. Ramsay's knee.[13]

The question changes. What has started out as a question about Mrs. Ramsay's essence, her quality, her property, turns into a question about her relation to Lily. Lily wants to be her and not to be her. Lily wants to be known to her and knows that Mrs. Ramsay can never truly see her. And Lily laughs.

It is in her laughter that we hear the echo of what Stern has called the infant's "emergent self."[14] It is in her laughter that we find the space between the mother and child where Kristeva locates the beginnings of discontinuity and ego boundaries. The infant's laughter erupts, she reminds us, when there is disruption:

when motor tension is linked to vision (a caricature is a visualization of bodily distortion, of an extreme, exaggerated movement, or of an un-mastered movement); when a child's body is too rapidly set in motion by the adult (return to motility denying its fixation, space and place); when a sudden stop follows a movement (someone stumbles and falls). . . . The *chora* is indeed a strange "space": the rapidity and violence of the facilita-tions are localized at a point that absorbs them, and they return like a boomerang to the invoking body, without, however, signifying it as sepa-rate; they stop there, impart the jolt-laughter.[15]

Drawn back from the postoedipal violation of the superego in Kris-teva's theory, laughter has a homecoming in preoedipal, prelinguistic communication as sound and breath are mustered to absorb and pro-ject the shock and relief of our earliest intimations of separateness. "We have," Kristeva suggests, "either a riant, porous boundary, or a block-ing barrier of earnest sullenness—the child gets one or the other from its mother."[16] It is in Lily's laughter that she resists and celebrates the temptation to sink into what Jessica Benjamin calls that "deepest level of feeling [where] there is not that sharp and clear sense, that vibrant aliveness of knowing that I am I and you are you."17

Chodorow tells us that we must see gender as processual, reflexive, and constructed. And that is what the passage that we have just read portrays, I believe. That is why it was almost impossible to abstract or reduce it. It is a dance to the tune of Mrs. Ramsay in which Lily resists and complies, blends and distinguishes, sinks and lifts, and laughs. The question of difference becomes the question of differentiation, and that becomes a question of sameness as well as separation. The reflection on this process comes to form in Lily's painting, "the triangular purple shape, 'just there.'" The power of *her*, who closes the windows and shuts the doors, is echoed in the power of the mother. Although Mrs. Ramsay mediates between what Maria Di Battista calls the "earthly child" and the "heavenly father," her mediation for all its comfort preserves the transitions to patriarchal culture.18 And it is the consolation of this mediation, its stability and comfort, that Lily both desires and repudiates. Mrs. Ramsay is a bulwark against the terror; to sink into her protection is to collapse into what Di Battista calls the

> conservatism of the eternal feminine [that] continually works to perpetuate, never to transcend or revise the eternal round of existence. In opposing the life she deems hostile and threatening to the human order, Mrs. Ramsay merely succeeds in becoming an instrument of its recreation. The presumption of Mrs. Ramsay's thoughts is in arrogating a power that properly resides in untransformed Nature—reproduction, symbolized in her mania for marriage and child-bearing—and having done so, imagining fairy tale existences for those she has willed into life.19

Lily turns her particular relation, the desire for and repudiation of Mrs. Ramsay's world, into a form that others can see. She studies the relation and paints her understanding of it. This is the art that women who teach must bring to our work, studying the relations in which we came to form, reflecting on those relations and creating new forms in the curriculum that express our appreciation, our critique and transformation of the processes that constituted our subjectivity (our identities) and objectivity (the world we share). Lily constructs the sense of herself in a process of differentiation that recognizes what it negates. She transforms the moment of bliss without repressing it or making it ugly so she won't miss it. This is the process of thinking back through our mothers. It is an archaeology not of them but of our relation to them. It is the question of how to be separate and still recognize them in us, us in them, and us in each other. For the boys are not the only ones who flee to second nature. More ambivalent than they, perhaps, we too sign up, indulging now and then in surreptitious sentimentalities behind the classroom door.

What would thinking back through our mothers mean to us, we the women who educate? It invites us to recollect, to re-collect the process of our own formation. Rarely does one hear a woman proclaim, "I made myself"; the defensive arrogance of the self-made man is not available to women, who cannot forget what men cannot remember. Because our separation from our mothers is rarely as defined as that of our brothers, we are more modest, a bit unsure. Beginnings and endings are not quite so clear to us, where one leaves off and another begins, Mrs. Ramsay, Mrs. Ramsay. But the ambivalence, that middle ground, should be the territory of our explorations. We have access, paths of feeling, of memory, into the gardens where our first worlds grew. That is the soil we need to turn over, as we study the relations within which subject and object, parent and child, ego and ego, person and world, come to form. Guarding our knowledge of differentiation in the wilderness of private reservation, we subordinate these questions to the malestream epistemologies that search for connections everywhere but in our own lived experience. They make connection into a mystery and we creep around after them with binoculars and scalpels, observing gorillas and left hemispheres, playing Doctor Watson to their Sherlock Holmes, pretending to discover what we can only recover.

But recovery is not a simple task. Lily's laughter comes only after she sits with her arms around Mrs. Ramsay's knees, as close as she can get. It is not just the task of trading stories. It is the task of recognizing unity in what we see as separate, the task of claiming exemption, as well, from the universal law and claiming separateness despite the wish for unity. Truth, Joan Cocks has argued, comes from thought, not from observation.[20] Thought can never coincide with immediate experience, and even the candid self-interpretation of the actors themselves is ideological, too often shaped around rules and conventions for thought that are not of their making or in their interest. Cocks reminds us that "women who restrict their insights to the immediacy of personally felt life are fated to be unwitting collaborators with the dominant order, in imposing debilitating rules of vision and narrow possibilities of action on themselves."[21] But here is the dilemma: If we relinquish our narcissism, accuse ourselves of false consciousness, and try to find the histories of differentiation that neither we nor our mothers ever told, will we not be replicating the process of radical separation in adult, theoretical practice that our male siblings have committed without the benefits of reflexivity? Benjamin is helpful here. She describes recognition and negation as the two basic relationships we can have with an other.[22] Every action that a subject performs on an object negates it, transforms it. Total negation, total transformation, is total control, for it violates the identity of the object as existing independently from the subject, whose way of knowing the object has literally swallowed it.

Mrs. Ramsay, Mrs. Ramsay. This is the triumph of that book; revealed in her arrogance, her conservatism, she is still Mrs. Ramsay, Mrs. Ramsay, the twisted finger of the glove. Woolf recognizes what she transforms; she continues to love what she cannot, will not be. For the object of our thought, our study, our theory, must retain its identity if we are to both recognize it and transform it, and if we negate it we negate ourselves, for we came to form in her smile. Securing recognition from her may be a more difficult matter. Though Mrs. Ramsay never sees Lily, Frances Rotter has caught a glimpse or two of me.

Too often we give up. We stop trying to tell our mothers who we are, and sometimes they leave us before we find out. That is what happened to Virginia, but as Ellen Hawkes has shown us, she and Ethyl Smith, and Vanessa Bell and Violet Dickenson, and Vita Sackville-West constructed a community of women who could recognize each other.[23]

We have been different too long. Separated from her, separated from each other, women in education have withheld recognition from our mothers and from each other. And in that isolation not only have we relinquished the middle ground, that relational ambivalent place of our own histories, we have relinquished schooling as a middle ground as well. For it need not be the anteroom for second nature; it can be the place where the defensive oppositions of first and second nature are mediated and transformed by women who think back through our mothers.

Notes

1 CONCEPTION, CONTRADICTION, AND CURRICULUM

1. Julia Kristeva, *About Chinese Women*, trans. Anita Burrows (London: Marion Boyars, 1977), p. 15.
2. Maurice Merleau-Ponty, *Phenomenology of Perception*, trans. Colin Wilson (New York: Humanities Press, 1962).
3. In Christine Froula's study of Christian doctrine and its interpretation in Milton's *Paradise Lost*, Eve's transgression is the claim of direct experience, rather than the mediated knowledge that imputes invisibility to authority. See "When Eve Reads Milton: Undoing the Canonical Economy," in *Canons*, ed. Robert von Hallberg (Chicago: University of Chicago Press, 1984).
4. Antonio Gramsci, *Selections from the Prison Notebooks*, trans. and ed. Quinton Hoare and Geoffrey N. Smith (New York: International Publishers, 1971).
5. Edmund Husserl, *Ideas: General Introduction to Pure Phenomenology*, trans. W. R. Boyce Gibson (New York: Collier Books, 1962).
6. Stephen Strasser, *The Idea of a Dialogic Phenomenology* (Pittsburgh: Duquesne University Press, 1969).
7. Ibid., pp. 61–63.
8. Nancy Chodorow, *The Reproduction of Mothering: Psychoanalysis and the Sociology of Gender* (Berkeley: University of California Press, 1978).
9. Ibid., p. 47.
10. In *The Politics of Reproduction* (Boston: Routledge and Kegan Paul, 1981), Mary O'Brien provides a philosophy of birth and brings each of these "moments" to its meaning in the generation of the human species and the human spirit: menstruation, ovulation, copulation, alienation, conception, gestation, labor, birth, appropriation, nurture (p. 47).
11. Shulamith Firestone's startling prophesy that women will seize control of our own bodies and of reproduction, in *Dialectic of Sex* (New York: Bantam Books, 1972), has, despite its specter of a totalitarian technology, challenged us to name the experience, meaning, and politics of heterosexual reproduction as we know it. See Jean Bethke Elshtain's critique of Firestone in *Public Man, Private Woman: Women in Social and Political Thought* (Princeton, N.J.: Princeton University Press, 1981).

12. Vangie Bergum, *Woman to Mother: A Transformation* (South Hadley, Mass: Bergin and Garvey, forthcoming).

13. Jürgen Habermas, *Knowledge and Human Interests*, trans. Jeremy J. Shapiro (Boston: Beacon Press, 1971), pp. 262–63.

14. Bernard Wishy, *The Child and the Republic* (Philadelphia: University of Pennsylvania Press, 1968).

15. Chodorow, *Reproduction of Mothering*, pp. 166, 167.

16. Ibid., p. 174.

17. Daniel Stern, *The Interpersonal World of the Infant* (New York: Basic Books 1985).

18. Constructivism is the epistemological theory described by Jean Piaget. See *The Grasp of Consciousness*, trans. Susan Wedgwood (Cambridge, Mass.: Harvard University Press, 1976).

19. Mary Field Belenky, Blythe McVicker Clinchy, Nancy Rule Goldberger, and Jill Mattuck Tarule, *Women's Ways of Knowing: The Development of Self, Voice, and Mind* (New York: Basic Books, 1986).

20. See Herbert Marcuse, *Eros and Civilization* (Boston: Beacon Press, 1955); and Christopher Lasch, *The Culture of Narcissism* (New York: W. W. Norton, 1979).

21. Kristeva, *About Chinese Women.*

22. This concept of negation is drawn from Jean-Paul Sartre's association of negativity with the *pour-soi,* the human responsibility to reject determination and shape its own essence, developed in *Being and Nothingness*, trans. Hazel E. Barnes (New York: Washington Square Press, 1966).

23. Extensive development of this distinction can be found in Julia Kristeva, *Revolution in Poetic Language*, trans. Margaret Waller (New York: Columbia University Press, 1984).

24. Philippe Aries, *Centuries of Childhood*, trans. Robert Baldick (New York: Random House [Vintage Books], 1965); Wishy, *Child and Republic.*

25. Although the contradictions as stated here appear to contain a simple opposition of thesis and antithesis, that simple polarity may mask other intervening terms. The polarization of racism and mandated integration masks the issue of economic class. "Back-to-basics" provides another example of an apparent opposition that masks a third term. The slogan responds to the alienating technology of our culture, to the specialized curricula of the fifties and the expressive curricula of the sixties, and to the perceived deficiencies of the high school graduates of the seventies. The compensatory thrust of "back-to-basics" addresses itself to the failure of the school curriculum to provide adequate instruction in reading, writing, and mathematics and focuses on the profound inadequacies of these high school graduates. The revelation of these inadequacies is used to justify the failure of the economy to provide meaningful work for these graduates while it distracts our attention from the material conditions that reduce their learning, schooling, and literacy to empty gestures.

26. Walter Doyle presents the process/product paradigm (which I am associating with the curricula associated with masculine epistemology) in contrast

to the mediating process and classroom ecology paradigms in teacher-effectiveness research. The mediating process paradigm acknowledges the interdependency of teacher and student behaviors. It mirrors the emphasis on context and process noted in the mother/child preoedipal relation and the subject/object reciprocity noted in constructivism. The classroom ecology paradigm is field-centered like object relations theory itself, as it attempts to ascertain those skills that continuous experience with classroom demands engenders in the students. See "Paradigms for Research on Teacher Effectiveness," in *Review of Research in Education*, ed. Lee Shulman (Itasca, Ill.: F. E. Peacock, 1978).

27. It is necessary to distinguish these studies and their findings from each other as they represent various interests, ask different questions, and come up with different answers. *The Paideia Proposal*, for example, calls for rigor in the traditional disciplines and active learning directed toward the development of civic virtues. *A Nation at Risk* associates poor schooling with the nation's economic and military vulnerability in international competition. Thirty-three studies are summarized in Marilyn Clayton Felt, *Improving Our Schools* (Newton, Mass.: Educational Development Center, 1985). In *Culture Wars* (Boston: Routledge and Kegan Paul, 1986), Ira Shor argues that economic malaise has inspired these critiques of education as well as the narrow projects of control that they offer as solutions.

28. Chodorow, *Reproduction of Mothering*, p. 179.

29. Chodorow cites Rosaldo's observation that men's work brings them into a social group of peers, dominated by a single generation that cuts across lines of kinship and is defined by universal categories where women's work is kin-related and cross-generational, tied to the nurturance of both her children and, later on, her parents. Ibid., p. 181.

30. Rachel Sharp and Anthony Green, *Education and Social Control* (London: Routledge and Kegan Paul, 1975), pp. 68–113.

31. Dorothy Dinnerstein, *The Mermaid and the Minotaur: Sexual Arrangements and Human Malaise* (New York: Harper and Row, 1976).

32. Ibid., p. 191.

33. Kim Chernin, *The Hungry Self: Women, Eating, and Identity* (New York: Times Books, 1985).

34. Chodorow, *Reproduction of Mothering*, pp. 201–2.

35. Kristeva, *About Chinese Women*, p. 37.

36. Ibid., p. 115.

2   PEDAGOGY FOR PATRIARCHY

1. Victor Turner, "Mukanda: The Rite of Circumcision," in *A Forest of Symbols* (Ithaca, N.Y.: Cornell University Press, 1967), p. 190.

2. All references to this Ndembu ritual, *Mukanda*, are drawn from Turner's study.

3. Turner, "Mukanda," p. 193.

4. Ibid., p. 266.

5. Catherine MacKinnon, "Feminism, Marxism, Method, and the State," in *Feminist Theory: A Critique of Ideology*, ed. Nannerl O. Keohane, Michelle Z. Rosaldo, and Barbara C. Gelpi (Chicago: University of Chicago Press, 1981), p. 6.

6. Curriculum theorists contributing to this discourse are Peter Taubman, "Gender and Curriculum: Discourse and the Politics of Sexuality," *Journal of Curriculum Theorizing* 4, no. 1 (Winter 1982): 12–87; Barbara Mitrano, "Feminist Theology and Curriculum Theory," *Journal of Curriculum Studies* 11, no. 3 (July–September 1979): 211–20; Janet Miller, "Feminist Pedagogy: The Sound of Silence Breaking," *Journal of Curriculum Theorizing* 4, no. 1 (Winter 1982): 5–11; James Macdonald and Susan Cohlbert Macdonald, "Gender Values and Curriculum," *Journal of Curriculum Theorizing* 3, no. 1 (Winter 1981): 299–304; William Pinar, "Curriculum as Gender Text: Notes on Reproduction, Resistance, and Male–Male Relations," *Journal of Curriculum Theorizing* 5, no. 1 (Winter 1983): 26–52; Jo Anne Pagano, "The Claim of Philia," in *Curriculum Theory Discourses*, ed. William Pinar (Scottsdale, Ariz.: Gorsuch Skarisbrick, forthcoming); Mary Kay Tetreault and Patricia Schmuck, "Equity, Educational Reform, and Gender," *Issues in Education* 3, no. 1 (Summer 1985): 45–65; Patti Lather, "Research as Praxis," *Harvard Educational Review* 56, no. 3 (August 8, 1986): 257–77. Margo Culley and Catherine Portuges, eds., *Gendered Subjects: The Dynamics of Feminist Teaching* (Boston: Routledge and Kegan Paul, 1985), addresses teaching as a "complex and emotional engagement" (p. 4). A more discipline-focused approach may be found in Elizabeth A. Flynn and Patrocinio P. Schweickart, eds., *Gender and Reading* (Baltimore: Johns Hopkins University Press, 1986). See also the special issue of *Teacher Education Quarterly*, "Women and Teacher Education," ed. Grace Grant, 14, no. 2.

7. "Correspondence" theories were conspicuous in the seventies. See Samuel Bowles and Herbert Gintis, *Schooling in Capitalist America* (New York: Basic Books, 1976); Joel Spring, *The Sorting Machine* (New York: David McKay, 1976); Martin Carnoy, ed., *Schooling in a Corporate Society* (New York: David McKay, 1972). Some of the essays in Michael Apple's collection, *Cultural and Economic Reproduction in Education* (London: Routledge and Kegan Paul, 1982), acknowledge the determinism of the correspondence theories and call for less reductive work that grants the complexity of schools and the agency of students and teachers.

8. Kathryn K. Sklar, *Catharine Beecher* (New Haven: Yale University Press, 1973), p. 180.

9. This portrait of the period of industrialization is drawn from W. Elliot Brownlee, *Dynamics of Ascent: A History of American Economy* (New York: Alfred A. Knopf, 1979).

10. Redding S. Sugg, Jr., *Motherteacher: The Feminization of American Education* (Charlottesville: University Press of Virginia, 1978), p. 15.

11. David Nassaw, *Schooled to Order* (New York: Oxford University Press, 1979), pp. 49–50.

12. Ann Douglas, *The Feminization of American Culture* (New York: Avon Books, 1977).
13. Robert V. Bullough, Jr., "Teachers and Teaching in the Nineteenth Century: St. George, Utah," *Journal of Curriculum Theorizing* 4, no. 2 (Summer 1982): 199–206.
14. Ibid., pp. 201–2.
15. Ibid., p. 202.
16. Ibid., p. 203.
17. Arthur O. Norton, ed., *The Journals of Cyrus Peirce and Mary Swift* (Cambridge, Mass.: Harvard University Press, 1926).
18. Thomas Morain, "The Departure of Males from the Teaching Profession in Nineteenth Century Iowa," *Civil War History* 26, no. 2 (1980): 161–70.
19. Richard M. Bernard and Maris A. Vinovskis, "The Female Teacher in Antebellum Massachusetts," *Journal of Social History* 10, no. 3 (1977): 332–45.
20. Catharine Beecher to Horace Mann, originally published in the *Common School Journal* vol. 5 (1843). Cited in Sklar, *Catharine Beecher*, pp. 312–13.
21. Sheila Rothman, *Woman's Proper Place* (New York: Basic Books, 1978), p. 59.
22. Morain, "Departure of Males from Teaching," p. 165.
23. Sklar, *Catharine Beecher*, p. 182.
24. See Walter Feinberg, *Reason and Rhetoric* (New York: John Wiley, 1975), and Nassaw, *Schooled to Order*.
25. Nassaw, *Schooled to Order*, p. 33.
26. Ibid., p. 77.
27. Sklar, *Catharine Beecher*, p. 11.
28. Ibid., p. xii.
29. Douglas, *Femininization of American Culture*, pp. 11–12.
30. Elizabeth Peabody's foreword to Friedrich Froebel, *Mother-Play and Nursery Songs*, trans. F. E. Dwight and J. Jarvis (Boston: Lothrop, Lee, and Shephard, 1878), p. 7.
31. Cited in Mary J. Moffat and Charlotte Painter, eds., *Revelations* (New York: Random House, 1975), p. 32.
32. Cited in Rothman, *Woman's Proper Place*, p. 103.
33. In "Come Back to the Raft Agin, Huck Honey!" Leslie Fiedler locates the erotic icon of the myth of American innocence, "its implacable nostalgia for the infantile," in the homoerotic romances of Huck and Jim, Ishmael and Queequeg, carried by the river and the sea away from the racist, sexist culture of nineteenth-century America; *An End to Innocence* (Boston: Beacon Press, 1955), p. 144. See also Madeleine Grumet, "The Lie of the Child Redeemer," *Journal of Education* 168, no. 3 (1986): 87–89.
34. Douglas, *Feminization of American Culture*, p. 69.
35. David Tyack, *The One Best System* (Cambridge, Mass.: Harvard University Press, 1974), p. 54.
36. Ibid., p. 60.

37. Rothman, *Woman's Proper Place*, p. 57.
38. John Bennet, *Strictures on Female Education* (1795; New York: Source Book Press, 1971), pp. 99–100.
39. Douglas, *Feminization of American Culture*, p. 11.
40. See Susan S. Klein, ed., *Handbook for Achieving Sex Equity through Education* (Baltimore: Johns Hopkins University Press, 1985), for studies of sex equity in elementary and secondary education, the disciplines, and teacher education.
41. Jean Elshtain, "Against Androgeny," *Telos* 14, no. 1 (Spring 1981): 5–21.
42. Ibid., p. 16.
43. Merleau-Ponty, *Phenomenology of Perception*.
44. Raymond Williams, *Marxism and Literature* (New York: Oxford University Press, 1977), p. 122.
45. Bernard and Vinovskis, "Female School Teacher."
46. D. H. Lawrence, *The Rainbow* (New York: Modern Library, 1915).
47. Ibid., p. 334.
48. Ibid., p. 347.
49. Ibid., p. 362.
50. Ibid., p. 369.
51. Ibid., pp. 382–83.
52. Norton, *Journals of Peirce and Swift*, p. xxvii.
53. Ibid., p. iv.
54. Ibid., p. 54.
55. Ibid., p. 91.
56. W. W. Charters and Douglas Waples, *The Commonwealth Teacher-Training Study* (Chicago: University of Chicago Press, 1928), pp. 467–68.
57. Sugg, *Motherteacher*, p. 74.
58. Norton, *Journals of Peirce and Swift*, pp. 181–82.
59. Dan C. Lortie, *Schoolteacher* (Chicago: University of Chicago Press, 1975).
60. Virginia Woolf, *Three Guineas* (New York: Harcourt Brace, 1966), pp. 62–63.
61. I am grateful to Stanley Engerman for suggesting studies pertinent to this essay.

3   FEMINISM AND THE PHENOMENOLOGY
    OF THE FAMILIAR

1. Colin Greer, *The Great School Legend: A Revisionist Interpretation of American Public Education* (New York: Penguin Books, 1972), p. 38.
2. Stephen J. Ball and Ivor F. Goodson, eds., *Teachers' Lives and Careers* (Philadelphia: Falmer Press, 1985), pp. 6–7.
3. These critical essays can be found in William F. Pinar, ed., *Curriculum Theorizing: The Reconceptualists* (Berkeley, Calif.: McCutchan, 1975). See James Macdonald, "Curriculum Theory, Curriculum, and Human Interests"; Dwayne Huebner, "Curricular Language and Classroom Mean-

ings"; Maxine Greene, "Curriculum and Consciousness"; Michael Apple, "The Hidden Curriculum and the Nature of Conflict."

4. William F. Pinar, "The Analysis of Educational Experience," "*Currere*: Toward Reconceptualization," "Search for a Method," in Pinar, *Curriculum Theorizing*.

5. William F. Pinar and Madeleine Grumet, *Toward a Poor Curriculum* (Dubuque, Iowa: Kendell/Hunt, 1976).

6. Richard Rorty, *Philosophy and the Mirror of Nature* (Princeton: N.J.: Princeton University Press, 1982).

7. Compunctions concerning the use of autobiographical texts in educational research are addressed in Madeleine Grumet, "The Politics of Personal Knowledge," *Curriculum Inquiry* 17, no. 3 (1987).

8. Jean-Paul Sartre, *Kean* (London: H. Hamilton, 1954).

9. Erwin Straus, "The Upright Posture," in *Essays in Phenomenology*, ed. Maurice Natanson (The Hague: Martinus Nijhoff, 1966).

10. My reading of Oedipus's response to the Sphinx is influenced by Susan Griffin's gender analysis of the myth in *Pornography and Silence* (New York: Harper and Row, 1981).

11. O'Brien, *Politics of Reproduction*.

12. Ibid., pp. 42–43.

13. Phenomenological studies of childhood and family relations appear regularly in the journal *Phenomenology and Pedagogy*, edited by Max Van Manen and published by the University of Alberta. See also Nel Noddings, *Caring* (Berkeley: University of California Press, 1984).

14. Meredith A. Skura, *The Literary Use of the Psychoanalytic Process* (New Haven: Yale University Press, 1981), p. 26.

15. Emily Dickinson, "Letter to Maria Whitney," in *Mother to Daughter, Daughter to Mother*, ed. Tillie Olsen (Old Westbury, N.Y.: Feminist Press, 1984), p. 231.

16. I am grateful to Jane McCabe, first for writing these vivid stories and then for permitting me to carry their wonderful images and cadences to curriculum theory in this interpretation.

17. Joan Didion, "On Keeping a Notebook," in *Slouching Toward Bethlehem* (New York: Dell Books, 1961).

18. In *Autobiographical Consciousness* (Chicago: Quadrangle Books, 1972), William Earle asks, "Is not one's fidelity to objects really a fidelity to others and oneself about objects?" (p. 28). The relation of this position to literary interpretation and pedagogy is developed brilliantly by David Bleich in *Subjective Criticism* (Baltimore: Johns Hopkins University Press, 1978).

19. Earle, *Autobiographical Consciousness*, p. 58.

20. Autobiographical consciousness is that form of human existence, Earle claims, "where the *accidental is essential*." Ibid., p. 45.

21. Charles Altieri, "Ecce Homo: Narcissism, Power, Pathos, and the Status of Autobiographical Representation," *Boundary II* 9, no. 3 and 4 (Spring 1981): 394.

22. Robert Frost, "Birches," in *The Oxford Book of American Verse*, ed. F. O. Matthiessen (New York: Oxford University Press, 1950).

4   WHERE THE LINE IS DRAWN

1. Herbert Marcuse, *The Aesthetic Dimension: Toward a Critique of Marxist Aesthetics* (Boston: Beacon Press, 1977), pp. 9, 10.

2. I have explored the theatrical character of schooling in "In Search of Theatre: Ritual, Confrontation, and the Suspense of Form," *Journal of Education* 162, no. 1 (Winter 1980): 93–116. See Elliot Eisner, *The Educational Imagination* (New York: Macmillan, 1979).

3. Johan Huizinga, *Homo Ludens* (Boston: Beacon Press, 1955); Susanne Langer, *Feeling and Form* (New York: Charles Scribner's Sons, 1953); F. David Martin, *Art and the Religious Experience: The Language of the Sacred* (Lewisburg, Pa.: Bucknell University Press, 1972); Marcuse, *Aesthetic Dimension*.

4. See the work of Maxine Greene, *Landscapes for Learning* (New York: Teachers College Press, 1978); Elliot Eisner, ed., *The Arts, Human Development, and Education* (Berkeley, Calif.: McCutchan, 1976); Robert E. Stake, ed., *Evaluating the Arts in Education* (Columbus, Ohio: Charles E. Merrill, 1975); and Landon Beyer, "Aesthetic Theory and the Ideology of Educational Institutions," *Curriculum Inquiry* 9 (Spring 1979): 13–26.

5. Neil Harris, *The Artist in American Society: The Formative Years, 1790–1860* (Chicago: University of Chicago Press, 1982).

6. Ibid., p. 36.

7. Benjamin Franklin, *The Autobiography of Benjamin Franklin* (New York: Collier Books, 1962), p. 91.

8. Harris, *Artist in American Society*, p. 195.

9. Ibid., p. 23.

10. Ibid., pp. 46–47.

11. Ibid., pp. 173–74.

12. Ibid., p. 159.

13. A more detailed account of the feminization of teaching is provided in Chapter 2.

14. Cited in Herbert Read, *The Philosophy of Modern Art* (New York: New American Library [Meridian Books], 1955), p. 17.

15. This phrase describing phenomenological method is drawn from Maurice Roche, *Phenomenology, Language, and the Social Sciences* (London: Routledge and Kegan Paul, 1973).

16. Chodorow, *Reproduction of Mothering*, and Dinnerstein, *Mermaid and Minotaur*.

17. Chernin, *The Hungry Self: Women, Eating, and Identity*.

18. Judy Chicago, *Through the Flower: My Struggle as a Woman Artist* (New York: Doubleday, 1977), p. 74.

19. Maurice Merleau-Ponty, "Indirect Voices and the Language of Silence," in *Signs*, trans. Richard C. McCleary (Evanston, Ill.: Northwestern University Press, 1964), p. 46.

20. Jerzy Grotowski, *Toward a Poor Theatre* (New York: Simon and Schuster, 1968).

21. See Margaret Hunsberger, "Phenomenology of Reading: When Child and

Curriculum Meet in Reading Class," *Reading—Canada—Lecture* 3, no. 2 (1985): 101–8, for an insightful discussion of the place of silence in pedagogical discourse.

22. Tillie Olsen's text, *Silences* (New York: Dell, 1978), describes the conditions that encourage creativity and honors those silenced by social strictures, child care, housework, and wage labor.

23. John Dewey, *Art as Experience* (New York: Capricorn Books, 1934), p. 46.

24. Chicago, *Through the Flower*, p. 100.

25. The scripted character of teacher discourse is revealed in Arthur Woodward's study, "Taking Teaching Out of Teaching and Reading Out of Learning to Read: A Historical Study of Reading Textbook Teachers' Guides, 1920–1980," *Book Research Quarterly*, (Spring 1986): 53–73. Madeline Hunter's scripts for teaching, *Mastery Teaching* (El Segundo, Calif.: TIP Publications, 1982), are pervading in-service education as well as teacher evaluation programs.

26. Michael Apple, "Work, Gender, and Teaching," *Teachers College Record* 84, no. 3 (Spring 1983): 611–28. Although the concepts of "deskilling" and "reskilling" may serve to describe teachers' subordination to a highly rationalized and bureaucratic curriculum, they also bring language drawn from the task analysis of the factory to the classroom, draping the work and experience of women in the labor experience of men. In either case the narrow competencies implied by the terms denigrate the subjects they describe.

27. Ibid., p. 621.

28. Virginia Woolf, *Three Guineas*, cited in Chicago, *Through the Flower*, p. 197.

29. Didion, "On Keeping a Notebook," p. 136.

30. Nancy Hale, *The Life in the Studio* (New York: Avon Books, 1957), p. 80.

31. Cited in Olsen, *Silences*, p. 160.

32. Chicago, *Through the Flower*, p. 204.

33. Virginia Woolf, *A Writer's Diary* (New York: Harcourt Brace Jovanovich, 1953), pp. 30–31.

34. Merleau-Ponty, "Indirect Voices," p. 64.

35. Margaret Anderson is a painter now living in La Crosse, Wisconsin. We shared years when she, the painter, and I, the teacher, were busy having, nursing, changing, and rocking our babies. She painted my portrait in a few late afternoons while her daughters napped just a week or so before my first child was born. The portrait, never quite finished, understandably, speaks to me still of women's capacity to support and celebrate the creativity of other women. All that I have studied since merely confirms what her visions of our experience taught me then. This essay honors her work.

5   MY FACE IN THINE EYE, THINE IN MINE APPEARES

1. John Donne, "The Good Morrow," in *Seventeenth Century Verse and Prose: Volume I, 1600–1660*, ed. Helen C. White, Ruth C. Wallerstein, and Ricardo Quintana (New York: Macmillan, 1951), p. 80.

2. Ibid., lines 12–14.

3. Maurice Merleau-Ponty, "The Child's Relations with Others," in *The Primacy of Perception*, ed. James Edie, trans. William Cobb (Evanston, Ill.: Northwestern University Press, 1964), pp. 116–17.

4. Strasser, *Dialogic Phenomenology*.

5. Gerald W. Grumet, "Eye Contact: The Core of Interpersonal Relatedness," *Psychiatry* 46 (May 1983): 172–80.

6. Douglas, *Feminization of American Culture*.

7. Jean-Paul Sartre, "The Look," in *Being and Nothingness*, pp. 340–400.

8. Grotowski, *Toward a Poor Theatre*, p. 194.

9. Merleau-Ponty, "Child's Relations with Others," p. 119.

10. Ibid.

11. Wilhelm Reich, *Character-Analysis*, trans. Theodore P. Wolfe (New York: Noonday Press, 1961).

12. R. L. Fantz, reported in John Bowlby, *Attachment* (New York: Basic Books, 1969), p. 270.

13. Daniel N. Stern, cited in Joseph D. Lichtenberg, *Psychoanalysis and Infant Research* (Hillsdale, N.J.: Lawrence Erlbaum, 1983), p. 7.

14. P. H. Wolff, cited in Bowlby, *Attachment*, p. 274.

15. Lichtenberg cites studies of Klaus and Hales that indicate that extended and immediate contact with their newborn infants was shown to increase mothers' caretaking and attachment responses, even the greater tendency to hold infants *en face* during feedings. *Psychoanalysis and Infant Research*, pp. 18–19. Following Mary O'Brien's argument in *Politics of Reproduction* that the technology of reproduction alters male and female relations to each other, to the child, and to culture, one wonders what the ontological consequences of the images provided by ultrasound technology of infants in utero would be if that process became part of the universal birth experience.

16. See Chapter 1.

17. Henri Wallon, cited in Merleau-Ponty, "Child's Relations with Others," pp. 141–51.

18. Stern, *Interpersonal World of the Infant*, p. 17.

19. Jacques Lacan, *The Language of the Self*, trans. Anthony Wilden (New York: Dell, 1968).

20. Elizabeth Wright, *Psychoanalytic Criticism* (New York: Methuen, 1984), p. 107.

21. Ibid., pp. 108–9.

22. Stern, *Interpersonal World of the Infant*, p. 10.

23. Ibid., p. 21.

24. Wright, *Psychoanalytic Criticism*, p. 99.

25. Heinz Kohut, *The Analysis of the Self* (New York: International Universities Press, 1971).

26. Carl Frankenstein, *The Roots of the Ego* (Baltimore: Williams and Wilkins, 1966).

27. I can recall a few times when, meeting the parent of a troubled child whom I

taught, I was surprised at her way of describing the child when a cool objectivity would take the place of blind and irrational support. I would consider the possibility that this posture was being assumed to match the professional stance that I, as the teacher, would be expected to take, but always I was left with the suspicion that the detachment that permitted this mother to describe her child as a "liar" or a "spoiled brat" was more a cause than a consequence of the problems the child faced.

28. In *Phenomenology of Perception*, Merleau-Ponty talks at length about the significance of pointing and grasping as actions that reveal the distinction of the objective from the phenomenal body. The phenomenal body is known to us through what it can do: a repertoire of behavior profoundly influenced by others. See the chapter, "The Spatiality of One's Own Body and Motility." David Bleich's term "cognitive stereoscopy" names the process where, within the relation and perceptions of two persons, objects of knowledge come to form, just as binocular vision achieves the single image. *Subjective Criticism*, p. 50.

29. Martin Buber, *Between Man and Man* (New York: Macmillan, 1965).

30. Ibid., p. 89.

31. Ibid., p. 100.

32. D. W. Winnicott, *Playing and Reality* (New York: Basic Books, 1971).

33. Richard Kuhns cited in Wright, *Psychoanalytic Criticism*, p. 97.

34. I am grateful to Nel Noddings for alerting me to the patriarchal implications of some interpretations of object relations theory.

35. John Demos, *A Little Commonwealth* (New York: Oxford University Press, 1970), p. 11.

36. In *The Origin of the Theater* (New York: Hill and Wang, 1955), Benjamin Hunningher dismisses the contention that the origin of our theater lies in the medieval Christian church: "On one hand stands Christianity jubilant in its freedom from the material world and its participation in eternal invisible salvation; on the other, an art concerned only with what the eye can see and the ear can hear in our painful and glorious mortality" (p. 1).

37. Michel Foucault, *Discipline and Punish*, trans. Alan Sheridan (New York: Random House [Vintage Books], 1979), pp. 137–38.

38. In Jacob Kounin's well-known study, *Discipline and Group Management in Classrooms* (New York: Holt, Rinehart and Winston, 1970), the competent teacher is described as one who can see and take note of many interactions and behaviors going on at the same time. Teachers endowed with this roving and recording eye were identified as good managers.

39. Foucault, *Discipline and Punish*, p. 216.

40. Jacques Lacan, "The Eye and the Gaze," in *The Four Fundamental Concepts of Psycho-analysis*, ed. Jacques-Alain Miller, trans. Alan Sheridan (New York: W. W. Norton, 1981), p. 73.

41. John Berger, *Ways of Seeing* (New York: Penquin Books, 1972), p. 47.

42. John Goodlad and M. Frances Klein, *Behind the Classroom Door* (Worthington, Ohio: C. A. Jones, 1970).

43. "Sex Equity in Classroom Organization and Climate," in Klein, *Handbook for Equity through Education*, p. 197.
44. John Holt, *How Children Fail*, rev. ed. (New York: Delta/Seymour Laurence, 1982).
45. Stern, *Interpersonal World of the Infant*, p. 197.
46. D. Jean Clandinin, *Classroom Practice* (Philadelphia: Falmer Press, 1986).
47. Marie M. Clay, *Reading: The Patterning of Complex Behaviour* (London: Heinemann Educational Books, 1977).
48. Susan Stanford Friedman, "Authority in the Feminist Classroom: A Contradiction in Terms?" in Culley and Portuges, *Gendered Subjects*.
49. Buber, "Essay on Education," in *Between Man and Man*, pp. 94–98.
50. My colleague, Professor Joan Stone, reports that although duration is absent from most pedagogical relations it is sustained in many schools where deaf children are taught. "Teachers may work with the same kids every day, all day, for four or five years—touch comes back and the look is different. Interesting—I've seen many gentle women in the past few weeks as I visited these schools. They seem more like mothers than teachers; they don't seem to have sold out to the patriarchal structure, and they fight it with impressive energy. Same is true of some of the men." Personal correspondence. Clearly the more nurturant arrangements provided for those requiring "special education" would benefit those who escape its categories.

6   ON TEACHING THE TEXT

1. Susan Kappeler and Norman Bryson, eds., *Teaching the Text* (Boston: Routledge and Kegan Paul, 1983).
2. Witold Gombrowicz, *The Marriage*, trans. Louis Iribane (New York: Grove Press, 1969).
3. Kappeler and Bryson, *Teaching the Text*, p. viii.
4. Ibid., p. 18.
5. *The Compact Edition of the Oxford English Dictionary* (London: Oxford University Press, 1971), 1:1234.
6. See Raymond Williams, "Monologue in *MacBeth*," and John Barrell, "The Public Figure and the Private Eye: William Collins' 'Ode to Evening,'" in Kappeler and Bryson, *Teaching the Text*.
7. Langer, *Feeling and Form*.
8. Pinar and Grumet, *Toward a Poor Curriculum*, p. 77.
9. Jacqueline Rose, "Introduction II," in *Feminine Sexuality: Jacques Lacan and the "école freudienne,"* ed. Juliet Mitchell and Jacqueline Rose, trans. Jacqueline Rose (New York: W. W. Norton, 1982), p. 51.
10. Kappeler and Bryson, *Teaching the Text*, p. viii.
11. Terry Eagleton, *Literary Theory* (Minneapolis: University of Minnesota Press, 1983). He cites George Gordon, an early professor of English literature at Oxford: "England is sick and . . . English literature must save it. The churches (as I understand) having failed, and social remedies being slow,

English literature has now a triple function: still, I suppose, to delight and instruct us, but also, and above all, to save our souls and heal the state" (p. 23).

12. Ibid., p. 11.
13. I am indebted to Juliet Mitchell and Jacqueline Rose for whatever lucidity this presentation of Lacan's work may enjoy.
14. Lacan, cited in Rose, "Introduction II," p. 38.
15. Ibid.
16. Jane Gallop, "The Monster in the Mirror: The Feminist Critic's Psychoanalysis," manuscript.
17. Ibid.
18. Stephen Heath, "Writing for Silence: Dorothy Richardson and the Novel," in Kappeler and Bryson, *Teaching the Text*, p. 129.
19. Tony Tanner, "*Wuthering Heights* and *Jane Eyre*," in Kappeler and Bryson, *Teaching the Text*, p. 124.
20. Anita Kermode, "Ralph Waldo Emerson: An Introduction," in Kappeler and Bryson, *Teaching the Text*, pp. 86–87.
21. Frank Kermode, "Opinion in *Troilus and Cressida*," in Kappeler and Bryson, *Teaching the Text*, p. 178.
22. Susanne K. Langer, *Problems of Art* (New York: Charles Scribner's Sons, 1957), p. 8.

7 BODYREADING

1. Merleau-Ponty, *Phenomenology of Perception*.
2. Paul Ricoeur, *Interpretation Theory: Discourse and the Surplus of Meaning* (Fort Worth: Texas Christian University Press, 1976).
3. Ibid., p. 20.
4. Susan Suleiman, "Introduction: Varieties of Audience-Oriented Criticism," in *The Reader in the Text*, ed. Susan Suleiman and Inge Crossman (Princeton, N.J.: Princeton University Press, 1980), p. 38.
5. William Butler Yeats, "Sailing to Byzantium," in *Modern American and Modern British Poetry*, ed. Louis Untermeyer (New York: Harcourt Brace, 1955), p. 475.
6. Ferdinand de Saussure, *Course in General Linguistics*, ed. Charles Bally and Albert Sechahaye, trans. Roy Harris (London: Duckworth, 1983).
7. Merleau-Ponty, *Phenomenology of Perception*, p. 187.
8. Madeleine Grumet, "Songs and Situations," in *Qualitative Evaluation*, ed. George Willis (Berkeley, Calif.: McCutchan, 1978).
9. William Shakespeare, "Sonnet 18," in *The Riverside Shakespeare* (Boston: Houghton Mifflin, 1974), p. 1752.
10. *Encyclopaedia Britannica* (Chicago: William Benton, 1962), 19:657.
11. *The Compact Edition of the Oxford English Dictionary*, 2:2427.
12. Meyer Fortes, "Religious Premises and Logical Technique in Divinatory Ritual," *Philosophical Transactions of the Royal Society of London* 251, no. 722 (1966): 409–26.

13. Elizabeth Keim, Hobart and William Smith Colleges, manuscript. Frank Smith's theories of reading are supported by Keim's portrayal of reading competence as a gestalt that arises from a complex communication situation. See Smith, *Understanding Reading* (New York: Holt, Rinehart and Winston, 1971), and *Psycholinguistics and Reading* (New York: Holt, Rinehart and Winston, 1973).

14. Stanley Elkin, "Where I Read What I Read," *Antaeus* 45/46 (Spring/ Summer 1982): 57.

15. Marie-France Etienne, Hobart and William Smith Colleges, manuscript.

16. Walter Slatoff, *With Respect to Readers: Dimensions of Literary Response* (Ithaca, N.Y.: Cornell University Press, 1970), p. 54.

17. Stanley Fish, *Is There a Text in This Class?* (Cambridge, Mass.: Harvard University Press, 1980).

18. Smith, *Understanding Reading.*

19. Galway Kinnell, "Freedom, New Hampshire," in *What a Kingdom It Was* (Boston: Houghton Mifflin, 1960).

20. Schema theory addresses the relation between a particular interpretation or understanding of text and the expectations, assumptions, and particular experiences that readers bring to it. See the work of Richard C. Anderson, Jean Osborn, and Robert J. Tierney, *Learning to Read in American Schools* (Hillsdale, N.J.: Lawrence Erlbaum, 1984).

21. Mitford Mathews, *Teaching to Read* (Chicago: University of Chicago Press, 1966).

22. Chodorow, *Reproduction of Mothering.*

23. Smith, *Understanding Reading.*

24. Godfrey Lienhardt, *Divinity and Experience* (Oxford: Clarendon Press, 1961).

25. Julia Kristeva's writings explore the epistemology and politics of the "mother tongue." See *About Chinese Women* and "Women's Time," trans. Alice Jardine and Harry Blake, in *Feminist Theory: A Critique of Ideology,* ed. Nannerl O. Keohane, Michelle Z. Rosaldo, and Barbara C. Gelpi (Chicago: University of Chicago Press, 1981). In "From One Identity to Another," in *Desire in Language,* ed. Leon S. Roudiez, trans. Thomas Gora, Alice Jardine, and Leon S. Roudiez (New York: Columbia University Press, 1980), Kristeva warns against *psychosis*: "symbolic legality is wiped out in favor of arbitrariness of instinctual drive without meaning and communication: panicking at the loss of all reference the subject goes through fancies of omnipotence or identification with a totalitarian leader. On the other hand where *fetishism* is concerned, constantly dodging the paternal, sacrificial function produces an objectification of the pure signifier more and more emptied of meaning—an insipid formalism" (p. 139).

26. Remy Kwant, *The Phenomenological Philosophy of Merleau-Ponty* (Pittsburgh: Duquesne University Press, 1963).

27. Merleau-Ponty, *Phenomenology of Perception,* p. 10.

28. Harold Herber, *Teaching Reading in Content Areas* (Englewood Cliffs, N.J.: Prentice-Hall, 1978), p. 40.

29. Mark F. Goldberg, "An Update on the National Writing Project," *Kappan* 65, no. 5 (1984): 356–57.
30. See Bleich, *Subjective Criticism*, and Eugene Kintgen, "Reader Response and Stylistics," *Style* 11, no. 1 (Winter 1977): 1–18.
31. Ernst Kris, *Psychoanalytic Explorations in Art* (New York: International Press, 1952).
32. Eagleton, *Literary Theory*, p. 138.
33. Roland Barthes, *The Pleasure of the Text*, trans. Richard Miller (New York: Hill and Wang, 1975), p. 24.
34. In addition to the works of Bleich and Fish already cited, see Norman Holland, *The Dynamics of Literary Response* (New York: W. W. Norton, 1975).
35. See *New Literary History* 7 (1976) for articles by David Bleich, "The Subjective Paradigm," and Norman Holland, "The New Paradigm: Subjective or Transactive?"
36. Grotowski, *Toward a Poor Theatre*, p. 57.
37. Ricoeur, *Interpretation Theory*, p. 87.
38. Langer, *Feeling and Form*, p. 322.

8 REDEEMING DAUGHTERS

1. Isa. 11:6.
2. Isa. 11:7–9.
3. Maurice Natanson, *The Journeying Self* (Reading, Mass.: Addison-Wesley, 1970), p. 4.
4. Paulo Freire, *Pedagogy of the Oppressed*, trans. Myra Bergman Ramos (New York: Continuum, 1981), uses the term "malefic generosity" when he discusses those who attempt to aid the exploited: "These adherents to the people's cause constantly run the risk of falling into a type of generosity as malefic as that of the oppressors. The generosity of the oppressors is nourished by an unjust order, which must be maintained in order to justify that generosity" (p. 46). The term also appears in Maxine Greene's essay, "Pedagogy and Praxis: The Problem of Malefic Generosity," in *Landscapes for Learning*, where it describes the self-abnegating interest in the other that employs altruism to evade responsibility for one's own action.
5. Aries, *Centuries of Childhood*.
6. James Axtell, *The School upon the Hill* (New York: W. W. Norton, 1976).
7. One is tempted to wonder whether this history of infantilization and dependency accounts for the alcohol abuse inscribed in the traditions of so many college campuses.
8. Wishy, *Child and Republic*.
9. William Wordsworth, "Ode: Intimations of Immortality from Recollections of Early Childhood," in *Immortal Poems of the English Language*, ed. Oscar Williams (New York: Pocket Books, 1952).
10. Mark Twain, *The Adventures of Huckleberry Finn* (New York: Washington Square Press, 1962), p. 374.

11. Merleau-Ponty, *Phenomenology of Perception*, p. ix.
12. Robert Louis Stevenson, "Whole Duty of Children," in *A Child's Garden of Verses* (Cambridge: W. W. Heffler and Sons, 1922), p. 5.
13. Sissela Bok, *Lying* (New York: Random House [Vintage Books], 1979), p. 16.
14. Agnes Smedley, *Daughter of Earth* (New York: Feminist Press, 1973), p. 7.
15. Zora Neale Hurston, *Dust Tracks on the Road*, ed. Robert Hemenway (Urbana: University of Illinois Press, 1984), pp. 71–73.
16. Alice Walker describes her poignant search for Zora Neale Hurston's grave in the essay, "Looking for Zora," published in *In Search of Our Mothers' Gardens* (New York: Harcourt Brace Jovanovich, 1983).
17. Chodorow, *Reproduction of Mothering.*
18. It is impossible to read stories of talking birds without recalling that it was the talk of birds chattering in Greek that Virginia Woolf heard when she was ill. Roger Poole's study of her art and illness argues that this recurring hallucination is to be understood as her repudiation of the discourse that surrounded her, medical, military, manipulative, and male; see *The Unknown Virginia Woolf* (Cambridge: Cambridge University Press, 1978).
19. See Barbara Johnson, ed., "The Pedagogical Imperative: Teaching as a Literary Genre," *Yale French Studies* 63 (1982), special issue, for discussions of sadism in literary portrayals of pedagogy.
20. Mary McCarthy, *Memories of a Catholic Girlhood* (New York: Harcourt Brace Jovanovich, 1957), p. 71.
21. Wordsworth, "Ode: Intimations of Immortality," p. 260.
22. Kristeva, *Desire in Language.*
23. Marianne Moore, "Poetry," in *Immortal Poems of the English Language*, ed. Oscar Williams (New York: Pocket Books, 1952), p. 533.

9 OTHER PEOPLE'S CHILDREN

1. Ferdinand Schoeman, "Rights of Children, Rights of Parents, and the Moral Basis of the Family," *Ethics* 91 (October 1980): 8.
2. Marcuse, *Aesthetic Dimension*, p. 7.
3. Schoeman, "Rights of Children," p. 8.
4. Elshtain, *Public Man, Private Woman*, pp. 15–16.
5. If the Greeks were the first, they were not the last to conflate morality, masculinity and knowledge by establishing societies of young men to generate and contain ethical discourse. Benjamin Franklin designed such a society for this purpose, as described in his *Autobiography*: "My ideas at the time were, that the sect should be begun and spread first among young and single men only. . . . we should be call'd *The Society of the Free and Easy*: free, as being, by the general practice and habit of the virtues, free from the dominion of vice; and particularly by the practice of industry and frugality, free from debt, which exposes a man to confinement, and a species of slavery to his creditors" (p. 92).

6. Elshtain, *Public Man, Private Woman*, pp. 37–38.
7. Ibid., p. 45.
8. Ibid., pp. 190–95.
9. See Chapter 1.
10. Merleau-Ponty, *Phenomenology of Perception*, p. 83.
11. Mary Midgley, *Beast and Man: The Roots of Human Nature* (Ithaca, N.Y.: Cornell University Press, 1978), p. 291.
12. Freire, *Pedagogy of the Oppressed*, trans. Myra Bergman Ramos (New York: Continuum, 1981).
13. This aesthetic conception of curriculum is developed more fully in Grumet, "Songs and Situations."
14. See Gail McCutcheon, "How Do Elementary School Teachers Plan?" *Elementary School Journal* 81 (September 1980): 4–23.
15. Aaron Cicourel et al., *Language Use and School Performance* (New York: Academic Press, 1974).
16. Joseph Heller, *Something Happened* (New York: Alfred A. Knopf, 1974), pp. 246–49.
17. See Carol Gilligan, "In a Different Voice: Women's Conceptions of the Self and Morality," *Harvard Educational Review* 47, no. 4 (1977): 481–517.
18. Noddings, *Caring*, p. 19.
19. Jo Anne Pagano, "The Claim of Philia."
20. Ibid., p. 23.
21. Virginia Woolf, *The Years* (1937; London: Panther Books, 1977), pp. 288–89.

10   THE EMPTY HOUSE

1. This passage is drawn from the essay, "Professions for Women," written by Virginia Woolf in 1931, published in 1942, and quoted here from the collection, *Virginia Woolf: Women and Writing*, ed. Michele Barrett (New York: Harcourt Brace Jovanovich, 1979), p. 63.
2. Habermas, *Knowledge and Human Interests*.
3. O'Brien, *Politics of Reproduction*.
4. Strasser, *Dialogic Phenomenology*.
5. Chodorow, *Reproduction of Mothering*.
6. See Patricia Campbell, "Racism and Sexism in Research Methods," in *The Encyclopedia of Educational Research* (New York: Macmillan, 1983).
7. Woolf, "Professions for Women," p. 59.
8. Kristeva, "Women's Time," p. 52.
9. Ibid.
10. Jane Marcus, *New Feminist Essays on Virginia Woolf* (Lincoln: University of Nebraska Press, 1981), p. xx.
11. Nancy Chodorow, "Gender, Relation, and Difference in Psychoanalytic Perspective," in *The Future of Difference*, ed. Hester Eisenstein and Alice Jardine (New Brunswick, N.J.: Rutgers University Press, 1985), p. 8.

12. Virginia Woolf, *To the Lighthouse* (New York: Harcourt Brace and World, 1927), p. 76.

13. Ibid., pp. 77–79.

14. Stern, *Interpersonal World of the Infant.*

15. Kristeva, "Place Names," in *Desire in Language*, p. 284.

16. Ibid.

17. Jessica Benjamin, "The Bonds of Love: Rational Violence and Erotic Domination," in *The Future of Difference*, ed. Hester Eisenstein and Alice Jardine (New Brunswick, N.J.: Rutgers University Press, 1985), p. 46.

18. See "Virginia Woolf's Winter's Tale," in Maria Di Battista, *Virginia Woolf's Major Novels* (New Haven: Yale University Press, 1980).

19. Ibid., p. 79.

20. Joan Cocks, "Suspicious Pleasures: On Teaching Feminist Theory," in *Gendered Subjects*, ed. Margo Culley and Catherine Portuges (Boston: Routledge and Kegan Paul, 1985).

21. Ibid., p. 178.

22. Benjamin, "The Bonds of Love."

23. Ellen Hawkes, "Woolf's Magical Garden of Women," in *New Feminist Essays on Virginia Woolf*, ed. Jane Marcus (Lincoln: University of Nebraska Press, 1981).

Bibliography

Altieri, Charles. "Ecce Homo: Narcissism, Power, Pathos, and the Status of Autobiographical Representation." *Boundary II* 9, no. 3 and 4, 10, no. 1 (Spring and Fall 1981): 389–413.

Anderson, Richard C., Jean Osborn, and Robert J. Tierney. *Learning to Read in American Schools*. Hillsdale, N.J.: Lawrence Erlbaum, 1984.

Apple, Michael. "The Hidden Curriculum and the Nature of Conflict." In *Curriculum Theorizing: The Reconceptualists*, ed. William F. Pinar. Berkeley, Calif.: McCutchan, 1975.

———. "Work, Gender, and Teaching." *Teachers College Record* 84, no. 3 (Spring 1983): 611–628.

Apple, Michael, ed. *Cultural and Economic Reproduction in Education*. London: Routledge and Kegan Paul, 1982.

Aries, Philippe. *Centuries of Childhood*. Translated by Robert Baldick. New York: Random House (Vintage Books), 1965.

Axtell, James. *The School upon the Hill*. New York: W. W. Norton, 1976.

Ball, Stephen J., and Ivor F. Goodson, eds. *Teachers' Lives and Careers*. Philadelphia: Falmer Press, 1985.

Barrell, John. "The Public Figure and the Private Eye: William Collins' 'Ode to Evening.'" In *Teaching the Text*, ed. Susan Kappeler and Norman Bryson. Boston: Routledge and Kegan Paul, 1983.

Barthes, Roland. *The Pleasure of the Text*. Translated by Richard Miller. New York: Hill and Wang, 1975.

Belenky, Mary Field; Blythe McVicker Clinchy; Nancy Rule Goldberger; and Jill Mattuck Tarule. *Women's Ways of Knowing: The Development of Self, Voice, and Mind*. New York: Basic Books, 1986.

Benjamin, Jessica. "The Bonds of Love: Rational Violence and Erotic Domination." In *The Future of Difference*, ed. Hester Eisenstein and Alice Jardine. New Brunswick, N.J.: Rutgers University Press, 1985.

Bennett, John. *Strictures on Female Education* (1795). New York: Source Book Press, 1971.

Berger, John. *Ways of Seeing*. New York: Penguin Books, 1972.

Bergum, Vangie. *Woman to Mother: A Transformation*. South Hadley, Mass.: Bergin and Garvey, forthcoming.

Bernard, Richard M., and Maris A. Vinovskis. "The Female Teacher in Antebellum Massachusetts." *Journal of Social History* 10, no. 3 (1977): 332–45.

Beyer, Landon. "Aesthetic Theory and the Ideology of Educational Institutions." *Curriculum Inquiry* 9 (Spring 1979): 13–26.

Bleich, David. *Subjective Criticism.* Baltimore: Johns Hopkins University Press, 1978.

———. "The Subjective Paradigm." *New Literary History* 7 (1976): 313–334.

Bok, Sissela. *Lying.* New York: Random House (Vintage Books), 1979.

Bowlby, John. *Attachment.* New York: Basic Books, 1969.

Bowles, Samuel, and Herbert Gintis. *Schooling in Capitalist America.* New York: Basic Books, 1976.

Brownlee, W. Elliot. *Dynamics of Ascent: A History of American Economy.* New York: Alfred A. Knopf, 1979.

Buber, Martin. *Between Man and Man.* New York: Macmillan, 1965.

Bullough, Robert V., Jr. "Teachers and Teaching in the Nineteenth Century: St. George, Utah." *Journal of Curriculum Theorizing* 4, no. 2 (Summer 1982): 199–206.

Campbell, Patricia. "Racism and Sexism in Research Methods." In *The Encyclopedia of Educational Research.* New York: Macmillan, 1983.

Carnoy, Martin, ed. *Schooling in a Corporate Society.* New York: David McKay, 1972.

Charters, W. W., and Douglas Waples. *The Commonwealth Teacher-Training Study.* Chicago: University of Chicago Press, 1928.

Chernin, Kim. *The Hungry Self: Women, Eating, and Identity.* New York: Times Books, 1985.

Chicago, Judy. *Through the Flower: My Struggle as a Woman Artist.* New York: Doubleday, 1977.

Chodorow, Nancy. "Gender, Relation, and Difference in Psychoanalytic Perspective." In *The Future of Difference,* ed. Hester Eisenstein and Alice Jardine. New Brunswick, N.J.: Rutgers University Press, 1985.

———. *The Reproduction of Mothering: Psychoanalysis and the Sociology of Gender.* Berkeley: University of California Press, 1978.

Cicourel, Aaron, et al. *Language Use and School Performance.* New York: Academic Press, 1974.

Clandinin, D. Jean. *Classroom Practice.* Philadelphia: Falmer Press, 1986.

Clay, Marie M. *Reading: The Patterning of Complex Behaviour.* London: Heinemann Educational Books, 1977.

Cocks, Joan. "Suspicious Pleasures: On Teaching Feminist Theory." In *Gendered Subjects: The Dynamics of Feminist Teaching,* ed. Margo Culley and Catherine Portuges. Boston: Routledge and Kegan Paul, 1985.

Demos, John. *A Little Commonwealth.* New York: Oxford University Press, 1970.

Dewey, John. *Art as Experience.* New York: Capricorn Books, 1934.

Di Battista, Maria. "Virginia Woolf's Winter's Tale." In *Virginia Woolf's Major Novels.* New Haven: Yale University Press, 1980.

Dickinson, Emily. "Letter to Maria Whitney." In *Mother to Daughter, Daughter to Mother*, ed. Tillie Olsen. Old Westbury, N.Y.: Feminist Press, 1984.

Didion, Joan. "On Keeping a Notebook." In *Slouching toward Bethlehem*. New York: Dell, 1961.

Dinnerstein, Dorothy. *The Mermaid and the Minotaur: Sexual Arrangements and Human Malaise*. New York: Harper and Row, 1976.

Donne, John. "The Good Morrow." In *Seventeenth Century Verse and Prose: Volume I, 1600–1660*, ed. Helen C. White, Ruth C. Wallerstein, and Ricardo Quintana. New York: Macmillan, 1951.

Douglas, Ann. *The Feminization of American Culture*. New York: Avon Books, 1977.

Doyle, Walter. "Paradigms for Research on Teacher Effectiveness." In *Review of Research in Education*, ed. Lee Shulman. Itasca, Ill.: F. E. Peacock, 1978.

Eagleton, Terry. *Literary Theory*. Minneapolis: University of Minnesota Press, 1983.

Earle, William. *Autobiographical Consciousness*. Chicago: Quadrangle Books, 1972.

Eisner, Elliot. *The Educational Imagination*. New York: Macmillan, 1979.

Eisner, Elliot, ed. *The Arts, Human Development, and Education*. Berkeley, Calif.: McCutchan, 1976.

Elkin, Stanley. "Where I Read What I Read." *Antaeus* 45/46 (Spring/Summer 1982): 57.

Elshtain, Jean Bethke. "Against Androgeny." *Telos* 14, no. 1 (Spring 1981): 5–21.

———. *Public Man, Private Woman: Women in Social and Political Thought*. Princeton, N.J.: Princeton University Press, 1981.

Feinberg, Walter. *Reason and Rhetoric*. New York: John Wiley, 1975.

Felt, Marilyn Clayton. *Improving Our Schools*. Newton, Mass.: Educational Development Center, 1985.

Fiedler, Leslie. *An End to Innocence*. Boston: Beacon Press, 1955.

Firestone, Shulamith. *Dialectic of Sex*. New York: Bantam Books, 1972.

Fish, Stanley. *Is There a Text in This Class?* Cambridge, Mass.: Harvard University Press, 1980.

Flynn, Elizabeth A., and Patrocinio P. Schweickart, eds. *Gender and Reading*. Baltimore: Johns Hopkins University Press, 1986.

Fortes, Meyer. "Religious Premises and Logical Technique in Divinatory Ritual." *Philosophical Transactions of the Royal Society of London* 251, no. 722 (1966): 409–26.

Foucault, Michel. *Discipline and Punish*. Translated by Alan Sheridan. New York: Random House (Vintage Books), 1979.

Frankenstein, Carl. *The Roots of the Ego*. Balitmore: Williams and Wilkins, 1966.

Franklin, Benjamin. *The Autobiography of Benjamin Franklin*. New York: Collier Books, 1962.

Freire, Paulo. *Pedagogy of the Oppressed.* Translated by Myra Bergman Ramos. New York: Continuum, 1981.

Friedman, Susan Stanford. "Authority in the Feminist Classroom: A Contradiction in Terms?" in *Gendered Subjects: The Dynamics of Feminist Teaching,* ed. Margo Culley and Catherine Portuges. Boston: Routledge and Kegan Paul, 1985.

Froebel, Friedrich. *Mother-Play and Nursery Songs.* Translated by F. E. Dwight and J. Jarvis. Foreword by Elizabeth Peabody. Boston: Lorthrop, Lee, and Shephard, 1878.

Frost, Robert. "Birches." In *The Oxford Book of American Verse,* ed. F. O. Matthiessen. New York: Oxford University Press, 1950.

Froula, Christine. "When Eve Reads Milton: Undoing the Canonical Economy." In *Canons,* ed. Robert von Hallberg. Chicago: University of Chicago Press, 1984.

Gallop, Jane. "The Monster in the Mirror: The Feminist Critic's Psychoanalysis." manuscript.

Gilligan, Carol. "In a Different Voice: Women's Conceptions of the Self and Morality." *Harvard Educational Review* 47, no. 4 (1977): 481–517.

Goldberg, Mark F. "An Update on the National Writing Project." *Kappan* 65, no. 5 (1984): 356–57.

Gombrowicz, Witold. *The Marriage.* Translated by Louis Iribane, New York: Grove Press, 1969.

Goodlad, John, and M. Frances Klein. *Behind the Classroom Door.* Worthington, Ohio: C. A. Jones, 1970.

Gramsci, Antonio. *Selections from the Prison Notebooks.* Translated and edited by Quinton Hoare and Geoffrey N. Smith. New York: International Publishers, 1971.

Greene, Maxine. "Curriculum and Consciousness." In *Curriculum Theorizing: The Reconceptualists,* ed. William F. Pinar. Berkeley, Calif.: McCutchan, 1975.

———. *Landscapes for Learning.* New York: Teachers College Press, 1978.

Greer, Colin. *The Great School Legend: A Revisionist Interpretation of American Public Education.* New York: Penguin Books, 1972.

Griffin, Susan. *Pornography and Silence.* New York: Harper and Row, 1981.

Grotowski, Jerzy. *Toward a Poor Theatre.* New York: Simon and Schuster, 1968.

Grumet, Gerald W. "Eye Contact: The Core of Interpersonal Relatedness." *Psychiatry* 46 (May 1983): 172–80.

Grumet, Madeleine. "The Lie of the Child Redeemer." *Journal of Education* 168, no. 3 (1986): 87–97.

———. "The Politics of Personal Knowledge." *Curriculum Inquiry* 17, no. 3 (1987).

———. "In Search of Theatre: Ritual, Confrontation, and the Suspense of Form." *Journal of Education* 162, no. 1 (Winter 1980): 93–116.

———. "Songs and Situations." In *Qualitative Evaluation,* ed. George Willis. Berkeley, Calif.: McCutchan, 1978.

Habermas, Jürgen. *Knowledge and Human Interests.* Translated by Jeremy J. Shapiro. Boston: Beacon Press, 1971.

Hale, Nancy. *The Life in the Studio.* New York: Avon Books, 1957.

Harris, Neil. *The Artist in American Society: The Formative Years, 1790–1860.* Chicago: University of Chicago Press, 1982.

Hawkes, Ellen. "Woolf's Magical Garden of Women." In *New Feminist Essays on Virginia Woolf,* ed. Jane Marcus. Lincoln: University of Nebraska Press, 1981.

Heath, Stephen. "Writing for Silence: Dorothy Richardson and the Novel." In *Teaching the Text,* ed. Susan Kappeler and Norman Bryson. Boston: Routledge and Kegan Paul, 1983.

Heller, Joseph. *Something Happened.* New York: Alfred A. Knopf, 1974.

Herber, Harold. *Teaching Reading in Content Areas.* Englewood Cliffs, N.J.: Prentice-Hall, 1978.

Holland, Norman. *The Dynamics of Literary Response.* New York: W. W. Norton, 1975.

———. "The New Paradigm: Subjective or Transactive?" *New Literary History* 7 (1976): 335–46.

Holt, John. *How Children Fail.* Rev. ed. New York: Delta/Seymour Laurence, 1982.

Huebner, Dwayne. "Curricular Language and Classroom Meanings." In *Curriculum Theorizing: The Reconceptualists,* ed. William F. Pinar. Berkeley, Calif.: McCutchan, 1975.

Huizinga, Johan. *Homo Ludens.* Boston: Beacon Press, 1955.

Hunningher, Benjamin. *The Origin of the Theater.* New York: Hill and Wang, 1955.

Hunsberger, Margaret. "Phenomenology of Reading: When Child and Curriculum Meet in Reading Class." *Reading—Canada—Lecture* 3, no. 2 (1985): 101–8.

Hunter, Madeline. *Mastery Teaching.* El Segundo, Calif.: TIP Publications, 1982.

Hurston, Zora Neale. *Dust Tracks on the Road.* Edited with an introduction by Robert Hemenway. Urbana: University of Illinois Press, 1984.

Husserl, Edmund. *Ideas: General Introduction to Pure Phenomenology.* Translated by W. R. Boyce Gibson. New York: Collier Books, 1962.

Johnson, Barbara, ed. "The Pedagogical Imperative: Teaching as a Literary Genre." *Yale French Studies* 63 (1982).

Kappeler, Susan, and Norman Bryson, eds. *Teaching the Text.* Boston: Routledge and Kegan Paul, 1983.

Kermode, Anita. "Ralph Waldo Emerson: An Introduction." In *Teaching the Text,* ed. Susan Kappeler and Norman Bryson. Boston: Routledge and Kegan Paul, 1983.

Kermode, Frank. "Opinion in *Troilus and Cressida.*" In *Teaching the Text,* ed. Susan Kappeler and Norman Bryson. Boston: Routledge and Kegan Paul, 1983.

Kinnell, Galway. *What a Kingdom It Was.* Boston: Houghton Mifflin, 1960.

Klein, Susan S., ed. *Handbook for Achieving Sex Equity through Education.* Baltimore: Johns Hopkins University Press, 1985.

Kohut, Heinz. *The Analysis of the Self.* New York: International Universities Press, 1971.

Kounin, Jacob S. *Discipline and Group Management in Classrooms.* New York: Holt, Rinehart and Winston, 1970.

Kris, Ernst. *Psychoanalytic Explorations in Art.* New York: International Press, 1952.

Kristeva, Julia. *About Chinese Women.* Translated by Anita Burrows. London: Marion Boyars, 1977.

―――. *Desire in Language: A Semiotic Approach to Literature and Art.* Edited by Leon S. Roudiez. Translated by Thomas Gora, Alice Jardine, and Leon S. Roudiez. New York: Columbia University Press, 1980.

―――. *Revolution in Poetic Language.* Translated by Margaret Waller. New York: Columbia University Press, 1984.

―――. "Women's Time." Translated by Alice Jardine and Harry Blake. In *Feminist Theory: A Critique of Ideology,* ed. Nannerl O. Keohane, Michelle Z. Rosaldo, and Barbara C. Gelpi, Chicago: University of Chicago Press, 1981.

Kwant, Remy. *The Phenomenological Philosophy of Merleau-Ponty.* Pittsburgh: Duquesne University Press, 1963.

Lacan, Jacques. "The Eye and the Gaze." Translated by Alan Sheridan. In *The Four Fundamental Concepts of Psycho-analysis,* ed. Jacques-Alain Miller. New York: W. W. Norton, 1981.

―――. *The Language of the Self.* Translated by Anthony Wilden. New York: Dell, 1968.

Langer, Susanne K. *Feeling and Form.* New York: Charles Scribner's Sons, 1953.

―――. *Problems of Art.* New York: Charles Scribner's Sons, 1957.

Lasch, Christopher. *The Culture of Narcissism.* New York: W. W. Norton, 1979.

Lather, Patti. "Research as Praxis." *Harvard Educational Review* 56, no. 3 (August 8, 1986): 257–77.

Lawrence, D. H. *The Rainbow.* New York: Modern Library, 1915.

Lichtenberg, Joseph D. *Psychoanalysis and Infant Research.* Hillsdale, N.J.: Lawrence Erlbaum (Analytic Press), 1983.

Lienhart, Godfrey. *Divinity and Experience.* Oxford: Clarendon Press, 1961.

Lortie, Dan C. *Schoolteacher.* Chicago: University of Chicago Press, 1975.

Macdonald, James. "Curriculum Theory, Curriculum, and Human Interests." In *Curriculum Theorizing: The Reconceptualists,* ed. William F. Pinar. Berkeley, Calif.: McCutchan, 1975.

Macdonald, James, and Susan Cohlbert Macdonald. "Gender Values and Curriculum." *Journal of Curriculum Theorizing* 3, no. 1 (Winter 1981): 299–304.

MacKinnon, Catherine. "Feminism, Marxism, Method, and the State." In *Feminist Theory: A Critique of Ideology,* ed. Nannerl O. Keohane,

Michelle Z. Rosaldo, and Barbara C. Gelpi. Chicago: University of Chicago Press, 1981.

Marcus, Jane. *New Feminist Essays on Virginia Woolf.* Lincoln: University of Nebraska Press, 1981.

Marcuse, Herbert. *The Aesthetic Dimension: Toward a Critique of Marxist Aesthetics.* Boston: Beacon Press, 1977.

———. *Eros and Civilization.* Boston: Beacon Press, 1955.

Martin, F. David. *Art and the Religious Experience: The Language of the Sacred.* Lewisburg, Pa.: Bucknell University Press, 1972.

Mathews, Mitford. *Teaching to Read.* Chicago: University of Chicago Press, 1966.

McCarthy, Mary. *Memories of a Catholic Girlhood.* New York: Harcourt Brace Jovanovich, 1957.

McCutcheon, Gail. "How Do Elementary School Teachers Plan?" *Elementary School Journal* 81 (September 1980): 4–23.

Merleau-Ponty, Maurice. "The Child's Relations with Others." Translated by William Cobb. In *The Primacy of Perception*, ed. James Edie. Evanston, Ill.: Northwestern University Press, 1964.

———. "Indirect Voices and the Language of Silence." In *Signs.* Translated by Richard C. McCleary. Evanston, Ill.: Northwestern University Press, 1964.

———. *Phenomenology of Perception.* Translated by Colin Wilson. New York: Humanities Press, 1962.

Midgley, Mary. *Beast and Man: The Roots of Human Nature.* Ithaca, N.Y.: Cornell University Press, 1978.

Miller, Janet. "Feminist Pedagogy: The Sound of Silence Breaking." *Journal of Curriculum Theorizing* 4 no. 1 (Winter 1982): 5–11.

Mitchell, Juliet. *Psychoanalysis and Feminism.* New York: Random House (Vintage Books), 1975.

Mitrano, Barbara. "Feminist Theology and Curriculum Theory." *Journal of Curriculum Studies* 11, no. 3 (July–September 1979): 211–20.

Moffat, Mary J., and Charlotte Painter, eds. *Revelations.* New York: Random House, 1975.

Moore, Marianne. "Poetry." In *Immortal Poems of the English Language*, ed. Oscar Williams. New York: Pocket Books, 1952.

Morain, Thomas. "The Departure of Males from the Teaching Profession in Nineteenth Century Iowa." *Civil War History* 26, no. 2 (1980): 161–70.

Nassaw, David. *Schooled to Order.* New York: Oxford University Press, 1979.

Natanson, Maurice. *The Journeying Self.* Reading, Mass.: Addison-Wesley, 1970.

Noddings, Nel. *Caring.* Berkeley: University of California Press, 1984.

Norton, Arthur O., ed. *The Journals of Cyrus Peirce and Mary Swift.* Cambridge, Mass.: Harvard University Press, 1926.

Obeyesekere, Gananath. *Medusa's Hair.* Chicago: University of Chicago Press, 1981.

O'Brien, Mary. *The Politics of Reproduction*. Boston: Routledge and Kegan Paul, 1981.

Olsen, Tillie. *Silences*. New York: Dell, 1978.

Pagano, Jo Anne. "The Claim of Philia." In *Curriculum Theory Discourses*, ed. William F. Pinar. Scottsdale, Ariz.: Gorsuch Skarisbrick, 1988.

Piaget, Jean. *The Grasp of Consciousness*. Translated by Susan Wedgwood. Cambridge, Mass.: Harvard University Press, 1976.

Pinar, William F. "The Analysis of Educational Experience." "*Currere*: Toward Reconceptualization." "Search for a Method." In *Curriculum Theorizing: The Reconceptualists*. Berkeley, Calif.: McCutchan, 1975.

————. "Curriculum as Gender Text: Notes on Reproduction, Resistance, and Male–Male Relations." *Journal of Curriculum Theorizing* 5, no. 1 (Winter 1983): 26–52.

Pinar, William F., and Madeleine Grumet. *Toward a Poor Curriculum*. Dubuque, Iowa: Kendell/Hunt, 1976.

Poole, Roger. *The Unknown Virginia Woolf*. Cambridge: Cambridge University Press, 1978.

Read, Herbert. *The Philosophy of Modern Art*. New York: New American Library (Meridian Books), 1955.

Reich, Wilhelm. *Character-Analysis*. Translated by Theodore P. Wolfe. New York: Noonday Press, 1961.

Ricoeur, Paul. *Interpretation Theory: Discourse and the Surplus of Meaning*. Fort Worth: Texas Christian University Press, 1976.

Roche, Maurice. *Phenomenology, Language, and the Social Sciences*. London: Routledge and Kegan Paul, 1973.

Rorty, Richard. *Philosophy and the Mirror of Nature*. Princeton, N.J.: Princeton University Press, 1982.

Rose, Jacqueline. "Introduction II." In *Feminine Sexuality: Jacques Lacan and the "école freudienne*," ed. Juliet Mitchell and Jacqueline Rose, trans. Jacqueline Rose. New York: W. W. Norton, 1982.

Rothman, Sheila. *Woman's Proper Place*. New York: Basic Books, 1978.

Sartre, Jean-Paul. *Being and Nothingness*. Translated by Hazel E. Barnes. New York: Washington Square Press, 1966.

————. *Kean*. London: H. Hamilton, 1954.

Saussure, Ferdinand de. *Course in General Linguistics*. Edited by Charles Bally and Albert Sechahaye. Translated by Roy Harris. London: Duckworth, 1983.

Schoeman, Ferdinand. "Rights of Children, Rights of Parents, and the Moral Basis of the Family." *Ethics* 91 (October 1980): 8.

Shakespeare, William. "Sonnet 18." In *The Riverside Shakespeare*. Boston: Houghton Mifflin, 1974.

Sharp, Rachel, and Anthony Green. *Education and Social Control*. London: Routledge and Kegan Paul, 1975.

Shor, Ira. *Culture Wars*. Boston: Routledge and Kegan Paul, 1986.

Sklar, Kathryn K. *Catharine Beecher*. New Haven: Yale University Press, 1973.

Skura, Meredith A. *The Literary Use of the Psychoanalytic Process*. New Haven: Yale University Press, 1981.

Slatoff, Walter. *With Respect to Readers: Dimensions of Literary Response*. Ithaca, N.Y.: Cornell University Press, 1970.

Smedley, Agnes. *Daughter of Earth*. New York: Feminist Press, 1973.

Smith, Frank. *Understanding Reading*. New York: Holt, Rinehart and Winston, 1973.

Spring, Joel. *The Sorting Machine*. New York: David McKay, 1976.

Stake, Robert E., ed. *Evaluating the Arts in Education*. Columbus, Ohio: Charles E. Merrill, 1975.

Stern, Daniel N. *The Interpersonal World of the Infant*. New York: Basic Books, 1985.

Stevenson, Robert Louis. "Whole Duty of Children." In *A Child's Garden of Verses*. Cambridge: W. W. Heffler and Sons, 1922.

Strasser, Stephen. *The Idea of a Dialogic Phenomenology*. Pittsburgh: Duquesne University Press, 1969.

Straus, Erwin. "The Upright Posture." In *Essays in Phenomenology*, ed. Maurice Natanson. The Hague: Martinus Nijhoff, 1966.

Sugg, Redding S., Jr. *Motherteacher: The Feminization of American Education*. Charlottesville: University Press of Virginia, 1978.

Suleiman, Susan. "Introduction: Varieties of Audience-Oriented Criticism." In *The Reader in the Text*, ed. Susan Suleiman and Inge Crossman. Princeton, N.J.: Princeton University Press, 1980.

Tanner, Tony. "*Wuthering Heights* and *Jane Eyre*." In *Teaching the Text*, ed. Susan Kappeler and Norman Bryson. Boston: Routledge and Kegan Paul, 1983.

Taubman, Peter. "Gender and Curriculum: Discourse and the Politics of Sexuality." *Journal of Curriculum Theorizing* 4, no. 1 (Winter 1982): 12–87.

Tetreault, Mary Kay, and Patricia Schmuck. "Equity, Educational Reform, and Gender." *Issues in Education* 3 no. 1 (Summer 1985): 45–65.

Turner, Victor. "Mukanda: The Rite of Circumcision." In *The Forest of Symbols*. Ithaca, N.Y.: Cornell University Press, 1967.

Twain, Mark, *The Adventures of Huckleberry Finn*. New York: Washington Square Press, 1962.

Tyack, David. *The One Best System*. Cambridge, Mass.: Harvard University Press, 1974.

Walker, Alice. "Looking for Zora." In *In Search of Our Mothers' Gardens*. New York: Harcourt Brace Jovanovich, 1983.

Williams, Raymond. *Marxism and Literature*. New York: Oxford University Press, 1977.

———. "Monologue in *MacBeth*." In *Teaching the Text*, ed. Susan Kappeler and Norman Bryson. Boston: Routledge and Kegan Paul, 1983.

Winnicott, D. W. *Playing and Reality*. New York: Basic Books, 1971.

Wishy, Bernard. *The Child and the Republic*. Philadelphia: University of Pennsylvania Press, 1968.

Woodward, Arthur. "Taking Teaching Out of Teaching and Reading Out of Learning to Read: A Historical Study of Reading Textbook Teachers' Guides, 1920–1980." *Book Research Quarterly*, Spring 1986, pp. 53–73.

Woolf, Virginia. "Professions for Women." In *Virginia Woolf: Women and Writing*, ed. Michele Barrett. New York: Harcourt Brace Jovanovich, 1979.

———. *Three Guineas*. New York: Harcourt Brace, 1966.

———. *To the Lighthouse*. New York: Harcourt Brace and World, 1927.

———. *A Writer's Diary*. New York: Harcourt Brace Jovanovich, 1953.

———. *The Years* (1937). London: Panther Books, 1977.

Wordsworth, William. "Ode: Intimations of Immortality from Recollections of Early Childhood." In *Immortal Poems of the English Language*, ed. Oscar Williams. New York: Pocket Books, 1952.

Wright, Elizabeth. *Psychoanalytic Criticism*. New York: Methuen, 1984.

Yeats, William Butler. "Sailing to Byzantium." In *Modern American and Modern British Poetry*, ed. Louis Untermeyer. New York: Harcourt Brace, 1955.

Index